Microsoft HoloLens Developer's Guide

Create stunning and highly immersive 3D apps for your Microsoft HoloLens

Dennis Vroegop

BIRMINGHAM - MUMBAI

Microsoft HoloLens Developer's Guide

First published: July 2017

Production reference: 2020817

Published by Packt Publishing Ltd.
Livery Place
35 Livery Street
Birmingham
B3 2PB, UK.

ISBN 978-1-78646-085-1

www.packtpub.com

Credits

Author
Dennis Vroegop

Reviewers
Jason M. Odom
Vangos Pterneas

Commissioning Editor
Amarabha Banerjee

Acquisition Editor
Larissa Pinto

Content Development Editor
Roshan Kumar

Technical Editor
Murtaza Tinwala

Copy Editors
Dhanya Baburaj
Safis Editing

Project Coordinator
Devanshi Doshi

Proofreader
Safis Editing

Indexer
Tejal Daruwale Soni

Graphics
Jason Monteiro

Production Coordinator
Shraddha Falebhai

About the Author

Dennis Vroegop is a managing director at Interknowlogy Europe, a software architect, a speaker, and ten-time winner of the Microsoft MVP Award (C#, Surface, Hardware Interaction Design and Development, Kinect for Windows, and Emerging Experiences). He is a designer and developer of new ways to interact with people using multi-touch systems and camera-based solutions.

Dennis feels most comfortable when leading teams to a better way of working. Software development teams on the Microsoft platform, including but not limited to stakeholders, product owners, product managers, developers, and customers, benefit from his knowledge of good teamwork, quality assurance, and professional software development. He has been developing software since the early 80s, starting out on the Commodore 64. He taught himself to program the games that his friends ended up playing. He writes software in a large number of languages and environments. After graduating in the field of computer science from Amsterdam, Dennis started to work as a developer, but quickly took over the role of a lead R&D engineer. After a couple of years, he started his own company, seeing how most developers back then were not treated the way he wanted them to be treated. By always mixing his technical skills with his management style, he quickly became someone with whom people actually wanted to work.

In 2007, Dennis started to get into the world of Natural User Interfaces, driven by his passion to provide everyone with access to information. His goal is to enable everyone, regardless of income, capabilities, social background, and so on, to be able to get in touch with computers. This led to the formation of Interknowlogy Europe, a company that aims at getting great and easy-to-use software using technologies such as HoloLens into the world.

Dennis is the coauthor of the LinkedIn Learning video, *Developing for Microsoft HoloLens*. He is also a proficient professional speaker at smaller and large events. He is the chairman of the largest Dutch .NET usergroup--dotNed.

Acknowledgments

Even though there is only one name on the cover, a project such as this cannot be done without the help of a lot of other people. I am forever grateful for all those who have helped me get this project off the ground. First, a big thanks to all the people in the original Emerging Experiences MVP group--Josh, Tim, Andras, Andreas, Nicolas, Gian Paolo, Joanna, Bronwen, Dwight, and David. You guys rock! We were there where it all started.

A big thank you to my buddy James Ashley, another Rockstar EE MVP. We shared the stage, we did the training, and we shaped the future while having a nice steak and a couple of drinks. You've been a great source of inspiration for me. We need to spend more time together.

Of course, my parents, who bought me my first computer even though they couldn't really afford it--you got me on this path that I still love to travel on every single day.

My partner in crime at Interknowlogy Europe, Frank, whose passion for the HoloLens matches mine, and that says something!

Last but most definitely not least--my wonderful and amazing daughter, Emma, and my smart and beautiful wife, Diana--you were there all the time. All those days I was locked up writing this book, leaving you alone, all those time I didn't see the point anymore, you got me through. You always believed in me, no matter what I did. This book is as much yours as it is mine. I will love you forever!

About the Reviewer

Jason Odom is a game developer with nearly 20 years of experience working on titles for companies such as Activision and Take 2 Interactive, along with years of game development teaching and mentoring experience. He is the founder of Thought Experiment, a start-up mixed reality studio, currently working on HoloQuest and CrossTrainMR properties for HoloLens. He recently authored the *HoloLens Beginner's Guide* for Packt. When he is not making software and applications, he is a loud and proud mixed reality evangelist with a highly active YouTube channel, and he is a prolific technology blogger for Next Reality.

www.PacktPub.com

For support files and downloads related to your book, please visit www.PacktPub.com.

Did you know that Packt offers eBook versions of every book published, with PDF and ePub files available? You can upgrade to the eBook version at www.PacktPub.com and as a print book customer, you are entitled to a discount on the eBook copy. Get in touch with us at service@packtpub.com for more details.

At www.PacktPub.com, you can also read a collection of free technical articles, sign up for a range of free newsletters and receive exclusive discounts and offers on Packt books and eBooks.

https://www.packtpub.com/mapt

Get the most in-demand software skills with Mapt. Mapt gives you full access to all Packt books and video courses, as well as industry-leading tools to help you plan your personal development and advance your career.

Why subscribe?

- Fully searchable across every book published by Packt
- Copy and paste, print, and bookmark content
- On demand and accessible via a web browser

Customer Feedback

Thanks for purchasing this Packt book. At Packt, quality is at the heart of our editorial process. To help us improve, please leave us an honest review on this book's Amazon page at `https://www.amazon.com/dp/1786460858`.

If you'd like to join our team of regular reviewers, you can e-mail us at `customerreviews@packtpub.com`. We award our regular reviewers with free eBooks and videos in exchange for their valuable feedback. Help us be relentless in improving our products!

Table of Contents

Preface

With the introduction of the Microsoft HoloLens, the world has started to think about computing in a whole new way. Now, we are not locked inside a virtual world in either an enclosed device or on a screen, but we are able to mix the real world with anything that our minds can come up with in a virtual world. This opens up a lot of new exciting ways to create new immersive experiences.

The big question is, of course, how do you as a developer, designer, or an out-of-the-box thinker create these experiences? In this book, you will learn all you need to know to create stunning three-dimensional apps that run on the mixed reality platform. We will cover the basics, but will also show you how to get advanced work done. We will start simple but work our way deep into the inner workings of HoloLens. After reading this book, you will be ready to surprise the world with apps that do what most people consider still to be science fiction.

What this book covers

Chapter 1, *Let's Begin!*, examines the device, and sees what it does and how it works. After that, we get our first taste of developing and creating our first simple holographic app.

Chapter 2, *Designing Your App*, is all about how to get the best workflow for writing a holographic app. We discuss design techniques and start working on RockOn, the app that is the basis for all chapters in the book.

Chapter 3, *Gestures and Events*, explains how to deal with gestures when controlling your apps. We talk about why gestures are important, and how we can get the events when the user performs those gestures, while reading these chapters. We also explain how to track hand movements and other input methods.

Chapter 4, *Make Some Noise - Sounds*, is the chapter where we dive into the sound capabilities of the Mixed Reality world. This chapter introduces HRTF and spatial sounds, and how we can create those in our own apps.

Chapter 5, *Be Heard - Voice Interactions*, is the place where we dive into voices. This chapter covers how to synthesize voices and how to interpret voice commands. It also covers making the device sound less robot like and, of course, adding voice commands to RockOn.

Chapter 6, *Take a Look around You - Spatial Mapping*, is where we define the differences between VR, AR, and MR. Here, we take a look at how the HoloLens is able to scan the world around us and how we can get that depth data into our own apps.

Chapter 7, *Let's Talk! Communications between Devices*, is the chapter where we investigate the options to have two or more devices talk to each other. We discuss networking and the discoverability of devices. We also discuss world anchors and why they matter.

Chapter 8, *Speed Up Your Development - Advanced Unity3D*, is the chapter where we teach you some advanced topics, such as performance improvements and ways to streamline your workflow in Unity. We also introduce the HoloToolkit, a set of open source components you can use in your own apps.

What you need for this book

In order to work with the code samples in this book, you need some software installed on your machine. You need to have a machine running Windows 10 Professional with Hyper-V enabled. Make sure Windows is set to Developer mode by going to **Settings** | **For developers** | **Developer Mode**.

Besides that, you will need the following:

- Unity3D Personal or Professional, version 5.5 or higher
- Visual Studio 2015 with Update 3 or higher; this can be downloaded automatically for you when you install Unity3D
- A HoloLens Emulator

You can find these tools and instructions on the official HoloLens site, which can be found at `https://developer.microsoft.com/en-us/windows/mixed-reality/install_the_tools`.

Who this book is for

If you are a developer who wants to create augmented reality apps for the Microsoft HoloLens platform, then this is the book for you. Coding experience with C# is assumed.

Conventions

In this book, you will find a number of text styles that distinguish between different kinds of information. Here are some examples of these styles and an explanation of their meaning.

Code words in text, database table names, folder names, filenames, file extensions, pathnames, dummy URLs, user input, and Twitter handles are shown as follows: "The numbers you see in `MinVersion` and `MaxVersionTested` may differ."

New terms and **important words** are shown in bold. Words that you see on the screen, for example, in menus or dialog boxes, appear in the text like this: "Here, you can switch the **Developer Mode** on."

A block of code is set as follows:

```
<Dependencies>
 <TargetDeviceFamily Name="Windows.Holographic" MinVersion="10.0.10240.0"
MaxVersionTested="10.0.10586.0" />
 </Dependencies>
```

 Warnings or important notes appear in a box like this.

 Tips and tricks appear like this.

Reader feedback

Feedback from our readers is always welcome. Let us know what you think about this book—what you liked or disliked. Reader feedback is important for us as it helps us develop titles that you will really get the most out of.

To send us general feedback, simply e-mail `feedback@packtpub.com`, and mention the book's title in the subject of your message.

If there is a topic that you have expertise in and you are interested in either writing or contributing to a book, see our author guide at `www.packtpub.com/authors`

Customer support

Now that you are the proud owner of a Packt book, we have a number of things to help you to get the most from your purchase.

Downloading the example code

You can download the example code files for this book from your account at `http://www.packtpub.com`. If you purchased this book elsewhere, you can visit `http://www.packtpub.com/support` and register to have the files e-mailed directly to you.

You can download the code files by following these steps:

1. Log in or register to our website using your e-mail address and password.
2. Hover the mouse pointer on the **SUPPORT** tab at the top.
3. Click on **Code Downloads & Errata**.
4. Enter the name of the book in the **Search** box.
5. Select the book for which you're looking to download the code files.
6. Choose from the drop-down menu where you purchased this book from.
7. Click on **Code Download**.

You can also download the code files by clicking on the **Code Files** button on the book's webpage at the Packt Publishing website. This page can be accessed by entering the book's name in the **Search** box. Please note that you need to be logged in to your Packt account.

Once the file is downloaded, please make sure that you unzip or extract the folder using the latest version of:

- WinRAR / 7-Zip for Windows
- Zipeg / iZip / UnRarX for Mac
- 7-Zip / PeaZip for Linux

The code bundle for the book is also hosted on GitHub at `https://github.com/PacktPublishing/Microsoft-HoloLens-Developers-Guide`. We also have other code bundles from our rich catalog of books and videos available at `https://github.com/PacktPublishing/`. Check them out!

Downloading the color images of this book

We also provide you with a PDF file that has color images of the screenshots/diagrams used in this book. The color images will help you better understand the changes in the output. You can download this file from `https://www.packtpub.com/sites/default/files/downloads/MicrosoftHoloLensDevelop ersGuide_ColorImages.pdf`.

Errata

Although we have taken every care to ensure the accuracy of our content, mistakes do happen. If you find a mistake in one of our books—maybe a mistake in the text or the code—we would be grateful if you could report this to us. By doing so, you can save other readers from frustration and help us improve subsequent versions of this book. If you find any Errata, please report them by visiting `http://www.packtpub.com/submit-Errata`, selecting your book, clicking on the Errata submission form link, and entering the details of your Errata. Once your Errata are verified, your submission will be accepted and the Errata will be uploaded to our website or added to any list of existing Errata under the Errata section of that title.

To view the previously submitted Errata, go to `https://www.packtpub.com/books/conten t/support`and enter the name of the book in the search field. The required information will appear under the Errata section.

Piracy

Piracy of copyrighted material on the internet is an ongoing problem across all media. At Packt, we take the protection of our copyright and licenses very seriously. If you come across any illegal copies of our works in any form on the internet, please provide us with the location address or website name immediately so that we can pursue a remedy.

Please contact us at `copyright@packtpub.com` with a link to the suspected pirated material.

We appreciate your help in protecting our authors and our ability to bring you valuable content.

Questions

If you have a problem with any aspect of this book, you can contact us at `questions@packtpub.com`, and we will do our best to address the problem.

1
Lets Begin!

Welcome to the HoloLens!

Welcome to the future. We have been waiting for a long, long time but it is finally here. The book you hold in your hands would not have been possible half a decade ago. Well, that is not quite true; it was possible, but it would have been placed in the science fiction area, but not anymore. The fact that you are reading this right now is proof that changes are taking place at a tremendous pace, and before you know it you will be in a place you never thought possible.

Take a look at the famous quote by Arthur C. Clarke:

Any sufficiently advanced technology is indistinguishable from magic.

This is true for HoloLens as well. Nobody was able to predict this device a decade ago, and now you have it within your reach.

However, no matter how cool the device itself is, it needs a bit of magic to come alive, and that piece of magic is the software that we are going to write. The software and the software your peers think of is going to be the lifeblood of the device. Without it, the device is just a nice looking piece of hardware. With it, the device is capable of changing the world view for a lot of people. That being said, it is also a lot of fun to write software for the device, so why not get started?

The device

Before we delve globally into the code, let's first examine what we are talking about. I assume you have the machine somewhere near. If you do not have access to one, I suggest that you try to get it. Although the software we are going to build will run on the emulator, you will find that the experience is below par. It just is not the same as developing your software on a real device. Of course, we will use the emulator quite extensively in real-world scenarios; a typical company will have a team of somewhere between 5 and 15 professionals working on the software. It would be rather expensive to buy a device for all of them. One device per team or maybe two devices per team would be enough to make sure that the software does what it should do and that the experience is as magical as it can be.

Let's examine the hardware for a bit. What are we talking about? What is a HoloLens? What parts does it consist of?

In case you have never seen a HoloLens before, this is what it looks like:

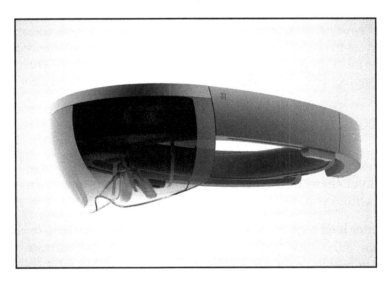

The device

A wearable computer

The HoloLens is a wearable computer. That is something that we have to keep in mind all the time when we write software--people will walk around with the device on their head, and we need to take that into account. It is not only wearable, it is also head mounted.

The device works without any cables attached to it, and the six built-in (non-replaceable unfortunately) batteries make sure that you can use it for 3-4 hours. They designed it like this because the device is meant to be worn on the head and be walked around with. I know, I just said that but this is so fundamentally different from what you are used to that I cannot stress this enough. If you have developed applications for mobile platforms, such as mobile phones or tablets, you might argue those are wearable as well. Well, technically they are, but those devices generally do not interact with their environment. They are location-agnostic. They might know where they are, but they do not really care, but the HoloLens does and so your software should care about the location as well.

The sensors

The HoloLens communicates with the environment and with its user using a whole lot of sensors and output devices. Let's go through them.

Cameras

How does the HoloLens know its location? If you look at the device and take a closer look at its front, you will see five tiny cameras. These are the eyes of the device; these are what make the device aware of its surroundings.

The camera you see in the middle is a normal, 2 megapixel RGB style camera, like the ones you will find in your mobile phone. The four cameras to the sides, two to the right and two to the left, are the environment cameras. They look at the area around you and are partially responsible to produce the knowledge the device needs to know what the room you are in looks like. I said partially, because there is another camera in the middle and front of the device. You cannot really see it since it is hidden behind the see-through visor. This camera is the IR camera. The device emits infrared light that is detected by this piece of hardware. By calculating the time it takes for the light to return, the HoloLens can measure depth and thus create a 3D image of your room. If you are familiar with Microsoft Kinect, you will recognize this; essentially, you will be wearing a tiny Kinect controller on your head. If you are not familiar with that amazing device, I suggest you look at `https://developer.micro soft.com/en-us/windows/kinect` for more information. It is worth getting to know the background of a lot of the principles described in this book.

Microphones

Next to vision-based input devices, there is also a microphone. Actually, there are four of these in a microphone array. This means that you can give the device spoken commands. The device itself listens to what you are saying, but we can also use this capability in our own software.

Holographic lenses

So, we have all the input parts. Now, we also need to get data out to the user. The most obvious part of this is the way the HoloLens displays the images. Since the HoloLens is a see-through device, meaning that it is transparent, the device only needs to provide you with the graphics the game or application needs to perform. This is done by the use of what Microsoft calls **Holographic lenses**. These two lenses are basically two tiny transparent computer screens in front of your eyes, where the device projects its images. Yes, I said transparent screens; these tiny computer screens are almost completely see-through. The resolution of the screens is 1268 x 720 pixels per eye, which seems low, but in reality is enough to generate good-looking graphics. Remember that the screens are tiny, so a lot more pixels will not make a lot of difference. In my experience, the graphics are just great and I noted that this low resolution was not a problem.

Spatial speakers

Next to the graphics part, there are also some speakers on the device. Microsoft calls them spatial sound speakers, meaning that they are capable of placing sounds in a three dimensional world. The speakers are quite obvious when you look at the device; they are the two red bars in the middle of the headband that will be just above your ears when you wear it. The effect is remarkably good--even with the use of just two tiny speakers, the sound quality is great, and you really feel the sound coming from a place in the room around you. Of course, this can be something we can use in our software. When we place items in our scene that we want the user to look at, we can have it make some noise and people will instinctively turn in the direction the sound is coming from, and this works even if we place the sounds behind the users. In practice, this works really well, and we will use this later on. The reason they decided to place the speakers in this location is that by putting them in front of your ears instead of on top of them, you will not be able to hear the actual real world around you anymore. This way, the virtual sounds blend in nicely with the real-world sounds.

Processors

All these input and output devices have to be connected to some sort of computer. With competing products in the virtual reality world, this is done by hooking up the device to some sort of an external computer. This could be a mobile phone, desktop, or laptop computer. Of course, with that last option, you lose the possibility of walking around, so the engineers at Microsoft have not gone down that route. Instead, they put all computing parts inside the device. You will find a complete Windows 10 computer and a special piece of hardware that Microsoft calls the **Holographic Processing Unit**, or **HPU** in short, inside the device. So, the computer consists of a CPU, a GPU, and an HPU, making it quite powerful.

The HPU is there for a reason--the computer itself is not that powerful. The machine basically is a 32-bit machine with 2GB of memory (the HPU has 1GB of its own), so the computing power is somewhat limited. If the CPU or the GPU would also have to do the processing of all the raw camera data it receives, it would be too slow to be practical. Having a more powerful general-purpose CPU will help of course, but that would mean the batteries will have to be bigger as well. Next, there would be a problem with heat--a faster computer generates more heat. At some point, it will need active cooling instead of the passive cooling the HoloLens currently has. By having a dedicated processing unit that decodes all the data before passing the results on to the rest of the device, Microsoft is able to have a relatively lightweight, but still fast machine, an impressive piece of engineering, if you ask me.

The power for all of this comes from three nonreplaceable batteries, located at the back of the device. The reason that they are in the back is so that they can act as a counter weight to all the hardware in front, thus delivering a nicely balanced device that is comfortable to wear. The batteries are good for 2-3 hours of usage, depending on the applications you run on it. Recharging is done by plugging a micro-USB cable attached into a power source in it, and takes about 4 hours to complete.

The device in a nutshell

There is a lot we know about the device. However, this is the state of the hardware as it is at the time of writing this book. This might change without notice. However, let me sum up the device for you anyway:

- **Computing power**:
    - A 32-bit Intel processor
    - 2 GB RAM
    - Microsoft Holographic Processing Unit

- **Sensors**:
    - Four environment-understanding cameras (two left and two right)
    - Depth camera (center front)
    - 2-megapixel photo or high-definition video camera (center front)
    - Four microphones
    - Ambient light sensor

- **Input and output**:

  - Two spatial sound speakers
  - An audio 3.5 mm jack for headphones
  - Volume up and down buttons
  - Brightness up and down buttons
  - A power button
  - Battery status LEDs (five in total, each representing 20% of the charge)
  - Wi-Fi 802.11ac
  - Bluetooth 4.1
  - Micro USB 2.0 (used for power and debugging)

- **Optics**:

  - Two see-through Holographic lenses
  - Two HD 16:9 light engines, running 1268 x 720 pixels each
  - Automatic pupillary distance calibration
  - Holographic Resolution, 2.3 million total light points
  - Holographic Density, more than 2,500 radiants

- **Miscellaneous**:

  - Weight: 579 grams
  - Storage: 64 GB flash memory

Displaying 3D images

Let's dive more deeply into the last three points in the optics part.

First is the **automatic pupillary distance calibration**. Let's be honest--no device except for a 3D printer can generate true 3D objects. It will always be a two-dimensional graphic, but presented in such a way that our brain gets tricked into seeing the missing third dimension. To achieve this, the device creates two slightly different images for each eye. We will get into that in later chapters, but for now let's just take this for granted. Our brain will see the difference between those two images and deduce the depth from that. However, the effect of this depends on one big factor--the images have to be exactly right. The position of each pixel has to be at exactly the right spot.

This means that we cannot just put a pixel in a X-Y coordinate on the display--a pixel that is meant to be in the middle of our view has to be presented right at the center of our pupils, and since no two eyes are the same, the device has to shift the logical center of the display a bit. In the early prototypes of the HoloLens, this was done manually by having a person look at a dot on the screen and then adjust the dials to make sure that the subject only sees on a single, sharp defined point. The automatic pupillary distance calibration in HoloLens now takes care of this, ensuring that every user has the same great experience.

The holographic resolution and density also need a bit more explaining. The idea here is that the actual number of pixels is not relevant. What is relevant is the number of radiants and light points. A light point is a single point of light that the user can see. This is a virtual point we perceive floating somewhere in mid-air. In reality, pixels are made out of these light points. There are many more light points than pixels. This makes sure that the device has enough power to produce pixels the person can actually see. *The higher the number of light points you have, the brighter and crisper each pixel seems. The radiant is the number of light points per radian.* As you probably know, a radian is a measure of angles, just like degrees. One radian is about 57.2958 degrees. Then, 2,500 radiants mean that for each radian, or 57.2958 degrees angles, we will have 2,500 light points. From this, you can deduce that objects closer by will have a better density of light points than objects far away.

Wearing the device

Wearing the device is something that needs some love and attention. The displays I mentioned earlier are actually pretty small. In practice, that is okay. Since they are so close to your eyes, you will not notice their size, but it does mean that a user has to position them fairly precisely in order to have a great experience. The best way to do this is to adjust the band so that is big enough to fit over your head. There is a cogwheel at the back of the head strap that you can turn to make the band wider or narrower. Place the band over your head and make sure that the front of the band is in the middle of your forehead. Then, turn the wheel to make it as tight as you can without making it uncomfortable. The reason that it has to be this tight is that the device--although it is nicely balanced, will shift around when you move about the room. When you move, the display will be unaligned and that can cause a narrower field of view and even can lead to nausea.

When you have balanced the device, you can move the actual visor about. It can move forward and backward to accommodate people wearing glasses and can also tilt up and down a bit. Make sure that your eyes are in the center of the screen, something that is easily done since you will notice images being cut off.

Turning the device on for the first time

Let's turn the device on--at the back, you will find the power button. Next to that are five LEDs that indicate whether the device is active and the state of the batteries. Each LED stands for 20% of the remaining power; so, assuming your device is fully charged, you will see five LEDs that are switched on. When you wear the device and press the power button, you will be greeted by a friendly "Hello", followed by either a "Scanning your environment" message or the start menu. The "Scanning your environment" message means that the device is looking at the environment. It will map all surfaces and will see if it recognizes them. If it does, it will load the known environment and use that, otherwise it will store a new one.

If this is the first time you have turned on the device, you have to personalize it. The steps necessary are simple, and the wizard will walk you through it, I will not go into that here. However, it is important to note that one step really should not be skipped--the network configuration. The device does not have a built-in GPS receiver and will rely on the network to identify the place it is in. It will store the meshes that make up the rooms and identify those with the network identifier. This way, it will know whether you are using it in your house or in your office, for instance. Next to that, applications, such as Cortana, need network connectivity to run, so the device can only really reliably be used in areas with a decent Wi-Fi reception.

One of the steps required is entering your Microsoft account. If you do not have one, I advise you to set one up before starting the device.

Learning the gestures

The usage of the device takes some getting used to. In the center of your view, you will see a tiny bright dot--this is your pointer. This dot will remain in the center of your view, so the only way to move it about is to move your head. A lot of first-time users of HoloLens will move their hands in front of the device as if they are trying to persuade the dot to move but that will not work. You need to look at something in order to interact with it.

There are two sorts of pointers in the default HoloLens world--one is the aforementioned dot, the other one is a circle. When the device sees your finger or hand in front of the sensors, it will let you know this and inform you that it is ready to receive commands--the dot will turn into this circle. Now, you can use one of the two default gestures. One is the air tap. Some people struggle with this one, but it is fairly straightforward.

You make a fist, point an index finger toward the sky and then move that finger forward without bending it, all the time leaving the rest of your hand where it is; that is it, tapping with a finger. Ensure that you don't bend the finger, do not move the whole hand, do not turn the hand, or just use one finger. It does not really matter if you use your right or left hand; the device will pick it up.

Next to the air tap gesture, we have the bloom gesture. Although this is slightly more complicated, people seem to have fewer issues with this one. Start with a closed fist in front of the device, palm upward. Next, open your hands and spread your fingers wide--just imagine your hand is a flower opening up.

This gesture is used to go back to the Start menu or the main starting point of an application.

That is it! There are no more gestures. Well, there is the tap-and-hold gesture (move your finger down and keep it there while moving your hand up and down, right and left or back and forth to move stuff about) but that is just a variation of the airtap.

Calibrating the device

The first time someone puts on the device, it should be calibrated. Calibration means that the screens need to be aligned to the center of the wearer's pupils. Obviously, each person has a different number for this; this number is called the **interpupillary distance** (**IPD**). Mine, for instance, is 66.831 millimeters, meaning that my pupils are almost 67 millimeters apart. This is important since this determines how effective the three dimensional effect is. A lot of people skip this step or do it only once for the initial user, but that is a big mistake. If this number is not correctly set, you will have a slightly offset image that just *doesn't feel right*.

The calibration is done with the calibration tool, one of the applications preinstalled on the device. This application will guide you through the process. The tool first shows a blue rectangle and asks whether you can see all corners. Ensure that the rectangle is in the center of your view by adjusting the device on your head. If you got it right, you can say the word next to move to the next stage. Yes, this is voice controlled, which makes sense--the device is still calibrating your vision, so it cannot rely on airtaps. The next phase consists of showing you outlines of a finger in a circle; you are supposed to place your finger in that outline. You have to do this five times for each eye, with the other eye closed. This process should not take very long, but it is extremely important that you do this for every new user.

The resulting IPD number is not visible in the device, but can be read out in the device portal. The number is unique for the combination of this user for this device--you cannot use that number for the same user on another device. I suggest that you write down that number for users who will be using the device more than once. That way, you can enter it in the device portal without having to go through the calibration process every time.

One word of warning--the device is not meant to be used by children under the age of 13 years. The reason for this is that their eyes tend to be rather close to each other and thus need IPD values too small to work. There are limits to what this number can be, although Microsoft has not yet disclosed these numbers. Having a wrong IPD could result in motion sickness during its use, so it is recommended that you have this set right and prevent children from playing with the device.

The device portal

Let's take a look at the device portal. Each HoloLens has a built-in web server that serves up pages that tell you things about your device and the state it is in. This can be very useful, as the device itself will give almost no information beside the fact that the network it is connected to, the volume of the sound, and the battery level. The portal gives a lot more information that can be very useful. Besides that, the portal also gives a way to see what the user is seeing, through something called **Mixed Reality Capture**; we will talk more on that later.

Overview of the portal

In the HoloLens device portal main screen, you can see the main screen of the device portal. There is quite a lot of information here that will tell you all sorts of things you need to know about the device. However, the first question is, How do we get here?

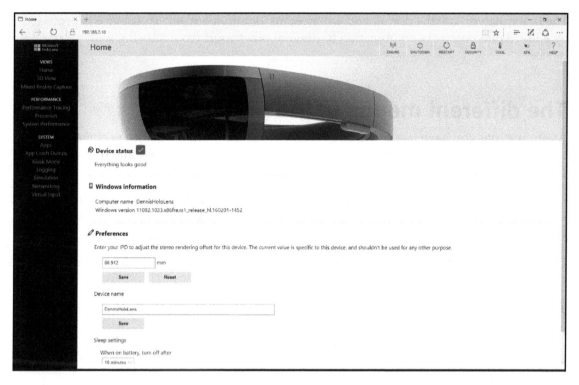

The HoloLens device portal main screen

The device portal is switched off by default. You have to explicitly enable this option by going to the settings screen; once there, select the **Update** option and you have the option to choose the **For Developers** page. Here, you can switch the **Developer Mode** on, which is a necessity if you want to deploy apps from your development environment to the device. You can pair devices; again, you need this to deploy apps and debug them, and you enable or disable the device portal.

If you set up your device correctly and have it hooked up to a network, you can retrieve the IP address of the device by going to the settings screen, selecting **Network**, and then selecting the **Advanced settings** option. Here, you will see all network settings, including the IP address the device currently uses.

When you enter that IP address in a browser, you will be greeted with a security warning that the certificate that the device uses is not trusted by default. This is something we will fix later on.

The first time you use the portal, you will need to identify yourself. The device is protected by a username/password combination to prevent other users from messing with your device.

The different menus in the portal

Assuming that you have taken care of all this, you can now see the device portal main screen, just like the one I showed you before. The screen can be divided into three distinct parts.

At the top, you will see a menu bar that tells you things about the device itself, such as the level of the batteries, the temperature the device is running at (in terms of cool, warm, and hot), and the option to shut down or reboot the device.

On the left-hand side, there is a menu where you choose the different options you want to do or control.

The menu is divided into three submenus:

- Views
- Performance
- System

The Views menu in the portal

The Views menu deals with the general information screen and the things your device actually sees. The other two, Performance and System, contain detailed information about the inner workings of the device and the applications running on it. We will have a thorough look at those when we get to debugging applications in later chapters, so for now I will just say that they exist.

The options are as follows:

- Home
- 3D View
- Mixed reality capture

By default, you will get the home screen. At the center of the screen, you will see information about the device. Here, you can see the following items:

- **Device status**: This is indicated by a green checkmark if everything is okay or a red cross if things are not okay. The next point confirms it.
- **Windows information**: This indicates the name of the device and the version of the software it runs.

- **The preferences part**: Here, you can see or set the IPD we talked about earlier. If you have written down other people's IPD, you can enter them here and then click on **Save** to store it on the device. This saves you from running the calibration tool over and over again. You can also change the name of the device here and set its power behavior: for example, when do you want the device to turn itself off?

The 3D view gives you a sense of what the depth sensor and the environment sensors are seeing:

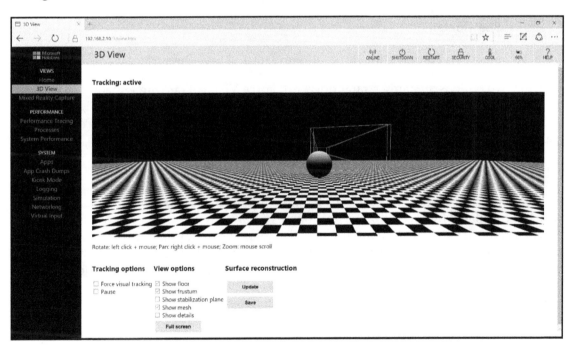

The 3D view

There are several checkboxes you can check and uncheck to determine how much information is shown. In the preceding screenshot, you can see an example in **3D View**, with the default options checked.

The sphere you see represents the user's head and the yellow lines are the field of view of the device. In other words, the preceding screenshot is what the user will see projected on the display, minus the real world that the user will see at all times.

You have the following checkboxes available to fine-tune the view:

- **Tracking options**
- **Force visual tracking**
- **Pause**
- **View options**
- **Show floor**
- **Show frustum**
- **Show stabilization plane**
- **Show mesh**
- **Show details**

Next, you have two buttons allowing you to update and save the surface reconstruction.

The first two options are fairly straightforward; **Force Visual Tracking** will force the screen and the device to continuously update the screens and data. If this is unchecked, the device will optimize its data streams and only update if there is something changing. Pause, of course, completely pauses capturing the data.

The View options are a bit more interesting. The **Show floor** and **Show frustum** options enable and disable the checkerboard floor and the yellow lines indicating the views, respectively. The stabilization plane is a lot more interesting. This plane is a stabilized area, which is calculated by averaging the last couple of frames the sensors have received. Using this plane, the device can even out tiny miscalculations by the system. Remember that the device only knows about its environment by looking through the cameras, so there might be some errors. This plane, located two meters from the device in the virtual world, is the best place to put static items, such as menus. Studies have shown that this is the place where people feel the most comfortable looking at items. This is the "Goldilocks zone," not too far, not too close but just right.

If you check the **Show mesh** checkbox, you can see what the devices see. The device scans the environment in infrared. Thus, it cannot see actual colors. The infrared beam measures distances. The grayscale mesh is simply a way to visualize the infrared information.

The depth image from the device

As you can see in the screenshot, I am currently writing this sitting on the right most chair at a table with five more chairs. The red plane you see is the stabilization plane, just in front of the wall I am facing. The funny shape in front of the sphere you see is actually my head--I moved the device in my hands to scan the area instead of putting it on my head, so it mistakenly added me as part of the surroundings.

The picture looks messy, but that is the way the device sees the world. With this information, the HoloLens *knows* where the table top surface is, where the floor is, and so on.

You can use the **Save** button to save the current scene and use that in the emulator or in other packages. This is a great way for developers to use an existing environment, such as their office, in the emulator. The Update button is there because, although the device constantly updates its view of the world, the portal page does not. Sometimes, it misses updates because of the high amount of data that is being sent, and thus you might have to manually update the view. Again, this is only for the portal page--the device keeps updating all the time, around five times per second.

The last checkbox is **Show details**. When this is selected, you will get additional information from the device with regards to the hands it sees, the rotation of the device, and the location of the device in the real world. By location, I am not talking about the GPS location; remember that the device does not have a GPS sensor, but I am talking about the amount of movement in three dimensions since the tracking started.

By turning this option on, we can learn several things. First, it can identify two hands at the same time. It can also locate each hand in the space in front of the device. We can utilize this later when we want to interact with it.

The data we get back looks like this:

Details

Hands

ID	X	Y	Z	ISPRESSED
895	-0.191912	0.096869	-0.252249	false
670	0.134939	-0.098979	-0.483796	false

Head Rotation Quaternion

CONST	I	J	K
0.991173	0.112653	0.004208	-0.069765

Origin Translation Vector

X	Y	Z
-0.030576	0.002437	-0.212598

Detailed data from the device

In the preceding table, we have information about the hands, the head rotation, and the origin translation vector.

Each hand that is being tracked gets a unique ID. We can use this to identify when the hand does something, but we have to be careful when using this ID. As soon as the hand is out of view for a second and it returns just a moment later, it will be assigned a new ID. We cannot be sure that this is the same hand--maybe someone else standing beside the user is playing tricks with us and puts their hand in front of the screen.

The coordinates are in meters. The X is the horizontal position of the center of the hand, the Y is the vertical position. The Z indicates how far we have extended our hand in front of us. This number is always negative--the lower is it, the further away the hand is. These numbers are relative to the center of the front of the device.

The head rotation gives us a clue as to how the head is tilted in any direction. This is expressed in a quaternion, a term we will see much more in later chapters. For now, you can think of this as a way to express angles.

Last in this part of the screen is the **Origin Translation Vector**. This gives us a clue as to where the device is compared to its starting position. Again, this is in meters and X still stands for horizontal movement, Y for vertical, and Z for movement back and forth.

The last screen in the Views part is the **Mixed Reality Capture**. This is where you can see the combined output from both the RGB camera in front of the device and the generated images displayed on the screens. In other words, this is where we can see what the user sees. Not only can we see but we can also hear what the user is hearing. We have options to turn on the sounds the user gets as well as relay what the microphones are picking up.

This can be done in three different quality levels--high, medium, and low.

The following table shows the different settings for the mixed capture quality:

Setting	Vertical Lines	Frames per second	Bits per second
High	720	30	5 Mbits
Medium	480	30	2.5 MBits
Low	240	15	0.6

Several users have noticed that the live streaming is not really live--most users have experienced a delay, ranging from two to six seconds. So be prepared when you want to use this in a presentation where you want to show the audience what you, as the wearer, see.

If you want to switch the quality levels, you have to stop the preview. It will not change the quality midstream.

Besides watching, you can also record a video of the stream or take a snapshot picture of it.

Below the live preview, you can see the contents of the video and photo storage on the device itself--any pictures you take with the device and any video you shoot with the device will show up here, so you can see them, download them to your computer, or delete them.

Now that you have your device set up and know how to operate it and see the details of the device as a developer, it is time to have a look at the preinstalled software.

The HoloLens Start screen

When the device is first used, you will see it comes with a bunch of apps preinstalled. On the device, you will find the following apps:

- **Calibration**: We have talked about this before; this is the tool that measures the distance between the pupils
- **Learn gestures**: This is an interactive introduction to using the device that takes you through several steps to learn all the gestures you can use
- **Microsoft Edge**: The browser you can use to browse the web, see movies, and so on
- **Feedback**: A tool to send feedback to the team

- **Setting**: We have seen this one before as well
- **Photos**: This is a way to see your photos and videos; this uses your OneDrive
- **Store**: The application store where you can find other applications and where your own applications, when finished, will show up
- **Holograms**: A demo application that allows you to place holograms anywhere in your room, look at them from different angles, and also scale and rotate them. Some of them are animated and have sounds
- **Cortana**: Since the HoloLens runs Windows 10, Cortana is available; you can use Cortana from most apps by saying "Hello Cortana"; this is a nice way to avoid using gestures when, for instance, you want to start an app.

I suggest you play around a bit. Start with **Learn Gestures** after you have set up the device and used the **Calibration** tool. After that, use the Hologram application to place holograms all around you. Walk around the holograms and see how steady they are. Note the effect of a 3D environment--when you look at things from different sides, they really come to life. Other 3D display technologies, such as 3D monitors and movies, do not allow this kind of freedom, and you will notice how strong this effect is.

Can you imagine what it would be like to write this kind of software yourself? Well, that is just what we are about to do.

Writing your first holographic application

It is about time we start writing some code. I will show you the different options you have when you want to write software for the HoloLens and give you some helpful pointers for setting up an ideal development environment for these kinds of projects.

The tools we need to write software

First of all, you will need Windows 10. The version you use does not matter if you have a device; however, when you want to use the emulator, you need to have the professional edition of Windows 10. The home edition does not support Hyper-V, the virtualization software that the emulator uses to run a virtual version of the HoloLens software.

Next, you need a development environment. This is Visual Studio 2015 Update 2 at least. You can use the free community edition, the most expensive and compete enterprise edition, or any version in between--the code will work just fine no matter what version you use.

When you install Visual Studio, make sure that you have the **Universal Windows Platform (UWP)** tools (at least version 1.3.1) and the Windows 10 SDK (at least version (10.0.10586) installed. If you want to use the emulator, and trust me, you do want this, you have to download that as well. Again, in this case, you need to have Hyper-V on your machine and have it enabled.

Your very first application

I assume that you have your environment set up and you have Visual Studio running. Let's start with our first program. Just follow along:

1. Choose **File** | **New** | **Project**. In the templates, select **Visual C#** | **Windows** | **Universal** | **Holographic** | **Holographic DirectX 11 App (Universal Windows)**:

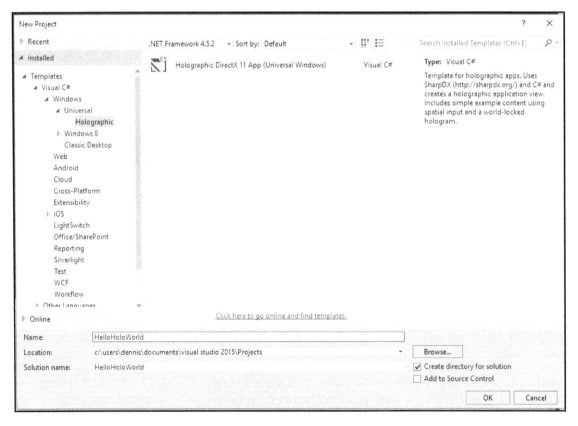

New Project wizard in Visual Studio

2. After this, you will get a version selector. The versions displayed depend on the SDKs you have installed on your machine. For now, you can just accept the defaults, as long as you make sure that the target version is at least build 10586.

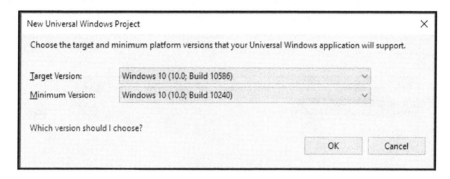

SDK version selector

3. Name the project and the solution `HelloHoloWorld`.

That's it! Congratulations! You have just created your very first HoloLens application. Granted that it is not very spectacular, but it does what it needs to do.

 As a side note, I will use the term "app" from now on to distinguish mobile or holographic applications from-full-blown applications that run on desktop computers. The latter are usually called "applications", whereas the former, usually smaller items, are called apps.

Deploying your first app to the emulator

To make sure that everything works fine, we will first see if we can deploy the app to the HoloLens emulator. If you have decided not to install this and choose to use a physical device instead, please skip to the next part.

In the menu bar, you can choose the environment you want to run the app on. You might be familiar with this, but if you are not, this is where you specify where the app will be deployed. You have several options, such as the local machine and a remote machine. Those two are the most used in normal development, such as if you are writing a universal Windows platform application or a website, but that will not work for us. We need to deploy the app to a Holographic capable device such as the emulator. If you have installed that, it will show up here in the menu, as follows:

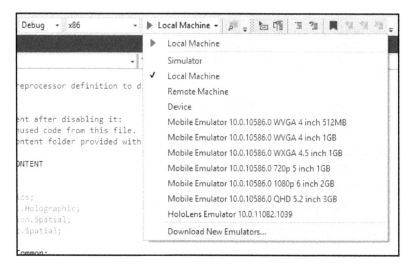

The deployment options

The version of the emulator might be different on your system--Microsoft continuously updates its software, so you might have a newer version. The one shown here is the latest one that was available during the writing of this book.

Now that you have selected this, you can select Run (through the green arrow, pressing *F5*, or through the **Debug | Start Debugging** menu). If you do that the emulator will start up. This might take some time. After all, it is starting up a new machine in the Hyper-V environment, loading Windows 10, and deploying your app.

However, after a couple of minutes, you will be greeted with the following view:

Our first HoloLens app in the emulator!

You will see a rotating multicolored cube on a black background.

How to use the emulator

Before we can dive into the code, it would be worthwhile to learn to use the emulator a bit. Obviously, you cannot use the gestures we have talked about before--it will not see what you are doing and you have to emulate these. Fortunately, it is not too hard to get used to the controls. You can use the mouse or the keyboard, or you can attach an Xbox controller to your machine and use that as well. We will cover the main controls; the more advanced options will be discussed when we need them in later chapters.

The following table shows the Keyboard, mouse, and Xbox controls in the emulator:

Desired gesture	Keyboard and mouse	Xbox controller
Walk forward, back, left, and right	*W, S, A*, and *D*	Left stick
Look up, down, left, and right	Click and drag the mouse; use arrow keys on the keyboard.	Right stick
Air tap	Right-click on the mouse. Press *Enter* on the keyboard	A button
Bloom gesture	Windows key of *F2*	B button
Hand movement for scrolling, resizing, and zooming	Press *Alt* key + right mouse button, then move the mouse.	Hold right trigger and A button, then move the right stick

In the center of your view, you will see a dot; this is the cursor. Do not try to move this dot-- this will always be in that spot. Move the emulator with the walk and look options to position the dot on the menu item you want to choose, then perform the air tap with the options mentioned above. This takes some practice, so try it out for a little while; it will be worth the effort.

When you are using the emulator, you will note that *Alt + Tab* does not get you back. This does make sense since you are working in a separate computer and *Alt + Tab* does not work on HoloLens. You really have to click somewhere out of the emulator screen to redirect the input back to your own computer.

Deploying the app to the device

Using the emulator can be a great tool in your toolbox, especially when you are working in a team; having a device for each developer is usually not an option. The devices are pretty expensive, and you don't need one to develop your app. Of course, when you are working on a project, it is invaluable to deploy to the device every now and then and see how your code behaves in the real world. After all, you can only experience the true power of the HoloLens by putting it on.

So, we need to deploy the code to the device. First of all, you need to make sure that you have the **Developer Mode** switched on. You can do this by going to the Settings app and selecting the *For Developers* option in the **Update** part. There, you can switch the Developer mode on.

Once you have done this, you can start the deployment from Visual Studio to the device. To do this, you have two options:

- **Use Wi-Fi deployment**
- **Use USB deployment**

Since you already have set up the device to use the network, you can use the option. This one tends to be slightly slower than using the USB deployment, but it has the advantage that you can do this without having a wire attached to the device. Trust me--this has some advantages. I have done a deployment through USB only to discover I could not immediately stand up and walk around my holograms--I forgot the cable was still attached to the device.

Deploying through Wi-Fi

If you chose the Wi-Fi deployment option, you can choose **Remote** as your deployment target. If you do this the first time, you will get a menu where you can pick the device out of a list of available devices. The autodiscovery method does not always work--every now and then, you need to enter the IP address manually.

You can find this IP address in the **Settings** | **Network & Internet** | **Advanced Options** menu on the device. This is the same IP address you use to launch the device portal.

The Remote Connections dialog

Make sure that you have the **Authentication Mode** set to **Universal**, otherwise your device will not accept the connection.

You need to take an additional step to deploy--your device needs to pair with your computer. This way you can be sure that no other people connect to it without you knowing it. If you start the debugger using the **Remote Machine** option or try to deploy to the Remote Machine, you will get a dialog box asking you for a PIN.

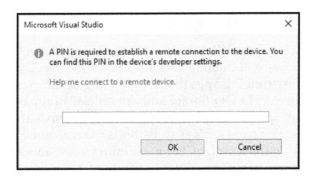

Visual Studio asking for the PIN to pair

This pin can be obtained in the device by navigating to the Settings app, then to **Update,** and then selecting *For Developers.* Here, you can pair the device. If you select this, you will get a PIN globally for each machine you want to connect. Enter this pin in the dialog and you are all set to go--the device should receive your app now. If you choose Deploy in Visual Studio, the app will show up in your list on the device. You can find it by starting the Start screen with the Bloom gesture, then select the + on the right-hand side of the menu. There, you will find the list with all the installed apps, including your new `HelloHoloWorld` project. Air-tap this to start it. If you are done with it, you can do the Bloom again to go back to the main menu.

 If you happen to forget the pin, do not worry. All you have to do is enter a wrong number three times in a row. After that, the device will ask you to reconnect once again from scratch, enabling you to think of a new pin.

If you choose Debug, the app will start automatically--you do not have to select it in the device.

Deploying through USB

Since the device has a USB port, we can connect it to the computer. Unfortunately, it does not show up in the explorer--we cannot access the filesystem, for instance. However, we can use this to deploy our app to the device. All you have to do in Visual Studio is select as target Device and it will deploy it through the USB cable. As I said before, this is slightly faster than using the Wi-Fi connection, but it gives you fewer options to walk around during debugging.

Let's have a look at the code

The code you just wrote is a C#, UWP Windows 10 app using DirectX through the SharpDX library. In later chapters, we will examine this much more closely. DirectX is the technology that allows us to write fast-running apps that use a lot of graphics, such as the holograms we create. However, DirectX is a C++ library and can officially only be used in C++ programs. Luckily, the people at SharpDX have written a wrapper around this, so we can use this in our C# applications and apps as well, this is the reason why the HoloLens SDK developers included this in the template. For more information about SharpDX, I suggest that you have a look at their site at `http://sharpdx.org/`.

The app uses some libraries from the Windows SDK. However, if you look closely at the References part in the solution, you will note that there are no *Holographic*-specific libraries included. The reason for this is that the APIs needed to run Holographic apps are standard in the Windows 10 runtime. That is right; your Windows 10 computer has all the code it needs to run Holographic apps. Unfortunately, the hardware you have will not support these APIs, so they are not available to use. If you try to deploy this app to a normal machine, you will get errors--the required capabilities are not available and the runtime will refuse to install the app.

This means that our app is a standard Windows 10 UWP app with some extra capabilities added. If you right-click on the `Package.appxmanifest`, you will find the following tag somewhere:

```
<Dependencies>
    <TargetDeviceFamily Name="Windows.Holographic"
MinVersion="10.0.10240.0" MaxVersionTested="10.0.10586.0" />
  </Dependencies>
```

This is what makes sure that our device accepts our app and other systems do not--the app is marked for usage in Windows. holographic-capable device. The numbers you see in `MinVersion` and `MaxVersionTested` may differ--these depend on the SDK versions that you have installed and chose when you created the project.

The structure of the project

If you have written UWP apps before, you will see that the structure of this app is quite different. This is mostly because of the code SharpDX needs to start up. After all, a Holographic app needs a different kind of user interface than a normal screen-based app. There is no notion of a screen, no place to put controls, labels, or textboxes, and no real canvas. Everything we do needs to be done in a 3D world. An exception to this is when we create 2D apps that we want to deploy to the 3D environment. Examples of this are the Edge Browser and the now familiar Settings app. Those are standard UWP apps running on HoloLens. We will see how to build this later on.

The project should look like this:

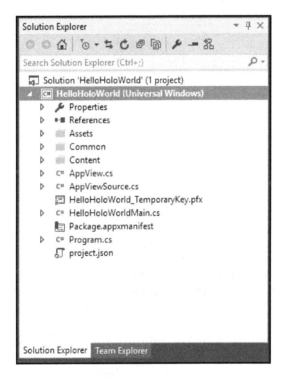

The project structure

As you can see, we have the normal Properties and References parts. Next, we have the expected `Program.cs` and `Assets` folder. That folder contains our logos, start screen, and other assets we usually see with UWP apps. `Program.cs` is the starting point of the app. We also can identify the `HelloHoloWorld_TemporaryKey.pfx`. The app needs to be signed in order to run on the device, and this is the key that does this. You cannot use this key to deploy to the store, but since we have set our device in developer mode, it will accept our app with a test key such as this one. `Package.appxmanifest` we have already looked at.

The other files and folder might not be that familiar.

The Common folder contains a set of helper classes that help us use SharpDX. It has some camera helpers that act as viewport to the 3D world, timers that help us with the animation of the spinning cube, and so on.

The Content folder has the code needed to draw our spinning cube. This has the shaders and renderers that SharpDX needs to draw the cube we see when we start the app. We will have a closer look at how this works in later chapters.

Inside the AppView class

The `AppViewSource.cs` and `AppView.cs` files contain the `AppViewSource` and `AppView` classes, respectively. These are the boilerplate code files that launch our scene in the app. `AppViewSource` is used in Program.cs, and all it does is start a new `AppView`. `AppView` is where most of the Holographic magic happens.

The following are the five different things this `AppView` class does:

- **Housekeeping**: The constructor and the `Dispose()` method live here. The code needs to be IDisposable since most DirectX-based code is unmanaged. This means we need to clean things up when needed.

- **IFrameworkView members**: IFrameworkView is the interface DirectX uses to draw its contents to. This contains the methods to load resources, run the view, and set a window that receives the graphics, and so on.

- **Application Lifecycle event handlers**: If you have developed Store apps before, you will recognize these; this is where we handle suspension, reactivating, and other lifecycle events.

- **Window event handlers**: Next to the lifecycle events, there are some other events that can occur during runtime: `OnVisibilityChanged` and `OnWindowClosed` can happen. This is where they are handled.

- **Input event handler**: I mentioned before that you can hook up a Bluetooth keyboard to the device. If you do that, the user can press keys on that keyboard and you need to handle those. This is where that part is done. I would recommend against using this in normal scenarios. People walking around with a HoloLens will not normally carry a keyboard with them. However, in certain use cases, this might be desirable.

In the `IFrameworkView.Initialize` method, the app creates a new instance of the `HelloHoloWorldMain` class. This class is where our custom code is placed, so basically this is our entry point. The rest can be considered as boilerplate code, stuff the app needs to do anything at all.

In the following chapters, we will adapt this class heavily, but for now I want to show you another way to create HoloLens apps that will give you much nicer results much more easily. We will start to use Unity3D.

Using Unity3D to create great holographic apps

Microsoft says the best way to build HoloLens apps is to use Unity3D. Unity3D, or Unity as some people call it, is a cross-platform game engine. This application was first used to create OS X applications in 2005, but has grown to support more than 15 platforms at the moment. Since one of those platforms is Direct3D on Windows, this was an obvious choice for the HoloLens team as the way to build 3D worlds.

Next to being a game engine, it also is a development environment for this engine, making it a great tool with which to create HoloLens apps. Unity3D natively supports HoloLens as a platform, so you do not need to install plugins.

Unity is not free. However, the Unity Personal license is all you need if you want to develop HoloLens apps and is free if you fulfill the requirements. I suggest that you go to their website to look up the exact license agreement, but basically it says that if the company using Unity has less than $100,000 in annual gross revenue, you are free to use the tool.

If you are unfamiliar with Unity I can reassure you that there is nothing magical about it and the tool is not that hard to learn. In this and in the following chapters, I will show you all you need to know to work with it.

When you install Unity from their website, you also need to install the Unity plugin for Visual Studio. There is a very good reason for this. Unity allows you to deploy to all their platforms from within the Unity editor itself, with one notable exception--the HoloLens. The final compile and build and the deployment still need to be done through Visual Studio.

Next to the Build and Deploy scenarios, we will also need Visual Studio to write scripts. Although you can use MonoDevelop, a free independent development tool based on the Mono framework, I still recommend using Visual Studio. You need Visual Studio anyway, so why not take advantage of the power of this IDE?

One word of warning--you should make sure that you have enough memory in your machine to have two instances of Visual Studio running at the same time. You will use one instance to edit your scripts, and the other to do the building and deploying of the UWP application.

Scripts in Unity are pieces of code that enhance or change the behavior of objects or add new behavior to them. Unity itself is more a 3D design environment and leaves the writing of the scripts to other tools. So you will find yourself switching between the Unity editor and the Visual Studio editor quite a lot.

Our first HoloApp in Unity3D

When you have all the tools installed, it is time to start up Unity. Immediately, you will notice a big difference between Unity projects and Visual Studio projects. The latter has solution files and project files that determine what goes together to create a project. Unity, however, uses a folder to determine what a project is.

When you start up Unity, you will be greeted by a screen that gives you the option to open a previous project or to create a new one. When you select **New Project**, you will get this:

The Unity new project screen

Unity wants you to give the project a name, a folder where the files will be stored, and an organization to which the license is assigned.

We can choose to have a 3D or 2D application, which we will leave to the default 3D option. The **Add Asset Package** gives you the option to add additional packages, but we will not use that here for now. The **Analytics** option is quite handy to debug your app.

Press **Create project** to have Unity create the necessary folders and files for you.

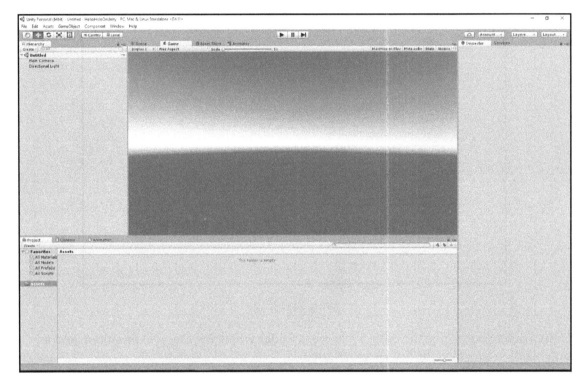

The default Unity screen

The screen we see is what the game looks like. For now, this is an empty screen with some sort of ground and sky above it. In the left-most panel, you see the objects currently available. Unity maintains a hierarchy of objects, and this is where you can see them. In the lower part of the screen, you see the Assets we have in our project. Currently, we do not have any assets, so this is empty, but we will later add some.

The two items we do have are a camera and a light source. The light is important--without light there is nothing to see in our virtual world. The camera is usually the way we look at the scene, but in the HoloLens this works slightly different--we need two cameras. One for each eye, remember? Fortunately, the tool takes care of this for us, so we do not need to worry about it.

Fixing the camera

We need to fix the camera a bit though. Remember when we started up the emulator and everything was black? The reason for this is that anything that is rendered black in the device is going to be transparent. The reason for this is quite straightforward--the device adds light points to the real world and black would mean it removes light points from the real world. This is unfortunately physically impossible. So anything that is black will not get any light point and is, therefore, transparent. We need to change this here as well. Select the **Main Camera** in the left side and see how the properties appear on the right-hand side in the inspector . This is where we can make changes to our assets, in this case, our camera.

Changing the position

First, we need to change the position. The default camera is placed at the coordinates {0, 1, -10}. In HoloLens, however, we are the camera. We are at the center of what is going on, so we need to change these to camera coordinates to {0,0,0}. You enter these values manually or you can click the cogwheel in the top-right corner and click on **Reset**. This will reset all values to the default which in our case is {0,0,0}.

Changing the background color

Another thing we need to change is the color of the virtual world. We do this by changing **Clear flags**. This is the color that is being used when no pixels need to be drawn for our scene. In a game, it would be nice to have a default background such as the one we see now, but in HoloLens, we want the default to be transparent and thus black.

Change Clear Flags from **Skybox** to **Solid color** and change the background color underneath this to black (RGB--0,0,0).

Every now and then, Unity might show Skybox again when we select other objects, but this is something we can ignore.

The camera itself has a "**MainCamera**" tag. This means that the SDK will take this camera and use it as the point of view. You can have multiple cameras in a scene, but only one camera can be the main camera. By default, this tag is already assigned, so we do not need to change anything here.

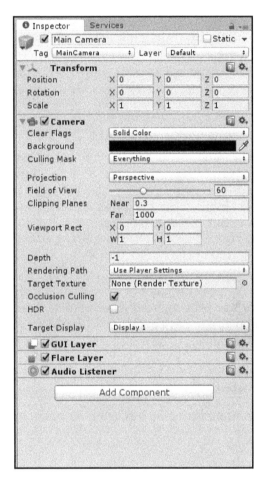

The properties of the main camera

Adding holographic objects

Our scene looks quite dull. We have nothing in our world besides a black background. So let's add something a bit more interesting to our world.

We will add a sphere in our world. To do this, take the following steps:

1. Make sure that the camera is not selected anymore--click anywhere in the hierarchy panel and verify that the inspector window is empty.
2. Click on the **Create** button at the top of the hierarchy window.
3. Select **Sphere**. You will note that the sphere is added to the hierarchy, although it is not visible. The reason for this is that, in order to make the whole system performant, the insides of our 3D objects are not rendered. Since the sphere is placed at location {0,0,0}, the camera is inside the sphere and we cannot see it.
4. Move the sphere by selecting it in the hierarchy panel and change its location in the inspector window. Move it about three meters away from the user and move it half a meter below the head of the user. Since the HoloLens is located at {0,0,0}, this means we have to place the sphere at {0,-0.5, 3}.
5. Scale the sphere (a sphere with a diameter of 1 meter is quite large) and make it 25 centimeters.

You will end up with something like this:

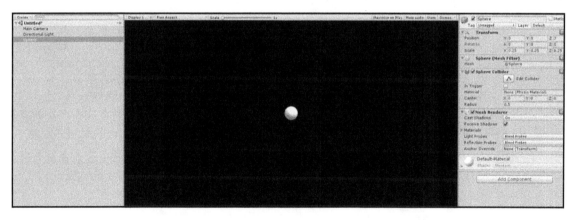

Our scene with the newly added sphere

Create a sample script

Like I have said before, scripting, an important part of Unity projects, is done in C#. I want to add an empty script here, just to show you how its done and what happens if you do so.

In the pane at the bottom, named Assets, right click and create a new folder named Scripts. Although this is not required, it is always a good idea to organize your project in logical folders. This way you can always find your components when you need them. Double-click on that folder to open it and see its contents. It should be empty. Right-click again and select **Create** -> C# Script. Name it PointerHelper. Unity will add the .cs extension to the file, so you should not do that.

Once you have added this empty script, take a look at the inspector pane on the right side. You will see it is not empty at all--the script contains a class named `PointerHelper`, derived from MonoBehaviour with two methods in it--Start and Update.

We will dive into this later on, but for now I will tell you that this is common with most scripts. The `Start()` method is called when the script is first loaded, and the `Update()` method is called each frame. We will discuss frames later on.

When you have created this script, we need to attach it to an object or an asset in our project. This particular script will later on allow us to create an object that shows the user where they are looking. Therefore, it makes sense to attach it to the camera. To do this, drag the script upward to the hierarchy pane and hover right above Main Camera. If you do this right, you will see that the Camera is selected in a light blue color. If it is a darker shade of blue, you will also see a line underneath the Camera object, stating that this script will be a child item of Camera instead of being a part of it. It needs to be a part of it, not a child.

You can always check whether you attached it correctly by selecting the camera and looking at the inspector pane. At the bottom of that pane, you will see the PointerHelper (Script) component being added to the cameras properties.

We will come back to this script later on.

Building the project

Of course, before building your project, it is a good idea to save it. If you click on Save or use the *Ctrl+S* key combination, Unity will ask you to save your scene. A scene is a collection of objects laid out in a 3D world. In our case, this is the collection containing the light source, the camera, and our sphere. Just give your scene a name, I used main and placed that in the subfolder Scenes under Assets (which is the default).

When you have saved your project, we can start to build the code. However, before we do that, we have to tell Unity that we are working on a Windows Holographic application. To do that, do the following:

1. Go the **File | Build** Settings or press *Ctrl + Shift + B*.
2. In the dialog you see now, press the **Add open scenes** button. This makes sure that our current scene is part of the package.
3. In the platform selection box, we can choose for which platform we would like to build our app. As you can see, there is quite a large choice of platforms, but we will choose **Windows Store** and then click on the **Switch Platform** button. You can tell we now have this platform as the default by the appearance of the Unity logo behind the **Windows Store** option.
4. On the right-hand side, we can set specific Windows Store options.
5. SDK: Windows 10.
6. UWP Build Type: D3D (meaning DirectX 3D).
7. Build and Run does not matter here; we can leave that.
8. Check Unity C# Projects.
9. Check Development Build.

Unity Build Settings for HoloLens

10. Now, before we press **Build**, we need to do one more thing--click on the **Player Settings...** button. This is where you set the properties for the Unity Player, thus the application that loads the scenes and performs the animations, interactions, and so on. We, however, do not use the Unity Player but use our own. Still, we need to set one very important property:

11. Click on **Player Settings**, and see that the Inspector changes.

12. Click on **Other Settings**.

13. Check **Virtual Reality Supported** and verify that the Virtual Reality SDK contains **Windows Holographic**. This makes sure that we have two cameras when we run the app.

14. Now, we can press **Build**. Unity will ask us for a place to put the C# and Visual Studio files. I usually create a folder in the current folder with the name **App**. Press Select Folder and Unity will build the code for us.

The first time you do this, you will notice this takes some time. It has to generate quite a lot of files, and it needs to package up all our assets. The next time only the changes need to be processed, so it will be much quicker.

When the building is done, Unity will open an Explorer window where our project is. You will see the newly created **App** folder. If you open that, you will find the `.sln` file, in my case `HelloHoloOnUnity.sln`. This is a Visual Studio solution file we can open in Visual Studio. Let's do this!

Continuing in Visual Studio after Unity

When you open the solution in Visual Studio, you will see three different projects. If you only see one, you have opened the `.sln` file in the root folder. Trust me, this will happen quite often. The names are the same and the folders look quite similar. However, the one with the three projects is the one we can use to build and deploy; so, open that one. Again, this is found in the App folder you created and pointed at in the last step of the Build in Unity.

The structure of a Unity HoloLens UWP app solution

As I said before, the solution contains three different projects:

- `Assembly-CSharp` (Universal Windows)
- `Assembly-CSharp-firstpass` (Universal Windows)
- `HelloHoloOnUnity` (Universal Windows)

The last project is our final project, the one we will deploy to the device. The first is a placeholder containing our scripts. If you look at it, you will see in the Scripts folder our `PointerHelper.cs` file:

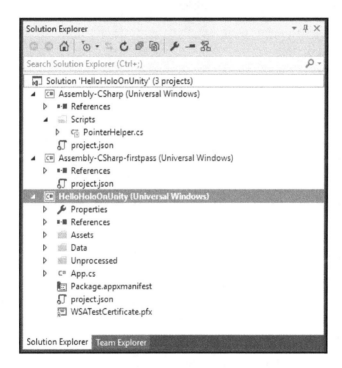

The solution structure for a Unity project

If you make changes to the scripts here, they will also be visible in Unity. So this is the place to write the specific code for your application.

The second project is a helper-like project that ties the projects together. We do not have to worry about that now.

The actual project itself, in our case, HelloHoloOnUnity, is nothing more than a loader. It loads the Unity3D player and launches our scenes. The player is deployed to the device and that takes care of running the application. There is not much we can do in this code base now.

Build configurations with Unity

Take a look at the configurations in the Build or Deploy drop-down. We have three configurations now, but although some names might seem familiar, they are not quite what you are used to. We have the following options:

Configuration name	Optimizations	Profiler enabled	Usage
Debug	No	Yes	Debug your scripts
Master	Yes	No	Deploy to the Store
Release	Yes	Yes	Test the application and test performance.

Also, note that the processor architecture is ARM, by default. This is a left-over from the Phone tooling on which the HoloLens SDK is based. However, the HoloLens uses a x86 processor, so you need to set this to x86 as well. I suggest that you use Debug/X86 for now. We also have the now familiar options for the deployment. You can use the emulator, the device through Wi-Fi (Remote Machine), or the device through USB (Device)--which one you choose is up to you.

Building and running your HoloLens Unity app

Build the project, and run the debugger. The build will take some time at first. It needs to get all the packages from the NuGet server. It will build all code; then deploy the whole app and all dependencies to the device or emulator; it then starts the app and attaches the debugger. This whole process can take a couple of minutes.

However, after this is done the first time, the next build and deployments will be much faster.

When it starts up, you will be greeted in the virtual world with a nice **Made With Unity** logo. After a little while, this goes away. In front of you, about three meters away and about half a meter below your eyes, you will see a white sphere floating in mid-air.

Walk around it! Look at it! Crawl underneath it! Try and grab it!

That last part doesn't work. The default near clipping plane in Unity is 30 centimetres, meaning that everything that is closer than that will not be rendered. Microsoft says it is best to set the clipping plane to 85 centimetre but, to be honest, 30 works just fine, and that is what they use in their own applications anyway. So I tend to keep it at that.

Of course, you can never grab the object; it is virtual. But to be honest -- you were tempted, right?

Summary

We have accomplished a lot. We have explored the device, and looked at it both on the inside and on the outside. We have seen what components there are. We have looked at the calibration and played a bit with the default apps. We have written a UWP app using DirectX and deployed it to both the emulator and the actual device. We have created our first Unity project and deployed that as well.

Now, it is time to take a step back and reflect a bit on how to create a great-looking holographic application. The first step in this process is always to have a great idea. I have one. We are going to build it together, but before we can do this, we need to design it and set things up. This is what we will do in the next chapter.

2
Designing Your App

The **HoloLens** is a great device. Everyone who puts it on is amazed. I always ensure that I explain how to use the device in detail before I allow people to put it on--the moment they wear it, they stop listening and are in awe of the experience.

Of course, once the initial wonder of seeing things float in mid-air in front of them wears off, they want to use apps and the experience should match the first moment of magic. Therefore, we need to ensure that our apps are just as good and deliver on that promise. To do that, we have to know how to design for the HoloLens. Guess what--this is what we will talk about right now!

Unique features of the device

The device is different from any other computing platforms you have seen before. If you are an experienced developer, you probably think that you know your way around computers and developing for Windows, but the truth is that HoloLens is not your average Windows 10 machine. There are some special and unique features that require another way of thinking about designing apps. Let's take a look at them again, and we will discuss what this means for your design process.

Thinking in three dimensions

First of all, normal Windows 10 applications are flat. It does not matter whether you write console applications, desktop applications, store applications, or mobile apps--all the action the users see is within a screen in front of them. Even if you write for the Xbox, which is a Windows 10 device with excellent graphics capabilities, you are still limited to the screen. The setup is always the same--the user looks at a screen in front of him.

In HoloLens, this is not the case. The user is placed in the middle of the scene. Sure, we can create two-dimensional apps and run them in the device but that is not what the device is made for. Most apps will have objects placed around the user and the user will navigate through the app by literally walking around, moving their head and looking in all directions. We need to ensure that we accommodate that. To do this, we need to do a couple of things:

- Ensure that objects are in a logical place
- Ensure that objects can be reached
- Ensure that objects can be found

Let's delve into these.

Making sure objects are in a logical place

Of course, the question is, What is a logical place? The key thing to remember here is that we are mixing the real world with the virtual world.

This means that people have certain expectations about the world around them. Things in mid-air drop to the floor if they are not supported, for instance. Unless, of course, they are floating balloons or robots. People do expect them to float about, but a table that is hovering 20 cm above the floor just does not feel right. Ensure that you place that table right on the floor.

If your app uses an information box that contains additional data about the app, we can have that hover in front of the user. This is a great way to show users some data they need at that moment, such as instructions they need to follow to go to the next phase of a game, for instance.

 Informational panels should float at a distance of two meters in front of the user. This is the best distance to be close enough to see and yet far enough to discourage trying to touch things.

However, if you want to give your users the ability to see their score, it would be a bad idea to have that box hover in front of them all the time. First of all, objects do not work like that in real life, and second, it gets in the way when the user wants to explore the environment.

A better way to do that is to place an information panel on a wall. People are used to having items on walls, such as paintings, forms, and information screens, so why not add a virtual monitor that shows the information you want to share?

That being said, the power of the virtual component in augmented reality is that we can do things that the user does not expect in real life. We can, as it were, give the user superpowers. The user can lift a heavy table and have it float about with a mere tap of the finger. If that fits your scenario, you should absolutely do so. However, in order to have the user feel at home in your app, ensure that most items behave as expected and are placed as expected.

Making sure objects can be reached

When we create a holographic scene, we determine where the objects are by putting them in our computer world. The HoloLens will later place these in the real world. The danger is that we do not know how the environment looks where the user is present. It can be a huge empty hall or it can be a small room in a student's dormitory. If we place an important object in our app four meters away from the user, and we expect the user to walk toward that object to interact with it, we might have a problem in that student's room. The object will somehow magically be visible through the solid wall of her room. The user, however, will not be able to go through that wall and is, thus, limited in the use of the app. Also, when this happens, the user will feel disconnected from the experience. What started out as an immersive experience, where she felt like a part of this augmented world, is suddenly just another app. The connection between her and the virtual objects is gone, and the app loses its appeal.

The HoloLens has an understanding of the rooms and the environment. So, we can ensure that the objects we present are within the confinements of that room. That way, we can ensure that the user is able to reach things and interact with them.

One word of warning--we cannot prevent items being projected out of reach when we have large glass window panes in the room. The depth sensor does not see the window and, thus, might consider walls and floors outside to be part of the room we are in. The result might be that the app will present items outside the room. Unfortunately, there is nothing we can do about that.

Making sure objects can be found

It is easy to get lost in a virtual world. In the real world, we have a sense of where objects are, especially if we are meant to deal with them. Imagine this scenario--you are at work, and you are told to go to a certain office to test out a new app your co-worker wrote. Of course, you comply. You know where the office is, so you walk there. You enter through the door, you look around the moment you step inside and see a laptop on the desk. You take one of the chairs you find at the small coffee table, pull it to the desk, and open the laptop.

This is so common that we do not immediately see the moments when we locate the things we are meant to be working with. Most of them are so obvious that we take them for granted:

- We know where the office of our co-worker is in the building
- We know where the door is
- We know where to find the desk in the office
- The laptops are usually found on the desk instead of hidden somewhere in a cupboard
- The chair behind the desk is the one your co-worker will sit in the moment he comes back to hear what you think, so you grab one of the other chairs
- Those coffee table chairs are movable, and you can place one near the desk
- And so on...

All these steps are so common that we never think about them. However, in the virtual world, nothing is so easy. We can ensure that the items we place are in positions the users expect them to be (again, tables usually are on the ground, not floating near the ceiling). However. the moment your user puts on the HoloLens and starts an app, he is immediately moved into a place he has never seen before. He has no references, he knows nothing about the layout of the place, and he has no idea whether his presumptions about the world are still valid.

Let's take a very simple example; we draw a layout like this:

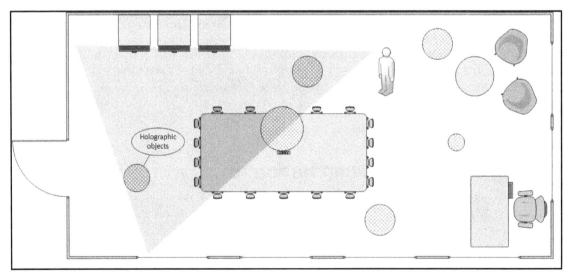

Field of view for a user

As you can see in the preceding diagram, we have placed the user in a room and surrounded him with holograms, shown here as circles. When the application starts up, the user will see the objects that are in front of him. This is indicated by the triangle in front of the user, depicting his field of view, but there are objects behind him as well, objects that might be important in the app; how do we tell the user to look around?

There are several ways of doing this, but the most used are as follows:

- Use a pointer or a special cursor to alert the user to look in a certain way
- Use sounds to notify the user about this

Pointers

Of course, part of the fun of playing games or using new apps lies in discovering new items in the new world we just stepped into. It can be part of the game play to discover new items. If that is the case, do not give too many pointers to the user as to where he needs to look. It is up to him to figure it all out.

However, in other cases, this is not desired at all. Imagine that you are playing a game, and you need to guide an avatar around the room. You can do this by looking at the avatar. In order to do that, you need to find it first. In that case, I would suggest that you use visual pointers to help the user find the avatar.

The user is probably used to having a pointer in the center of the screen. After all, this is the first thing the user sees when he turns on the device for the first time--a tiny white dot in the middle of his view that turns into a circle when the device sees his finger. Use this knowledge in your app, but enhance it.

You can use several icons or styles to do this. You can add a small arrow next to the dot, pointing in the direction the user needs to look, or you can make a colored disc that shows where the action is:

Look here, from Young Conkers, telling the user where to look

The size and presence of the icon depend on how important it is for the user to look in that direction. If you are creating an app in which there are several things that might be of interest for the user happening at once, use tiny markers around your cursor, which indicate that the user might be interested in looking in that direction. If the app is at a point where the user needs to do something in order to do anything at all, a big flashy sign saying **LOOK HERE** might be a better solution. It all depends on the situation, but ensure that the way you use this is proportional to the importance finding these objects has to the user.

Sounds

The pointer solution is a great way to, more or less, force the user to look in a certain way. Using a pointer is obvious to the user, so he is more inclined to follow the directions you give, but if you just want to make the user aware of the presence of an item in the space around him, you can consider using subtle spatial sounds.

Imagine that you are designing a game where the user has the option to pick up items from the scene around him. It would be helpful to have those items make subtle sounds. Since the spatial sound system of the HoloLens is extremely accurate, we can precisely place the origin of the sound at the location where the objects are, and the user will be able to find things this way. We, as people, are hardwired to find sources of audio by constantly slightly moving our heads to find where the sounds are coming from. The moment we hear something behind us, we will turn around to see what it is. We can use this to our advantage.

Having an item making sounds will draw the user toward it and help them find the object. Of course, this won't work anymore when we have dozens of objects, all happily chirping and bleeping away. The user will drown in the sounds and will not be able to identify the source anymore. However, when used in moderation, this can be extremely powerful and make the sense of realism even greater.

Dealing with limited input methods

People who develop software for desktop applications have a big advantage over people who develop for mobile devices--they can be sure that the user is able to use keyboards, mice, or pens to enter large amounts of data. Mobile app developers have to ensure that the input they need is limited; although most devices have virtual keyboards, they are not as friendly to use as physical keyboards. Therefore, the developer or designer must ensure that the input required is as little as possible and requires fewer keystrokes.

For HoloLens applications, this is even truer. Yes, we have a virtual keyboard. You used it to enter your credentials when you registered yourself with the device and probably, also when you set up the Wi-Fi connection, but you might have also noted that it is not so easy to use. To enter text, you are shown a keyboard, and you have to move your head to position the cursor on the correct keys and then tap at it while holding your head still to enter that key. This gesture is called an air-tap. We saw this in the last chapter. It takes very precise movements, and most people will not be able to do this for a longer period of time.

The HoloLens supports the use of a bluetooth keyboard, but most users will not have such a device. Also, relying on an external keyboard gets in the way of the wearable aspect of the device. If you have to carry a keyboard around all the time, using the HoloLens will be a lot less valuable.

Even if you have the need for a keyboard, be aware that most users are not proficient at typing and need to look at the keyboard to find the right keys. This means they are not looking at the holograms around them. I have noticed that people who do this follow a certain pattern:

1. Look at a hologram.
2. See that it needs input.
3. Look down at the keyboard.
4. Type some text.
5. Look up and notice that they don't immediately find the hologram with the input box.
6. Search a bit for the hologram.
7. See that they have made a mistake.
8. Return to the keyboard.
9. And so on...

Of course, this also happens with a regular application, but the head movement required to move from the keyboard to the object on screen is much easier and predictable. In the experiments I have done, people complained about the experience being tiring.

So, do not rely on keyboards being present except in some very specialized cases. HoloLens applications are not meant for data entry.

That being said, surely there are ways to interact with the objects around the user. Those ways are gestures and audio.

Gestures

Basically, we have two gestures, or three if you count variations on the air-tap. These gestures can be used to instruct the device to do something. Combined with the possibility of placing the cursor on objects by moving your head, we have ways to interact with objects.

First, we have the bloom gesture. As I have explained earlier, this is used to show the main start screen or hide that screen. This gesture is captured by the system and is not really available to us as developers. Compare this gesture with the use of the Windows key on a keyboard; this also generates a system-level command we cannot really use in our applications.

That leaves us with the air-tap. Officially, this is accomplished by having your finger move like a barrier. I have noted that it also works if you do a pinch movement, as if you want to grab an object out of the air.

There are two variations of this:

- Tap: Move the finger down and then immediately up again.
- Hold: Move the finger down, keep it there, and then move your hand about. This one is used to zoom, drag, and rotate items in the holographic space around us.

The device will recognize these special movements, and we can take advantage of this. In the later chapters, I will explain exactly how this works internally, but for now it is enough to know that we have these two modes.

To see this in action, start up the Hologram app that comes preinstalled with your device. We use the air-tap to start the app, to place the selection screen somewhere, and to select a hologram. Then, you move the hologram to a place you want it to be by moving your head; air-tap to place it:

The tiger hologram in my hallway at home

This is all done with the standard air-tap gesture we have used so many times earlier. However, there is more we can do. If you do half a tap, thus move your finger down and keep it there, you will see a circle of dots appear around the object. Now, if you move your hand slightly to the right or left, you will see the object rotate. Move your finger back up to set it to this position.

We use the same method to enlarge and move it; choose **Adjust** from the menu below the hologram and perform the same gesture--finger down, move it about, and then release by moving your finger up again.

We can design our app in such a way that we can move the cursor this way, but I really want you to think that through--users are not used to this. They expect to move their heads to move the cursor, and we should stick to that.

Audio

Using gestures is a great way to navigate around the app. However, it is not always practical. Sometimes, we need a set of commands the user can choose from. We can present the user with a list of buttons, but this can get rather confusing quickly. The buttons need to be quite large if you want the user to use them comfortably. If you have more than three buttons, the view area gets cluttered with buttons, and the user does not see anything besides these user interface controls.

One possible solution to this is to have a chain of buttons--one button opens up another screen with more buttons. Again, this is also not the best way--users tend to feel like they are getting lost in the user interface if they have to go more than three levels deep.

The best way to solve this is by using audio. HoloLens has four built-in microphones of very good quality. They pick up spoken commands while ignoring commands given by people a bit farther away. The software that does this is extremely good at identifying these commands, so most users will be recognized immediately--there is no need to train the software beforehand.

You might have noticed in the default apps that if you let your cursor hover over a button, such as the Remove or Adjust buttons in the hologram's app, a little box showing a microphone and the command you can use pops up. This is to show what you can say to do the same action. You can just say *remove* instead of placing the cursor in the top-right corner of the app and air-tapping it. This can be a great time-saver.

In your apps, this might come in handy as well. You can combine buttons with spoken commands so that the user can choose which way to interact, or you can have options that can only be used by either buttons or commands. It all depends on the scenario you have in mind. However, ensure that the user has a way of finding out about the existence of these commands. You can do this in the same way as the HoloLens does by default, showing a popup with the commands, or you use other ways.

In the Young Conkers game, the app starts with a training mode where the user is told how to perform actions. Here, the user hears how to use voice commands as well as gestures.

Whatever method you use, ensure that this spoken commands have the following characteristics:

- **Short and easy to remember**: Use *Start* instead of *Start the game now!*.
- **To the point**: Use *select* to have the app select something and do not use magical words to have that same effect (unless it fits in your app, of course).
- **Easily pronounceable**: Not all of your users might be native speakers of your language, so ensure that the words are easy. This also helps in recognizing your app.
- **Fewer words**: Use two or three words instead of long sentences, but do not limit to just one word, if necessary.
- **Consider using synonyms**: Allow the use of *Select*, *Active*, and *Do it* to perform an action.

Audio is not always an option; if your app is to be used in a quiet environment, it would not be a great idea to have your user walk around the place shouting commands. Also, in very noisy environments, the user might have to shout to make himself heard over the background noise, resulting in a sore throat. In these cases, it is better not to use audio or to use it sparingly.

All in all, using audio to navigate through your app is a great way to enhance the feeling of the user being in a magical place.

People do not expect sudden changes

One of the downsides of **Virtual Reality** is that people sometimes get motion sickness. This happens when the vestibular system feels movement but the eyes do not see this. Alternatively, of course, when the reverse happens, the eyes see that you are moving but your vestibular system says otherwise. The body will react to this by thinking that something's wrong, probably some kind of poisoning, and will try to resolve this by getting rid of this poison. This is not the kind of reaction you want your users to have when using your app.

When you limit the amount of movement in a virtual environment, users will probably be alright, but still there's a level of discomfort when scenery suddenly changes or when items move about.

In augmented reality, this does not happen that much. After all, the user still sees the physical world, so the motion sickness will not happen--the movements the user makes match what they see.

 In virtual reality, the scenery usually moves around the user; in augmented reality, the user moves around the scenery.

However, we have other issues that we need to take into account. The level of realism in HoloLens apps is quite high. This means that people can get startled by what they see. Of course, this could be intentional; if you are writing an app that is supposed to scare users, this can be really powerful, but most apps are not written for this kind of audience, and you need to be careful not to startle your users.

In the real world, objects never materialize out of thin air. It never happens that one moment a table is empty and the next moment, there's something there. Things can appear fast, but it is never instantaneous. There is always a transition, no matter how short the time period in which this may occur. Your apps should do that as well. This guideline is not only valid for HoloLens apps, but also for any other platform you might write for, and it is so much more important for the HoloLens. After all, we want to have the user feel as if the virtual world is an actual part of his universe and thus we need to ensure that things feel natural. Yes, we can have things happening that are not possible in real life, but they still need to follow some of the rules in our universe; not immediately appearing without a transition is one of those rules.

You can choose many ways to have a new object appear in your scene:

- You can have it move in from the left, right, top, or bottom. Do not use this too much; when objects suddenly appear from apparently behind the user, they will feel as if there is something or someone behind them who makes this happen. This will result in a paranoid-like feeling. Again, if this is your goal, this can be a strong effect, but it's better to not use this most of the time.
- Have an object appear by starting as a bright dot somewhere and grow from that dot into the object. This transition can be slow (several seconds) or it can be fast (under half a second), but this gives a more relaxed feeling to the user.
- Have the object change its transparency from completely see-through to completely opaque. Again, you decide on the speed this is done at.

When you want objects to disappear, you can reverse this, but ensure that you use the same technique you used when you had it appear. Do not mix this. Again, we want realism!

Another thing to consider is sounds. Things in the real world make a noise when they move about, so why not do the same thing in your virtual world? Having a very faint '*pwop*' sound when an object appears makes it more realistic, especially when you use spatial sound. This has the advantage that you automatically have you users' attention drawn to the object when it appears at the edge of his field of view or even outside it.

There are, of course, several other ways you can simulate the objects appearing, and you should, by all means, invent your own, but these three are the most used.

The social aspect in collaborative situations

We need to discuss something that you will not see discussed in any other book about software development--what happens when two users work together?

The first mass-produced computers were called PCs, personal computers. The wording kind of gives it away--they were personal devices. When this term was first used, it was meant to distinguish them from the big mainframes that could have dozens of users at the same time. However, each job on the big machines was running for one user only, so there was little a user would note about the other users, besides a drop in performance.

The PC was not so different. The user has the machine to themselves, but since all work done on the mainframe was also only visible to them, there was nothing new about this way of working.

Even the smartphone, a device most people consider to be a very private thing, is not different in this aspect. You don't share it, but you never did anyway, so there's nothing new here.

The first device to differ from this was the Microsoft Surface. The Surface was a big table with a vision-based interface; it could look at the surface of the table and see what happened there. It could recognize hands, fingers, coffee cups, and so on. You operated that device by touching it or placing objects on it:

The Microsoft Surface, the precursor to shared interfaces

Since it was basically a table, users could sit around it and work on it together. No longer was a computer a device used by one person; it could be used by four adults or six children at the same time.

This led to some interesting behavior. The way people interacted with the device and with each other became dependent on how well they knew the people around them. If the users were familiar with each other, they worked together on a job. If the users did not know each other, they all worked on their own little corner or side of the machine on their own part of the job. In the latter, there was little or even no collaboration. After a while, people got to know each other a bit more and they started working together.

Since this table had no way of knowing which user did what (we could trick it a bit by measuring the shadow of the finger and arms to guess which user the touch belonged to), all applications dropped the notion of a user altogether.

In HoloLens, we can see a similar sort of behavior. If there is only one device present or if your apps are not designed to be used collaboratively, we can apply the principles we all know--there is one user and they control the complete app.

Things get more interesting when we design our apps in such a way that we allow for multiple users to exist in the same augmented world. Now we have to take into account the way people behave when dealing with other people.

Surface computing gave us three models we can still apply to the HoloLens world:

- **Flying solo**: Each user has their own holograms, and they do not interact. Basically, this is the default way computer interfaces work.
- **Captain co-pilot**: One user is in charge; they control the holograms. The other users can see what happens but have little control over them. They can observe and occasionally take over but that's it. The co-pilot might be enabled to create objects of her own, but has no power over shared holograms.
- **Multiple pilots**: Each user has equal rights. Everything that is being done is visible to all users. There is one shared virtual world and all users see the action. They can all control their own objects and shared objects.

Which model you should choose depends not only on the sort of app you create, but also on the relationship you expect your users to have:

Model	Audience	Example(s)
Flying Solo	Passers-by in a store and occasional users on a trade show	Demo apps for a conference
Captain co-pilot	Co-workers, neighbors, and participants in a training camp	Surgery preparation and training for engine maintenance
Multiple pilots	Family members, friends, and team members in smaller teams	Gaming and simulations

As you can see, the level of familiarity between the people you expect to work with your app matters when it comes to the way you let them interact. If you ignore this, people will feel uncomfortable.

Another aspect is the physical distance you expect between the users. The flying solo model requires a lot more space since two strangers do not enjoy being close to each other. With the multiple-pilot model, this is not an issue; friends usually do not mind being closer.

One word of warning--this may not be true in other cultures, so ensure that you know your audience before applying these principles!

Give your user superpowers!

One of the fun things in virtual worlds is that the laws of nature do not need to apply. Sure, the user has certain expectations about the behavior of things in your world, and you should honor these as much as possible, but you can do things that give your users the feeling that they have superpowers.

Some things are so common that, these days, we pay no attention to them anymore. Take for instance, a smartphone with a built-in camera. In the old days, when you wanted to take a picture, you had to take a camera, take the picture, drop off the film at the local developer, have it developed, go back to the developer, and see the picture. Then, you find one picture where something interesting is happening in the background. You want to focus on that tiny part, so you have it enlarged. This takes another couple of days and is usually quite expensive, so you don't do this that much.

Now, however, things are different. You take a picture, and you see the results instantaneously. When you look at that picture, you see something interesting, and you use two fingers to enlarge the photo. This is something so common that we do not think about it anymore. However, in the preceding example, you could not do this. If you tried it, you would end up with two pieces of paper, each with half the picture. You still could not see what happened in the background.

We now take this enlarging of pictures for granted. With HoloLens, we can do even more. We can give the user the ability to move objects by just looking at them. We can let the user move items with one move of a single finger. We can give the user the power to lift an elephant with one spoken word. We can transport the user from his own home to a magical kingdom no one has ever seen before.

In other words, we can give the user the feeling that he is omnipotent. Of course, with great power comes great responsibility, so use this with moderation. If we do this too much in our apps, the user will feel discomfort. It will be too far removed from his normal frame of reference, and the user will stop using the app, but with just a bit of superpowers, the user will feel invited to explore your world more and more deeply.

Why should we care about this? The answer is simple, but let me ask you a question first. I assume that you have a smartphone, a tablet, or have used Windows 10 in tablet mode. If so, I am sure that you have also installed apps there. Now answer this--How often have you read the manual for these apps? I can guess the answer--never. Apps come with no manuals, or with very little guidance at most.

HoloLens apps should be like this as well. The user should feel at home in the app. The basic gestures, such as air-tap and air-drag-and-drop, should be enough to start using the app. Using these gestures, the user will learn a bit more about the app. He will see which voice commands he can use. If you give him superpowers, the user will feel more confident to explore the app. After all, there is this sense of invincibility you get when you are given special powers.

All jokes aside, this really helps to make the user want to explore and not be afraid to try out new things.

Forming a design team

Design is a specialized job that requires specialized skills. If you are lucky, you have access to professional designers and user experience experts. However, keep in mind that even those professionals probably have little or no experience designing holographic worlds. It is up to you to tell them what to design, how to design, and what things to keep in mind when designing.

I strongly believe in the Agile approach when it comes to developing software. This means that we form teams that are fully self-sufficient. In that philosophy, designers are part of the team, just like the developers, testers, and other professionals. Design is a very important part of developing software, and more so in a graphic-rich environment, such as apps for the HoloLens.

That being said, not all projects need graphical designers, user experience designers and, interaction designers, and so on. It all depends on the specific project.

Big projects need big teams

This is obvious--the bigger the project, the more people are involved and thus you will need dedicated designers, but there's a limit. In the agile world, it is common to have smaller teams, not more than seven, plus or minus two (so between five and nine) members in each team. If this is not sufficient, you can scale up by having more teams working in parallel. Again, each team needs to be able to work on its own, so you will have all the required skills in each team.

However, when your project is very big, this will not work anymore. You will have to scale by having more specialized teams. In that case, you might need a separate graphics team, a backend team, and a frontend team. It all depends on the size of your project, your budget, and the time to market you try to achieve. but remember that bigger teams do not necessarily deliver faster.

Scaling a software team is pretty complicated and is beyond the scope of this book. However, I believe it is vital that there is an expert who talks to everyone involved all the time. You, by reading this book, will be that expert, so you need to know a bit about the design rationales behind HoloLens apps.

Small projects need small teams

Smaller projects can benefit from a design team, but this is not feasible in most cases. Let's be honest, smaller projects are not backed by huge budgets and hiring a designer costs money. So, in smaller projects, the design job falls to the individual developers. If that is the case, it is even more important for you to know about the design ideas behind the HoloLens apps so that you can make apps that are as attractive as the samples, or even better than them, of course.

In small teams, each developer is responsible for all the work. You might have specialists in your team, people who tend to know more about one topic than their fellow teammates, but in general, everyone should be able to take over from everyone.

This means that developers have to get out of their comfort zone. Most developers think that the old battleship grey applications we had in the days of Windows 95 still look gorgeous. They tend to think in terms of functionality, not in design **aesthetics**. In their eyes, there's nothing wrong with a screen filled with buttons in a large grid. As long as you can find the things you want to do, the design is done.

I am exaggerating of course, but this is not that far from the truth in general. Developers think differently about software and user experience than graphical designers do. You need each point of view to make a project successful, though.

You cannot expect a user experience specialist to write code for the backend of a huge banking application. Everyone sees that. Yet, we do expect a developer to create a great looking, easy-to-use application on a mobile platform or on the HoloLens. Luckily, with a few pointers, it is not impossible to create acceptable applications when your team does not have dedicated designers, and that's what I will show you right now.

Using your experience

We have talked about the bigger principles in the earlier sections of this chapter. From this point on, I will give you some pointers that will help you do the design work even if you are not a designer. Keep in mind that all this has to fit the big ideas outlined earlier.

I assume that you are an experienced developer. I guess you have written software before you picked up this book. Even if you have not done so, I think it would be fair to assume that you have used software before. Think about the apps you use on your smartphone. Which ones do you like to use? Which ones do you not like? Which apps do you use because you have to but do not enjoy doing so? Why is that?

It can be tremendously helpful to look at the software you use every day and make a list of things you like and dislike about them. This list will be highly personal--the things you like might be the things I dislike and vice versa, but this can still be a very educational task to do.

Learn from other people's mistakes instead of committing the same ones yourself; this is something that can be very helpful in designing apps as well.

Where holographic apps are "just another app"

I will repeat what I said earlier--people do not read manuals when they are using mobile or holographic apps. The app should be easy to use and, if you need to explain things, do so in a tutorial style. Show the user how to do things, and then let them try it out for themselves.

When designing apps for the HoloLens, you can learn a lot from the lessons we learned when the industry started building apps for the mobile space. After all, there are a lot of similarities between the two spaces. Let's take a look at some of them:

- Limited ways to input data
- Limited hardware

- Fixed set of peripherals
- Wearable
- Location aware

There are five key points you have to take into account when designing apps. In no particular order, these are the following:

- **Usability**: The app has to be usable. I guess we all know this, but it is still worth mentioning. There are a lot of apps out there that are too hard to use, and therefore people will not use them at all.
- **Goal-driven design**: The app has to be designed with a certain goal in mind. Great apps have one goal and one goal only. If you want your users to achieve more, create more apps and eventually, you can bundle them into a suite. However, ensure that your apps are goal-driven and that the goal is clear to the user.
- **Discoverability**: The key to great discoverability is to ensure that users can navigate around the app and find the functions they need. For instance, in apps, hyperlinks are usually displayed as blue underlined text. Users will see this and recognize this for what it is. If you create your app in such a way that these things are obvious and consistent throughout the experience, the user will feel invited to explore your app.
- **Learnability**: If you happen to have a scenario where the usage is not so obvious, ensure that you leave the user some pointers as to how to use the app. You can do that by giving him labels, hints, or spoken text to explain what you want the user to do. However, be careful; regular users do not want to be taken by the hand every time they start the app. You have to ensure that tutorial items can be turned off, or, even better, automatically switch the tutorial off once the user seems to understand the goal. Don't let the user guess what he has to do, but guide him toward achieving this goal.
- **Feedback and response time**: A good app is responsive, which means that the user does not have to wait for a long time until the app does what the user wants it to do. Of course, the term long time is rather subjective, but on average, users ;do not want to wait for over 0.5 second before they are notified that the app understands their intention. If your app needs a longer time to perform a task, let the user know. Show a popup, hint, or play audio to explain that you have understood the user and that you are working on it, but it might take some time.

These design principles apply to both mobile apps and holographic apps, and are applicable to most desktop applications as well. It gets interesting when they differ. In other words, what are specific design points for holographic apps?

Where do holographic apps differ?

Due to the unique nature of the HoloLens device, it should be no surprise that the apps running on it are unique as well. Of course, certain principles apply across all sorts of devices; I have outlined them earlier. However, there are specific things you need to keep in mind when building apps for HoloLens. Here are the most important ones:

- **Do not use the color black**: Well, you can use it, but keep in mind that black is transparent. After all, the device works by adding light, and black is the absence of light. There is an exception; if you want to draw tiny details in black on a light background, you will find that it works just great. If you were to look closely, you will note that the black is still transparent, but to the human eye, this looks black. You can use black text on a bright background, and people will be able to see it. However, large dark areas will be more or less translucent, so avoid those.

- **Take care of the level of detail of your graphics**: In a normal app, something that will be displayed far away (represented on the screen by being quite small) does not need much detail--it is only a couple of pixels high, so users cannot see detail anyway. With holographic apps, this is quite different--the user can decide to physically walk toward the object and examine it up close. When you have drawn the item thinking that you do not need that much detail, the user will see this.

- **Use large enough user interface elements**: People will have a hard time positioning the pointer on a button and keeping it there while air tapping. If the button is too small, the pointer will move away from it. Usually, this results in the user using all the muscles in his neck to steady his head. This can get quite tiring very soon. It is better to avoid this and to have large buttons, text boxes, and so on. In general, a button should be on a plane about 2 meters away from the user and have about 15% of the screen estate.

- **Do not use scrollbars**: People will move themselves, so just present longer lists. If you need to scroll, use the scroll-gesture the system provides. The Edge browser shows how to do this. The same applies for zoom and move. Use gestures to accomplish this, not a button or any other user interface control.

- **Use a pointer**: Although it is possible to create apps without having a pointer, I would strongly suggest that you create a pointer. This helps the user focus and determines what he is looking at. Users who are inexperienced with the HoloLens might think that they can select objects just by looking at them, but in reality; the pointer is always in the middle of the screen. They cannot move it by moving their eyes, they have to move it by moving their head. Showing the pointer helps them remember this and discover actions.

- **Use the hover event**: In mobile apps, we have no hover event; there's no way to know whether the user is holding their finger over an element on the screen until they touch the actual control. With HoloLens apps, we can use this; the user can look at an item and that looking-at can be considered to be a hover. Use this to indicate that the user can or cannot do anything with this item. Change the pointer, change the color, animate the user interface a bit, anything to make it clear that the thing the user is looking at is special and deserves some exploration.
- **Use the physical world**: If you can, make good use of the existence of the walls, floors, and other surfaces in the user's environment. A great example of this is the **RoboRaid** app, which you can find in the store. This app will punch holes in the walls and let aliens creep out of them. The effect is incredibly strong and much stronger than when these aliens appear out of thin air. You can do similar things: placing holograms firmly on tables or attaching them to walls if you can. Alternatively, ensure that you hide your holograms when they are behind or under physical things. This helps in achieving a level of realism.

The workflow to identify your features

It is not easy to identify what your app needs to shine. I earlier stated that you have to ensure that your app is goal-driven, but how do you achieve that? To help you do this, I have created the following workflow that you might want to follow when thinking about your next project:

1. Write down your mission statement.
2. Brainstorm all ideas.
3. Remove ideas that don't support the mission statement.
4. Separate must-haves from nice-to-haves.
5. Prioritize must-haves.
6. Implement.

Writing down your mission statement

Think about your idea. Can you describe it in one line? To help you do that, I have created a template to fill in:

"My app [app name] is the best app to help [audience] [task it is achieving] in order to [reason to achieve this task]"

Fill in the app name, the audience, the task it is achieving, and the reason to achieve it, and you have a mission statement. I will give you some examples:

- My app *PlaneSpotter* is the best app to help plane spotters track planes in order to have a great overview of departing and incoming types of aircraft
- My app *FoodDesigner* is the best app to help amateur cooks identify what meal to create in order to make the best use of the leftovers in the fridge
- My app *BowlStrategy* is the best app to help bowlers select the curve to throw in order to hit the most pins possible in one throw

You get the idea.

Write down this statement, put it on a banner, print it in a large font, and stick it to the wall of your office. Ensure that you can see it whenever you work on your app. This helps you stay close to your goal. This is what you will make, who you make it for, and why you are doing it.

Brainstorming all ideas

Now comes the fun part. Take a piece of paper and a pencil, look at your mission statement, and write down ideas. Describe anything that your app might do. However, and this is vital, do not hold back. Write down anything that comes to your mind, no matter how crazy it might seem. We will clean this list later on, but for now, let your mind go wild. The reason to do it this way is that, by not limiting yourself, that one bad idea might lead to another bad idea, which might lead to a great idea. If you limit yourself beforehand to only writing down great ideas, you will miss out on a lot of things that might turn into great ideas. That list can quickly contain over 50 items. Do this over the course of a couple of hours. It is no use trying to do it in one go, the creative brain does not work that way; take your time.

If you look at the mission statement for the *PlaneSpotter* app, what do you think can be part of that list? To clarify, a plane spotter is someone who enjoys going to airfields and noting all the airplanes going and coming.

My list looks a bit like this. I have shortened it a little, but these are some typical items that could be on it:

- Note incoming plane type
- Note incoming airline
- Note outgoing plane type
- Note outgoing airline

- Note weather conditions
- Take pictures of the planes
- Warn friends about exciting plane arriving or going
- Check weather before spotting
- Order pizza when spotting planes
- Looking up date of first appearance of a plane type
- Note the runway planes use
- Share pictures with friends

The list can and should be much longer, of course, but you get the idea.

You should repeat this process a couple of times to ensure that all your ideas are on it, no matter how silly they may seem at first.

Removing ideas that don't support the mission statement

Now it's time to clean up the list. Remember that an app should be goal-oriented. So, look at your mission statement and remove all items from your list that do not support this goal.

My list looks like this now:

- Note incoming plane type
- Note incoming airline
- Note outgoing plane type
- Note outgoing airline
- Note weather conditions
- Take pictures of the planes
- Warn friends about exciting plane arriving or going
- Check weather before spotting
- Order pizza when spotting planes
- Looking up date of first appearance of a plane type
- Note the runway planes use
- Share pictures with friends

The weather conditions are not relevant when you want to keep track of what planes arrive or depart. They are very relevant to the pilots; they need to keep track of the wind and the direction they need to take, but for us this is less interesting. After all, certain wind directions cause the planes to depart from another runway. We have got that covered in the *Note the runway planes* use part.

The pizza function sounds great, I can imagine that you might get hungry when you are in a field all day long, but I am sure there are other apps that do that already. The same applies to the weather checking beforehand.

Warning friends and sharing pictures of planes with friends seem reasonable, but we can do this using the existing social networking apps, such as **Facebook** and **Twitter**. They are probably already available on your device, so why replicate this? We can, however, add an option to launch these apps from our app.

Separating must-haves from nice-to-haves

The best way to ensure that apps are actually finished and deployed, especially for smaller teams or one-person teams, is to ensure that the app will not be too big. A good rule to remember is--ship early, ship often. These days, with app stores for all sorts of platforms and devices, including the HoloLens, updating an app is easy. Most of the time, the user does not need to do anything. He will just be aware of a new functionality in his app all of a sudden. So, ensure that your app is in the store as fast as you can, and then start updating it.

To get the app in the store as quickly as possible, you have to trim your list down to the bare essentials. This is my attempt:

- Note incoming plane type
- Note incoming airline
- Note outgoing plane type
- Note outgoing airline
- Take pictures of the planes
- Look up date of first appearance of a plane type
- Note the runway planes use

I have removed the pictures function and the looking-up functionality. I believe that they can be strong features that really make my app shine, but I do not necessarily need them in the first version. Apart from this, I am not entirely sure how to take pictures from the device, so I want to investigate that later on, when I have a little more time. This way, I am removing all risks that might delay shipping version 1.

Prioritizing must-haves

Now comes the time to decide the order in which we will develop the features. I have put numbers behind each item to indicate when we will develop them:

- Note incoming plane type (1)
- Note incoming airline (3)
- Note outgoing plane type (2)
- Note outgoing airline (4)
- Note the runway planes use (5)

As you can see, I have decided to implement the feature to indicate the plane type first, for both incoming and outgoing flights. The reason for this is that I can easily create a set of buttons, each depicting certain types. Taking note of them is just a matter of clicking or the right button. Attaching the airline to it is slightly more work, so I postpone this. This way, I am sure that I am getting a minimal version working as soon as possible.

Implementing your app

Finally, we get to do some coding. Start up Visual Studio or Unity, and create that project. Build the frameworks you need, lay out the foundation of your app, and create item 1 on your list. Test it, play with it, and see that it does what it needs to do.

Once you have done that, you might get a feeling of the time it will take to implement the next item on the list, and thus how long, more or less, it might take to build all the features you have described in the last step.

Set a time goal for yourself. For instance, you might decide that you want your first version in the store three weeks from now. Now, you can estimate which items will fit in that schedule and which won't. Work on those features until your deadline has passed, and deploy to the store.

Once the first users start to use your app, you can implement the next batch of features. Update the app as soon as possible with new features and bug fixes. Also, take note of the feedback you are getting from your users--they will tell you what they like and do not like in your app. This might have an impact on your feature list, so pay close attention to that!

These steps are valid for both mobile apps as well as HoloLens apps. The best way to learn all these principles is by doing them. So, I invite you do tag along as I show you how to design a great app called *RockOn,* an app that helps stage directors prepare for the best possible rock show. In subsequent chapters, we will actually build this app, so it is time we start designing for it!

Introducing the RockOn app

Let's take a side step. We are no longer rock-star holographic app designers and developers, we are rock stars. We make a living standing on stages all over the world, playing our music to thousands, hundreds of thousands, or even millions of people from all walks of life. We are the centerpiece of a rock band and, as such, personally responsible for giving the best show we can.

For years, we have done this in the same way. We have a fixed setup on the stage. After all, having your own spot on the stage helps with stage fright. All those different venues can be intimidating; that feeling can be taken away with having your own spot.

However, when every show all over the world uses the same setup, it is not likely that we are using the possibilities of the venue to its fullest. Every room or stadium has its own acoustics and layout. In order to give the best sound possible and to give the audience the best view of each member of the band, we need to redesign the stage for every single show.

This is where the *RockOn* app comes into play. The goal of this app is pretty simple--*RockOn* app is the best app to help tour managers lay out a stage in order to give the best show with respect to acoustics and layout.

What do we want to achieve?

Taking the approach I showed you earlier, I have come up with the following prioritized list of features that we will implement:

1. Place instruments on a stage.
2. See stage layout.
3. Helicopter view.
4. Audience view.
5. Move the stage around in the concert hall.
6. Listen to each instrument in the setup.
7. Listen for unwanted echoes.

8. From the stage.
9. From the audience.
10. Work with band members to eliminate getting in each other's way.

Of course, there are many more things we can do but for now this sounds like a nice start for our app. In the following chapters we will implement each of these features. After each chapter we end up with a working version we might want to ship and put in the store. But first we need to get a basic version up-and-running. And that is what we will do now.

How do we get there?

In the first chapter, I showed you how to start developing with *HelloHoloWorld*. We took a simple program with one hologram and deployed that to the device and the emulator. This time we will do that again, but with a more realistic project. As we go along, I will also show you some best practices and explain the rationale behind some of the choices we have to make.

Decision time - tooling

As I explained, there are basically two ways you can develop apps for the HoloLens. The choices you have are as follows:

- Pure C# development with DirectX
- Hybrid development by mixing Unity3D and Visual Studio

Developing with DirectX

The pure-C#-with-DirectX route has some advantages. You can use the latest runtime Microsoft offers, and you have full control over anything that happens in your app. There is no dependency on external libraries or runtime besides the DirectX libraries. This means that you can do whatever you want to do.

The downside is that DirectX development has a very steep learning curve. It is not easy to create 3D objects in DirectX, and there are a lot of things you need to be aware of when starting with this platform.

Of course, this is always the trade-off--you have to do a lot of things yourself if you want power, you have less choice in how to do things if you want ease of development.

Developing with Unity3D

Unity3D is a game engine used to build three-dimensional worlds. It is one of the most used engines and development environments when it comes to gaming and 3D applications, and that's the reason Microsoft selected it as the preferred way to develop HoloLens apps. More and more applications are written in this platform. The good news is that there's a lot of documentation about Unity3D out there. However, this also means you have less control over how to do certain things.

Next to that, all code in Unity3D is written for the **Mono runtime**. Mono is not used in the final version, but the Unity3D tool does not understand this. This results in a lot of `#define` statements in your code to prevent errors from popping up all the time.

However, Unity3D is a great tool to get up-and-running pretty fast and create stunning apps on HoloLens that perform well.

For this book the RockOn app will be built in Unity3D but I will also explain how to achieve the same results using DirectX in each chapter.

To summarize--use Unity3D unless you have a very good reason not to.

One final note--you often will see the name Unity being used instead of Unity3D. There is however a very popular **Inversion of Control** (**IoC**) framework that has the same name. I will use the shorter name Unity from now on as well, but just remember that I am talking about Unity3D. We will not be using IoC here at all, so for now you can forget that it exists.

Creating a new project

Each project begins exactly the same way--by creating a new project in your development environment. For HoloLens, this is no different. We will first have to do the boring stuff--creating our project and setting it up just right.

First, ensure that you have all the tools you need. I have mentioned the requirements in the first chapter, so I will not repeat them here. Let's begin by opening Unity.

Getting started with Unity3D

When you start up Unity, you will get a screen such as this one:

The Unity3D startup screen

If you have tried Unity before, you will have a list of recently opened projects here, but in my case, this list is empty as I start with a clean install. Click on the **New project** button.

Fill in the name and location you want to save the project to and click on create. Unity is file-based and thus all files and folders needed will be in one location. Ensure that you back up this location later on and store it in a repository, such as Visual Studio Team System or Git, if you want to ensure that you do not lose your sources.

You will be greeted with the standard Unity screen. This is where we will put our holograms and other assets we might need, but for now we will just set up the environment.

I have already explained how to do this in Unity in the last chapter, so I will just outline the steps you need to take here:

1. Select the Main Camera in the **Hierarchy** panel.
2. Reset the coordinates of that camera to location (0,0,0). By default, this is (0, 0, -10), meaning that the user is 10 meters away from the center. In HoloLens apps, the user is always in the center of the application.

3. Set **Clear flags** to **Solid Color** and **Background** to black (RGB 0,0,0). Remember that black is transparent, and we want the user to see the real world as much as possible.

4. In your **Assets** panel, right-click and create a new folder. Name this Scenes.

5. Press *Ctrl + S* to save the scene in this newly created folder; name it main.

6. Go to **File | Build Settings**, or press *Ctrl + Shift + B* to open the **Build Settings** screen.

7. Click on the **Add Open Scenes** button to ensure that the current scene is part of the app.

8. Click on **Windows Store**, and then on **Switch Platform**. You should see the Unity logo next to the Windows Store line to indicate that this is our current platform.

9. Change the **SDK** to **Universal 10**.

10. Change the **UWP Build type** to **D3D**.

11. Check both **Unity C# Projects** and **Development Build** under debugging.

Your **Build Settings** screen should look like this:

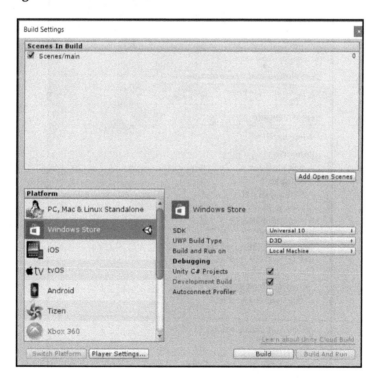

The Build Settings for Holographic applications

1. Press **Player Settings...**
2. In the Inspector panel, you should see the settings. They are organized in sections, one of which is called **Other Settings**. Under **Rendering**, you will find the **Virtual Reality Supported** option, and this needs to be checked. You will see the options you have, but there is only one SDK supported here--**Windows Holographic**. So, you do not need to do anything here:

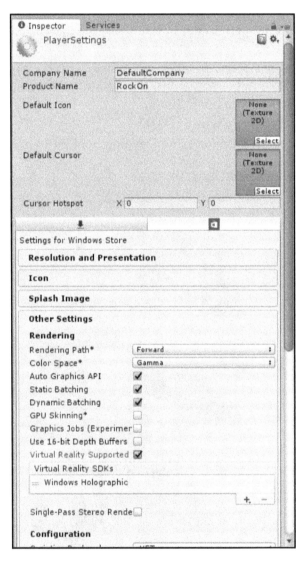

PlayerSettings for HoloLens Unity projects

3. Now, assuming that you still have the **PlayerSettings** opened, press **Build**. If not, open the **PlayerSettings** dialog again.
4. You will be asked for a location to store the Visual Studio Solution. Create a new folder called VS and select that.
5. Unity will now build your project. This might take some time when you do it for the first time.

After the building is done, Explorer will open to show you the results. It is time to explore them in Visual Studio!

The role of Visual Studio in developing for the HoloLens

You might have noticed another RockOn.sln file in the top-level folder. If you open that solution, you will see that it is empty. It contains no projects at all. The reason for this is that this solution will be a place for Unity to store all C# scripts that we will write. However, these scripts are not to be compiled in Visual Studio--it will not know how to deal with them. When we build our project in Unity, it creates a new RockOn.sln file in the VS folder. That is the one we need to open.

Later, when we add scripts to our app, you will see that the scripts are copied to the new VS folder as well. That's where we will edit them, debug them, and build them. So, this is the workflow:

1. Add objects and scripts to the *Unity* project.
2. Build the *Unity* project for the first time, giving it a unique folder.
3. Open the newly created .sln file in that new folder in Visual Studio.
4. Now, when you add scripts in Unity, rebuild the Unity project, leaving Visual Studio open in the background.
5. Go to Visual Studio and you will get the familiar **Files have changed; do you want to reload** dialog. Click **Yes**.
6. Edit the files in Visual Studio and verify in Unity that they are changed as well.

If you double-click a script file in Unity, it will open another instance of Visual Studio to edit it. That is a waste of resources--the procedure I described earlier works more quickly and is more memory-efficient.

Now, open the `RockOn.sln` file in the VS folder. Note the folder structure we already described before; it should look like this:

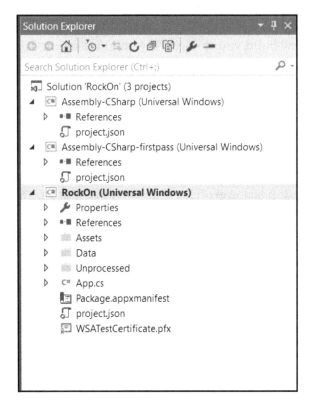

The Solution Explorer for our new project

We can build and deploy it now, but that will result in an empty scene, which I think is pretty boring, so it's time to add some items here.

Adding assets to the scene

Assets in Unity are everything in the scene. This is a pretty broad description, but that's basically true. Assets can be any of the following:

- 3D objects
- Scenes
- Scripts
- Sounds

- Animations
- Materials
- And so on...

You will see the assets in the Asset panel. You can select them there and drag them to the scene or the Hierarchy panel. You can import new assets from your own storage or from the Asset Store. The last one is interesting--a lot of people create assets to be used in Unity. These assets vary from simple objects to complex structures with scripts, animations, materials, and everything else you might need. Some of these assets are free, others require a fee. Some are to be used in any way you like, others require a license. Ensure that you explore the requirements before you use these assets in your project.

Open the Asset Store in Unity by clicking on **Window -> Asset Store** or by pressing *CTRL + 9*. The store should open, and you can now find items of interest. I want a simple object in our scene, so this is what my search looks like:

The Unity store with a guitar, free only

As you can see, I did a search on guitar and set it to only show me free assets. I will pick a nice electric guitar to use in our scene. Select something you like and press **download**. Unity will now download the asset from the store and give you a dialog showing you what is inside this asset. Remember that an asset might contain a lot of things such as objects, materials, and scripts. So, you may not want to include everything in your project.

By default, the **All** option is selected. Some assets have a sample scene, which you do not need, so uncheck that if you see it. When you have selected the things you want, click on **Import** to add it all to your project.

Depending on the layout of your asset, you might find the object in the root of your Asset panel, or in a subfolder the import has created. I choose the **Guitar and Amp** in the top-left corner of my store, which created a Prefab folder. Prefabs are assets you can reuse; think of them as components. So, I now have a prefab folder that contains a guitar and an amp object. I just drag the guitar into my scene to have it added. It does not matter where you put it; we will adjust the location anyway.

When you have added an object, you can look at the Inspector panel and see the properties. Just like we did with the camera, we can reset the position of the object. If you reset it, the location will be set to (0,0,0), the rotation will be set to (0,0,0), and the scale will be set to (1,1,1).

So, now we have a guitar, which is placed in the same spot the camera in. This will mean that the user's head is inside the guitar, something we need to change. Change the z-axis property of the object to something like 3 meters. This means that the guitar is 3 meters away from the user. If needed, you can also rotate the guitar to make it more visible. In my case, I need to rotate it (-90, 180, 0); a quarter circle over the horizontal axis and half a circle over the vertical axis to show it to the camera.

You can always check the view by selecting the **Game** view. If you select this and then move things about, you immediately see things as they will appear in the running app. You can also use the **Scene** view, which is the default view; select the camera first and then choose the **Align View To Selected** option in **Game Object**. This ensures that the view is the same as in the Game view, but leaves you with all the editing options you need.

Building the project

If you have placed your objects in the spot you want, save the scene and rebuild it using the **PlayerSettings** dialog. I assume that you still have Visual Studio open, so if you move there after the building is done, it will warn you about changes in the project. Just reload it and build the project in Visual Studio.

Before you build, however, ensure that you have set the configuration as described in the first chapter; set it to **Debug** for **x86**.

If you build the solution for the first time, it will load all the NuGet packages. Again, this might take some time the first time you do this. Also, the first build might take pretty long, but that's only the case the first time. It helps to do this as soon as possible in the project, so you are not bothered with this during development.

You can choose to build a Release build; in our case, this will not matter much. Release builds tend to be a bit faster, but you will miss the debug information in case something goes wrong.

If the build has succeeded, it's time to deploy.

Deploying the project

Deploying the project is the part where we take the bits Visual Studio has created for us and send them to the place where they will run.

When you are used to writing normal desktop or Windows Store applications, you might want to deploy the app to the local machine. You can do this. After all, the application is just a Universal Windows Platform app, and your Windows 10 machine you are working on supports this. Of course, the moment you require special capabilities from the device, the app will not start anymore, complaining about not meeting the requirements. It might be a better idea to deploy to the correct platform, such as the emulator or an actual HoloLens device.

Using the emulator

In the selector in Visual Studio, you can choose the target for the deploy and debug session:

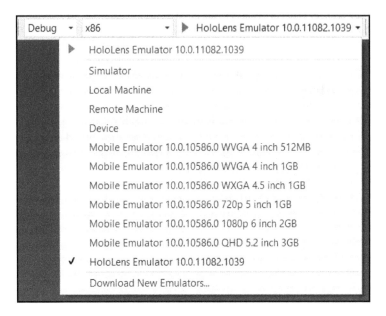

Deploy targets on my machine: yours might look different

You see the targets I have on my machine. I have several virtual machines I can deploy to, since I also have the mobile development tools installed. Your screen might be different, but you should have the Remote Machine, Device, and HoloLens Emulator options available. Remote Machine and Device connect to the actual HoloLens (through Wi-Fi and through USB respectively); the Emulator is a virtual machine that got installed when you installed the tools. This is what we use now. Select this and start a debug session by either pressing the play icon next to the selection, pressing *F5*, or going to **Debug** | **Start Debugging**. The project will build again and then deploy to the emulator. If it is not already running, it will start the emulator and load the OS first. Then, it will start your application. And if all goes well, you should see your guitar. Use the *A*, *W*, *S*, and *D* keys on your keyboard to move left, forward, backward, and right in the virtual world; use the arrow keys to move your virtual head around. Try to walk around your object and see what it looks like from all sides. Press *F2* to go back to the Start menu in the emulator.

Using the device

We have two options to deploy to a physical machine. Again, I am assuming that you set up the device for developer mode, as described earlier. This is necessary since the device will not accept apps that are signed with a temporary key. Since this is what Visual Studio does, it will not run your app. If you have set it to Developer Mode, you can deploy your apps.

The way you deploy is up to you. It does not really matter if you use the Wi-Fi connection or USB connection. Although USB is slightly faster, it restricts you in your movements. On the other hand, using Wi-Fi, you run the risk of your batteries running out pretty quickly. I leave it up to you.

In this case, I selected Wi-Fi deployment. I selected the right IP address and pressed **Debug** in Visual Studio.

After a couple of minutes, I was presented with a holographic guitar in my office:

The guitar, deployed to the HoloLens

Making some small adjustments

As you can see, my guitar is way too big to be realistic. We need to scale it down in order to make it more life-size. Now, Unity does not offer you the option to measure items in the editor. There are ways to achieve this, mainly by writing a custom script for this. However, in this case, it is easier to add a box to the editor screen of the size you want your object to be and use that as a reference. The scale options in the inspector are the way to do that. I have added a box with the scale of (0.275,0.93,0.10), which are more or less the dimensions of my own guitar. I have placed that box in the same spot as the guitar. Now, I scaled the guitar object so that it fits the box precisely.

Now it looks better, and it feels like a real guitar. It's time to make things more interesting though, by adding some interactivity!

Summary

In this chapter, we learned a lot about designing your app for HoloLens. Although the main steps we took when we started thinking about our app are not that different from normal app development, we identified some key areas that require more attention. We also talked about the way people interact with each other and how to design your app around that. This is something you usually do not take into account when designing your app.

We took our first steps in developing our *RockOn* app. We started developing in Unity3D, and we added some assets to our holographic world. Then, we deployed that to a device and saw our 3D objects come alive. We are now ready for the next step!

3
Gestures and Events

We have played a bit with the development environment. In the previous chapters, we added a multicolored cube, a white sphere, and even a guitar in the virtual world. Now, this is all very impressive when you do this for the first time. Even your users will be amazed at seeing a hologram floating in front of their eyes. They even might feel privileged; they see things no other people can see.

However, after a couple of minutes, it might get boring. It will be much more interesting if we allow our users to play around with the world, interact with it, and even control it in a way you cannot do in real life.

In this chapter, we will make that possible. We will enable users to touch objects and move them about, so the user can control the virtual world.

Before we do this, we must first talk about the ways HoloLens allows us to do this. We need to talk a bit more about the gestures we can use.

Working with gestures

To detect gestures, you have to do a lot of work. Recognizing hand movements and turning them into events for the application is not a trivial task. In order for the application to recognize a hand wave, for instance, you can take two approaches:

- **Procedural**: This is done in code. You detect a hand position, note its placement in 3D space, then see the movement and deduce from that what happens.
- **Machine learning**: This is a way to use the power of computing to learn about gestures. Basically, you feed an enormous number of images to a computer and try to teach it to recognize the gesture you want it to see.

Both approaches have advantages and disadvantages. For instance, the procedural way is relatively easy to get started with, but usually the results are less accurate. The machine learning way is hard to set up and takes a long time and a lot of training to get right, but results in much better recognition. Getting this right is a lot of tedious work and takes time and skill.

Luckily for us, however, Microsoft has done all the hard work for us beforehand. The basic gestures we need to get things going are built into the hardware. If we perform the bloom gesture in front of the device, the **Holographic Processing Unit**, or **HPU**, will see this and send the event to the operating system.

The same happens with the tap gesture, the tap-and-hold gesture, and the tap-release gesture. We do not have to do anything to recognize these gestures in our device, and in our code we get this for free.

Next, we do not only get hand recognition, but it also handles the clicker that comes with the HoloLens and even recognizes the voice command *select*. Yes, if you position the cursor on an object and say the word *select*, you will get the same results as if you had air-tapped. This is all done by the device; we do not have to do anything special.

Now, this is all great and nice, but what if this isn't enough? What if we need something special? The answer is, of course--write your own **gesture recognition**. The good news is that we can access the data the cameras see. The bad news is that this requires a lot of work. However, we can do this, so, if you really need this, the **SDK** will not stand in your way. Be warned though, there are some other considerations you have to take into account. For instance, how does the user respond to new and unfamiliar gestures?

Some UX considerations

A user who has been using the HoloLens for some time will know how to operate the device. They will be aware that the center of their view is where the cursor will be. They will know how to use the bloom gesture. They will use air-tap and related gestures to do the work that needs to be done.

I have seen a lot of users struggle with the air-tap gesture. It takes a little time to get used to it, to get it just right so to speak. Most people try to be creative and invent their own gestures to make a hologram do what they want it to do. Some people try to grab the holograms, and others tap with two, three, or even four fingers. Again others make some sort of wave gesture. Of course, none of these work. The device currently only sees the one-finger tap, and that is the way you control the apps. There is a very simple reason why people behave this way.

The holograms feel real enough to them to encourage them to try out real-world interactions. This is completely different from people using mice and keyboards for the first time. Those devices are designed in such a way that you cannot make a mistake about how to use it. The form defines the function, making the user change their behavior as to match the intended usage of the device. I have never seen anybody pick up a computer mouse and try to move it against a wall, or flip it upside down to control the sensors with their finger.

With holograms, this is different. The HoloLens is a natural user interface device, designed in such a way people will more or less feel free to experiment.

I think this is a good time to look at some of the ideas behind the natural user interface principles since this is what drives our interaction model.

A brief history of user interfaces

The **Natural User Interface**, or **NUI** in short, is another way of defining user interfaces in computer applications. The term NUI stems from the early 1990s, when Steve Mann published his work on user-interface strategies based on interaction with real objects. This was seen by a lot of people as the next step in the line of user interfaces--first, we had **command-line interfaces** (**CLI**), then we had **graphical user interfaces** (**GUI**), and now we had NUI. Of course, this is not true. Although most CLI applications have been replaced by GUI applications, a lot of people still use CLI. The reason for this is that with each step in this evolution, the user trades power for ease of use. A well-trained systems operator can do so much more work in much less time using a CLI than a user on a GUI system can do. With NUI, this is even more so.

Command-line interface

In CLI, users had to learn the language of the application. Using the system consisted of typing in all sorts of commands, usually without any help from the system. Since computing power was limited, most commands were abbreviated and used flags and options as well. A proficient user would have to memorize all these options. It would be quite common for users to have the manual of the system lying next to the keyboard, more often than not spanning hundreds of pages.

This is still in use today. Most system administrators prefer to use command line-based systems since that gives them much more power. An example of such a command is this:

```
Dir | Rename-Item -NewName { $_.name -replace " ", "_" }
```

This weird looking line is a `PowerShell` command that looks into the current directory on your disk and replaces all spaces in all filenames with an underscore. If you did that in a GUI, you were working for quite some time, if the number of files were big enough. With the power of the command line, you can achieve a lot of things with very little effort. Of course, first you will have to learn all the commands and all their variations, options, and parameters.

Graphical user interface globally

The CLI was one of the reasons people were afraid of computers. The users seemed like wizards to the casual observer as frantically typed in weird incantations to have the machine work the way they wanted it to. This appeared a bit like magic to the casual observer. This was not for mere mortals, this was only for the elite.

However, when computers became more powerful, companies began creating graphical user interfaces. These interfaces relied on using metaphors for actions. Users would be handling those metaphors and models instead of typing in commands. For instance, on a Windows computer, you can work with your directories by moving icons depicting folders about. The actual data on the hard disk is not a folder, of course. The data is a data structure somewhere in the operating system, but it is displayed as a folder since this is a metaphor users recognize and can work with.

The Apple Macintosh was one of the most famous systems to use this kind of interface. Of course, this was not the first--most of the ideas were first implemented in systems built by *Xerox PARC* in Palo Alto back in 1973, and even those ideas were not entirely new--the work done by Xerox was in turn based on ideas from Stanford Research Institute in THE 1960s.

Most GUI systems were based on the **WIMP** principles--they made use of **Windows**, **Icons**, **Menus**, and **Pointers**.

With the advent of the GUI, people felt less threatened by the technology. More and more people felt like they could handle this kind of system and were less afraid to try out things. Although the user has less control of the computer when using a GUI, they feel more welcome and thus will make better use of the system.

The touch devices that appeared later on formed another transition--the touch-based approach more or less invalidated the ideas behind the GUI. Instead of moving a mouse on your desk that resulted in moving something on the screen, people could now move the actual object itself. This led to a much more intuitive way of working since you could almost touch the object you wanted to manipulate.

The touch-based approach enabled other people to think about a more natural way of interacting with computer-based content,--something that would be even more easy than using simple touch as a replacement of the mouse. This led to the more widespread adoption of the NUI.

Natural user interface

The NUI is a way of designing interactions that makes the user feel like a natural. The goal is to eliminate the learning curve associated with the CLI and GUI ways of designing modes of interaction. The user should feel at home in the environment and feel invited to explore new ways of using the system.

Most features of the app will be quite straightforward, and users will discover them easily. If they are not so easily found, the app will guide the user toward them, offering some sort of in-app training. One of the hardest things to achieve in a good NUI system is to make the system adapt to the knowledge level of the user. The best examples of this kind of system are the ones that start off with a lot of guidance, telling the user what to do and how to do it. However, as the user gets more proficient, the system should notice this and slowly get out of the user's way. The guidance should slowly be reduced, and only pop up whenever it seems the user is lost or does things in a way that could be done better. Achieving this means measuring what the user does all the time, noticing patterns of usage and the path the user takes to achieve a goal.

One of the goals of NUI systems is to replace all metaphors with as many real-world objects as possible. I have referred to the Microsoft Surface table before; this device allowed actual real objects to be used and handled by the user. Instead of moving an icon depicting a button, we could place a physical button somewhere on the screen and let the user press that. Users immediately knew what to do with this button. After all, they have been using buttons all of their lives, and they recognized it for what it was.

There is a lot more to be said about NUIs and their implications, but for now I will just inform you that this is the preferred way of interacting with the HoloLens device. Let users play with holograms that resemble real-world objects. Let users interact with them, walk around them, and discover them just as they would with real physical objects in the space around them.

Feedback

There is a big difference between the virtual world and the physical world. Look around you. You probably have some items around you that you can touch; go ahead and touch them. You will feel the object and notice that it resists while pushing it a bit or that it moves when you push it. The object will react to what you do. This is nothing new, the laws of physics that describe this have been known for centuries. Push against something, and you will at least feel it and will probably result in action.

How different this is in a virtual world. When you click on something that is on your screen, by means of your mouse, nothing will physically happen. All interactions are done by the software, letting you know that you pressed the button. If you use your mouse to click on anything that is not part of the user interface, nothing will happen.

When people first start using computers and GUIs, they will need to learn what they can do with the system and which objects are to be clicked on or pressed on in a touch-based interface. Usually, they learn this quite quickly. Most buttons on screens are shaped in such a way people recognize them for what they are. Other user controls, such as scrollbars, might take a bit longer to learn to use, but eventually these will also be understood.

The important thing is to give feedback. Let the user know that the system has received the input and does something with it, even when the system cannot do anything useful with the input at this time.

Most touch-based interface show some sort of effect if you touch the screen, even if there are no user controls at that point. This is done with the above in mind. The system is telling the user: "Yes, I see what you did there. However, there is nothing I can do right now. Would you like to try again?".

Types of feedback in the HoloLens world

There are several different kinds of feedback we can think of when using the HoloLens apps. The kind you choose depends on a lot of factors, including but not limited to the following:

- The goal you want to achieve
- The amount of guidance you want to give the user
- Your personal preference
- The level of expertise of the user

As I have mentioned before, a good NUI is a system that adapts itself to the level of expertise of the user. So, the guidance you want to give should be getting less and less obtrusive as the user is using the app more.

Having said that, I believe there will always be a need for feedback in a HoloLens app. In traditional graphic-based software, there is always a mouse pointer on the screen. Even in applications where it is hidden, you can reveal the mouse pointer by moving the mouse a bit. A gentle nudge is usually all that it takes to show where the cursor is. Not only that, but the normal applications give all sorts of hints as to how to use the system. When you move your mouse pointer over screen items that can be interacted with, they usually show you that--buttons light up, items get a different color, and so on. This will give the user a signal they can do something interesting with that screen element.

In HoloLens apps, we do not have a mouse, but we do have gaze. We know how the user has positioned their head. We do not necessarily know where the user is looking at--the device does not have eye tracking capabilities. We can take an educated guess though by determining where the center of the device is pointing at. If there are items we generated underneath that point, this is probably the object of attention for the user.

I said probably because you cannot know this for sure. Therefore, it is important to utilize the same kinds of methods traditional applications use. Have the items light up, grow, and shrink or do something else to tell the user--, "Hey, this is probably worth exploring more!"

There are several ways to do this. The most common ones are as follows:

- Have a dot on the screen that turns into a circle whenever there is something to be done.
- Have no visible feedback until the device is pointed at an interactive element, then show some sort of mouse pointer.
- Draw controls in such a way that they are not very obvious and make them light up in brighter colors when they are in the focus of the device.
- Generate a sound whenever the device sees something worth looking at. Since we can use spatial sound, the user will be triggered to investigate this further.
- Use a pointer of some sorts. Whenever you want the user to look at something that is off-screen, generate a not-to-obvious arrow somewhere that guides the user.
- Have something off-screen generate a sound. Again, since we have spatial sound, we can place a sound effect on something, and the user will more or less automatically be drawn to the item you want them to look at.

Of course, there are many other ways you can think of. These, however, are the ones in use today, and thus are the ones users will be aware of and understand.

Getting to grips with gaze

Gaze is the technique of understanding where the device is pointed at, guessing where the user is looking at and feeding that information back to the user. We can use all sorts of techniques to give feedback, such as the ones mentioned above, but we need to build this into our applications. Let's give it a try.

We will draw a circle in front of the user. This circle will help the user to identify where the system is looking at, so the user can position this point.

Of course, you are not limited to using a center point. If you want, you can offset this cursor to another place on the screen, or have two points that the user must place in order to determine a distance, and so on. However, for now, we will use the most common scenario- placing a small circle in the middle of the screen.

To do this, we need to do a lot of work. We will go through the DirectX sample first, after that we will have a look at how to do this in Unity. Let me warn you beforehand--the DirectX sample is extremely complicated and takes an enormous amount of work while the Unity sample can be done in about four lines of code. Still, it is useful to have seen the actual work the computer needs to do in order to render something, so we will spend a lot of time on this sample.

Gaze in DirectX

We will do our DirectX sample in a new, separate project. So, let's begin by firing up Visual Studio and creating a new Holographic DirectX 11 app. We have done this before, so you should be able to do this by now.

DirectX requires you to do most of the work yourself. With DirectX, we will be programming the GPU to show the things we want to show, which means there is a lot of manual stuff we need to do, before we can actually show something. The resulting code is blazingly fast--we can optimize things for the hardware, and since we know what the hardware is, we can use that knowledge. So, the downside of using DirectX is that it is hard and complex work, but the upside is performance and complete control. In DirectX, we have to give the system all our vertices. Just a quick reminder, a vertex is a point in space. We define points and the HoloLens hardware, or rather, the GPU inside the HoloLens will determine what the actual image will look like.

Let's have a look.

The bare HoloCursor class

We will create a new C# file in the folder Content. This file will contain all code needed to render the circle, so I decided to call the class HoloCursor. I have called my project *GazeSampleDirectX,* so my resulting file looks like this:

```
using GazeSampleDirectX.Common;

namespace GazeSampleDirectX.Content
{
    internal class HoloCursor : Disposer
    {
        private readonly DeviceResources _deviceResources;

        public HoloCursor(DeviceResources deviceResources)
        {
            _deviceResources = deviceResources;
        }
    }
}
```

We need to derive our class from the Disposer class in order to be sure we are cleaning up after ourselves. Since DirectX uses a lot of COM calls, we need to remove all references. Disposer is a class that is part of the template for the Holographic applications, so we can use that to help us keep track of things to clear. Of course, you could use your own IDisposable interface, but that would require more work, and we already have so much to do.

We need a constructor that sets things up. As you can see, we pass in an instance of DeviceResources and store that in a private field. DeviceResources is a helper class that also comed with the template. This gives access to, as the name suggest, all resources of the device. The device in this case is the graphics card inside the HoloLens. Remember that DirectX is all about manipulating the hardware in a rather direct way.

Next, we need to add another private field to the class:

```
private bool _loadingComplete = false;
```

This flag will be used to determine whether all setting up, initialing, loading, and other things have been done so that we can use the graphics we want to see. The default setting is false of course, so we set this directly in this field.

Now, it is time to start initializing. In the constructor, we add the following call:

```
CreateDeviceDependentResourcesAsync();
```

This is the method we will use to allocate the memory for our graphics and where we will do all our vertex work. This will begin with a call to a clean-up function--if somehow this method gets called twice, we want to be sure that old memory has been cleaned up properly before reallocating it.

```
public async void CreateDeviceDependentResourcesAsync()
{
    ReleaseDeviceDependentResources();
}

public void ReleaseDeviceDependentResources()
{
    _loadingComplete = false;
}
```

We have marked the `CreateDeviceDependentResourcesAsync` function with the async keyword--we will make asynchronous calls later on, so it is handy to have it in place beforehand. We also created the stub for the `ReleaseDeviceDependentResources` function, which for now does nothing more than setting the `_loadingComplete` flag to `false`.

A word about shaders

Next, we need to create some shaders. Shaders are very important in graphical software, but most developers who have never had to work with them do not understand how they work and why they are so powerful. Now, this book is not about DirectX, it is all about HoloLens. If you want to know more about shaders, I suggest that you buy a book dedicated to DirectX or go online and find some tutorials on them. I will not describe them in detail, but I will tell you just enough so that you can use them in your own code and do things with them.

The first question that comes to mind is--what is a shader? Well, simply put, a shader is a piece of code that runs on the graphical card. Think about that for a while--we are writing software dedicated for another processor, not the normal CPU.

There are several kinds of shader you can write, each targeting a different part of the processing pipeline. To understand that concept, we have to talk about the way the graphics card and DirectX actually work.

The processing pipeline

Graphics that you see on your computer screen, or in our case in the HoloLens, are generated by the **Graphical Processing Unit**, or **GPU** in short. This is a device optimized for crunching large amounts of numbers in order to give you an image made up of millions of pixels. When you are dealing with animations that need 60 **frames per second** (**fps**), such as the HoloLens does, you can imagine that this requires some very sophisticated hardware. The GPU is exactly that--a device that can handle this kind of data.

Let's consider a normal computer screen. We will assume a fairly low resolution device, say 1266 times 720 pixels. This means the screen consists of 911,520 pixels. A pixel is a dot on the screen in a certain color, so we also have to store the color information. Usually, a color is represented in 3 bytes--one for red, one for green, and one for blue. So to make one screen, we need 911,520 times 3 bytes, or 2,734,560 bytes. To avoid number overload, we will say we need about 3 megabytes of data to draw one single screen.

This data is stored in a buffer somewhere. The GPU needs this data, so we need to allocate a buffer of 3 MB. The GPU will read this buffer to draw the pixels, every single time the screen needs refreshing. With a refresh rate of 60 fps, this means the GPU reads this buffer 60 times per second. However, what happens if we change the screen? When we want to show animations, the pixels change all the time. So it is very likely that halfway through reading the pixel data, suddenly the pixels will have changed, resulting in one half of the screen showing the old situation and the other half the new situation. Of course, this will only last for $1/60^{th}$ of a second, but still the next frame will probably be different as well. This results in a very messy screen--you will see all images blurred and mixed.

There is a way to prevent this. We can use buffers to make the transition smoother. A buffer is just a copy of the screen data, which we can use to write to. The GPU will use the original set of data to draw the screen, and we get to use the other set of data to write to. When we are done writing, we signal the GPU that it needs to switch. The moment the GPU is ready to drawn the screen again, it will now use that secondary copy of data to fill the first buffer. This way we always will have a full, steady screen in front of us.

We can even use more than one buffer--in theory, we could use dozens. We will not go into that here because it does not apply to the HoloLens, but a typical game might use more than two buffers.

The secondary buffer means we have to work with more than one set of data. We now need 6 MB of pixel information. As you can see, the numbers grow rather quickly when working with graphics. Luckily, the GPU is optimized for this. Note that this is why people write software that deals with large calculations to run directly on the GPU instead of on the CPU.

The GPU makes use of a pipeline. The DirectX implementation of this looks like this:

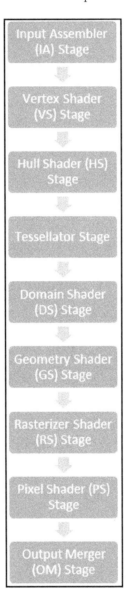

Whenever the GPU wants to process an image to be put on the screen, it goes through this pipeline. It starts with collecting all the information it needs in the **IA** stage, then pushes the data through all the other stages until it reaches the **OM** stage. This is where the actual data is written to the screen.

The great part about this is that we can replace each and every one of the stages with our own code. The bad part about this is that, it can become quite complicated.

Luckily for us, we only need to be concerned about the **Vertex Shader (VS)** and the **Pixel Shader (PS)**. The hardware inside the HoloLens is pretty sophisticated, which means we can skip the **Geometry Shader (GS)** stage as well. Most software written for DirectX needs to include this **GS** stage, but we do not need to.

Programming shaders

Shaders are pieces of code written in a special language. Fortunately for us, Visual Studio understands this and has the compilers for this installed, so we do not need to worry about that.

Let me illustrate this by showing you the most simple code for a Pixel Shader. Again, the shader is run on the GPU. The Pixel Shader is called for each and every pixel that needs to be drawn on the screen, so as you can imagine performance is key.

```
// Per-pixel color data passed through the pixel shader.
struct PixelShaderInput
{
    min16float4 pos   : SV_POSITION;
    min16float3 color : COLOR0;
};

// The pixel shader passes through the color data. The color data from
// is interpolated and assigned to a pixel at the rasterization step.
min16float4 main(PixelShaderInput input) : SV_TARGET
{
    return min16float4(input.color, 1.0f);
}
```

This is the default Pixel Shader code you get when you use the template in Visual Studio. The language used here resembles C or C++, but is actually called **High Level Shader Language (HLSL)**. Let's examine this a bit closer.

First, we define the format of the data we will use later on. We have a `PixelShaderInput` struct, which contains a position and a color. Thus, with this struct, we can identify the position of the pixel on the screen and the color we want it to have.

Below this, you will see the `main` method. This is what gets called whenever the shader is run. The method gets the input in the form of the previously defined `PixelShaderInput`. The return statement simply returns the color we want to have at this pixel. We do not do anything here, we just return the color we already had. So this shader code does not do anything useful.

The topic of writing shaders is beyond the scope of this book. If you want to know more about this, I suggest that you read the rather excellent documentation on the MSDN site or buy a dedicated DirectX 11 book, that deals with this.

However, you need to know that the code for the shader is given in HLSL, but the template associated with that code will compile this for us into a `.cso` file, which is a compiled shader object. This binary version is the one we will feed to the DirectX pipeline.

Adding shaders to our project

As I said before, the GPU in the HoloLens is sophisticated enough to not need a Geometry Shader. However, if in the future other devices are created on the Windows Holographic platform, this might no longer be the case. Other hardware might need this shader, so we have to check for this.

In our `CreateDeviceDependentResourceAsync` function, we add the following:

```
_usingVprtShaders = _deviceResources.D3DDeviceSupportsVprt;
```

Of course, you also need to create the `_usingVprtShaders` field in the file:

```
private bool _usingVprtShaders;
```

Aside from that, it is a good practice to use the `ReleaseDeviceDependentResources()` method to clean up after ourselves, so we add this line to that method:

```
_usingVprtShaders = false;
```

If this variable is true, we need to create and use the Geometry Shaders. Again, in the current version of the hardware, we do not need to do this; however, in future hardware, this might be different. It is better to be prepared.

First, we will create the Vertex Shader code. This shader will generate all the information to turn our vertices into vertices the GPU can use. We will have two different types of this shader:

- A version that sets the view id (thus, the index of which view to use when moving this to the next stage), so the Geometry Shader knows where this vertex belongs.
- A version that sets the same view id, but places it in the render target array, which is a job the Geometry Shader should take care of.

Version 2 is the one we need for our HoloLens app, but we will include both of them.

The code for the shaders is included in the template for our app, so I will not repeat it here. We will need to load the compiled code into our app first and add the following code to the class:

```
private async Task<byte[]> BuildVertexShader()
{
    var folder = Package.Current.InstalledLocation;

    var vertexShaderFileName = _usingVprtShaders
        ? "Content\\Shaders\\VPRTVertexShader.cso"
        : "Content\\Shaders\\VertexShader.cso";

    var vertexShaderByteCode =
        await DirectXHelper.ReadDataAsync(await
folder.GetFileAsync(vertexShaderFileName));

    _vertexShader = ToDispose(new VertexShader(_deviceResources.D3DDevice,
vertexShaderByteCode));
    return vertexShaderByteCode;
}
```

This code will simply load the compile .cso file from the correct location. We create an IDisposable object from the resulting block--we need to clean up afterward. The DirectXHelper class comes with a template.

Depending on the hardware capabilities, we will load one of the two given shaders. In HoloLens, the one in VertexShader.cso will be loaded.

Last in this method, we create a new VertexShader function and give it the variable vertexShaderByteCode we loaded. We will store this shader in an object named _vertexShader, a global field in our class.

Call this method from our initialization routine CreateDeviceDependentResourcesAsync():

```
var vertexShaderByteCode = await BuildVertexShader();
```

We need to return the bytecode object from the method since this is used later on. We store this in a local variable in our method.

Again, we might need a GeometryShader so we instantiate one next:

```
if (!_usingVprtShaders)
{
    await BuildGeometryShader();
}
```

The implementation of this method looks like this:

```
private async Task BuildGeometryShader()
{
    var folder = Package.Current.InstalledLocation;

    var geometryShaderByteCode =
        await DirectXHelper.ReadDataAsync(await
    folder.GetFileAsync("Content\\Shaders\\GeometryShader.cso"));

    _geometryShader = ToDispose(new GeometryShader(
        _deviceResources.D3DDevice,
        geometryShaderByteCode));
}
```

This is similar to the code we have seen before--we load the compiled shader and feed that to a field in our `_geometryShader` class. We will add that field to our class:

```
private GeometryShader _geometryShader;
```

It is now time to write our PixelShader. In our initialization method, add this line:

```
await BuildPixelShader();
```

This is the implementation:

```
private async Task BuildPixelShader()
{
    var folder = Package.Current.InstalledLocation;
    var pixelShaderByteCode =
        await DirectXHelper.ReadDataAsync(await
    folder.GetFileAsync("Content\\Shaders\\PixelShader.cso"));

    _pixelShader = ToDispose(new PixelShader(
        _deviceResources.D3DDevice,
        pixelShaderByteCode));
}
```

Do not forget to add the field to the class, if you want this to compile.

Additional data

We now have our shaders loaded into memory. The next step is to tell the system how to interpret the data and how to deal with the vertices. In other words, we need to tell the Input Assembler stage in the pipeline how to assemble the input.

Add the following code to the initialization routine:

```
InputElement[] vertexDesc =
{
    new InputElement("POSITION", 0, Format.R32G32B32_Float, 0, 0,
InputClassification.PerVertexData, 0),
    new InputElement("COLOR", 0, Format.R32G32B32_Float, 12, 0,
InputClassification.PerVertexData, 0)
};

_inputLayout = ToDispose(new InputLayout(_deviceResources.D3DDevice,
vertexShaderByteCode, vertexDesc));
```

Add the _inputLayout field to our class:

```
private InputLayout _inputLayout;
```

The input layout tells the GPU how the data looks like. It uses the vertex description we specify first. In this piece of code, we tell the GPU that the data consists of position data and color data. Remember the Pixel Shader we looked at? This is where we match up the parameters and the code we use in our app. We also give it the code for the vertex shader, the reason why we saved it in the first place.

There is one more thing to do to set the pipeline up. We need to have a place for the data telling the system what to draw:

```
_modelConstantBuffer = ToDispose(Buffer.Create(
    _deviceResources.D3DDevice,
    BindFlags.ConstantBuffer,
    ref _modelConstantBufferData));
```

This is added to the initialization. Again, we need the fields in our class:

```
private Buffer _modelConstantBuffer;
private ModelConstantBuffer _modelConstantBufferData;
```

That concludes the initial setup. This needs to be done, no matter what we draw. Of course, the drawing itself is where things get interesting. However, before we draw stuff, we need to determine how we can tell the GPU where to place the pixels. How do we create a 3D drawing?

Defining images in three dimensions.

We need to tell the GPU what we want our objects to look like. We cannot simply give the GPU a bunch of pixels. If we could do that, we would not need the GPU at all, but we would be doing all the calculations ourselves. That is something we do not want to do--it is extremely complicated and time-consuming and would result in a very slow code. The GPU in combination with DirectX knows how to transform 3D coordinates into pixels on a screen, so we only need to provide the system with our vertices.

A vertex has at least 3 parameters--an X, a Y, and a Z coordinate. X is the horizontal position, Y the vertical, and the Z is the direction forward or backward from the perspective of the user. Positive X goes to the right, whereas negative goes to the left. Positive Y goes up, whereas negative Y goes down. Positive Z goes toward the user in the direction of his back,whereas negative moves away from the user in the direction they look at initially. We can illustrate this as follows:

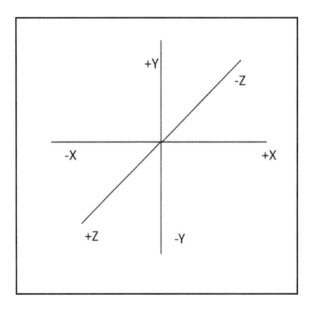

3D coordinate system in DirectX

In DirectX applications, the units are arbitrary--a 1 means one anything. You can make anything out of it you want. In HoloLens applications, the units are meters. If you position something two units away from the user, it will appear to be two meters away from her.

DirectX and the GPU are optimized for working with triangles. Basically, that is what graphical cards are great at--drawing lots and lots of triangles. It is up to us, the developer, to break up our drawing into those triangles. Let me show you what I mean by this using a two dimensional example--the basic square:

A square, one meter by one meter

I have defined this square with the dimensions of one by one meter. The bottom-left corner is in the origin (0,0). As we agreed earlier, the X to the right is positive, so the bottom-right corner has the coordinates (1,0). And so on.

We can break this up into two triangles:

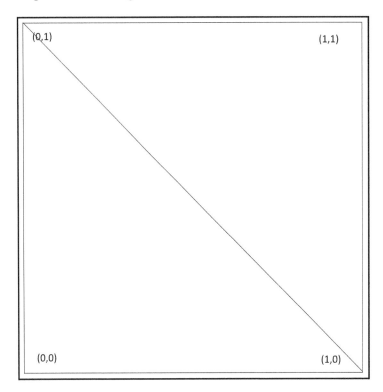

(0,1)

(1,1)

(0,0)

(1,0)

The square divided up in triangles

I have decided to draw a line from the top-left corner to the bottom-right corner, but I could just as easily have decided to go from-top-right to- the bottom-left corner. It does not matter, as long as I have two triangles.

Now that we have our triangles, we can describe this in a way a computer might understand. First, we define all vertices in this image. Remember, a vertex is a point in space. In this case, it is two dimensional, but the extra dimension is just another number here.

So we have the following vertices:

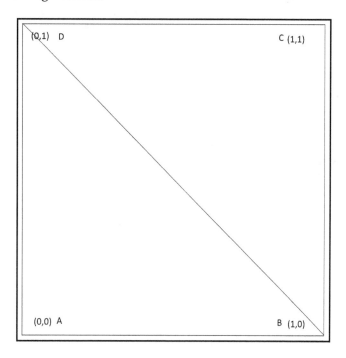

We have the following vertices:

Vertex A: (0,0)

Vertex B: (1,0)

Vertex C: (1,1)

Vertex D: (0,1)

In DirectX, we can pass these vertices onto the system. However, that is not enough; we need to tell the system how to combine these vertices into a triangle. After all, all sorts of combinations are possible.

We do this by forming a so-called triangle list. We give the system a list of vertices and tell the system to connect them in a certain order. It is very important to give these points in the right order--we need to define them in a clockwise manner.

The reason for this is that by defining them in this order, the system can tell which is the front of the triangle and which side is the back. It does so by determining the normal of the lines, which is just a line perpendicular to the lines drawn. The pixels on the front of a triangle get drawn, those on the back usually not.

So, we can tell the system that our triangles look like this:

Triangle 1: A -> D -> B (remember, we are going clockwise)

Triangle 2: D -> C -> B.

It does not matter where you start and which triangle you define first, as long as you use all points and use the right order.

Since we are programming computers, we do not give the vertices names but use their index instead. So in pseudocode, we might define our vertices like this:

```
public int[][] vertices =
    new int[][]
    {
        {0, 0}, // A
        {1, 0}, // B
        {1, 1}, // C
        {0, 1}  // D
    };
```

We have an array of vertex coordinates here. Our square then gets described as two triangles, again in pseudocode:

```
public int[][] indices = new int[][]
{
    // Triangle one
    {0,3,1}, // A -> D -> B -> A
    // Triangle two
    {3,2,1}  // D -> C -> B -> D
};
```

Since all triangles consist of three vertices, we can continue to define them after each set of three coordinates. The system knows that, after the third vertex, it needs to close the triangle by going back to the first. So we only need to specify the three points in the right order.

If we give these two datastructures to the DirectX pipeline, it will draw a nice square, one meter wide and one meter high.

Let's see what that looks like in real life.

Our square cursor

In our `CreateDeviceDependentResourcesAsync()` initialization method, we add the call to the following to methods:

```
BuildVertexBuffer();
BuildIndexBuffer();
```

The first one will define our coordinates for each vertex, and the second method will tell the system in which order these vertices are to be used to draw the triangles. I have chosen to make the object a bit more interesting by making it a diamond shape. Try to see if you can see the shape without running it, by looking at the numbers.

The implementation is as follows:

```
private void BuildVertexBuffer()
{
    VertexPositionColor[] cubeVertices =
    {
        new VertexPositionColor(new Vector3(0.0f, 0.0f, 0.0f), new
Vector3(1.0f, 1.0f, 1.0f)),
        new VertexPositionColor(new Vector3(0.0f, 0.05f, 0.0f), new
Vector3(1.0f, 1.0f, 1.0f)),
        new VertexPositionColor(new Vector3(0.05f, 0.00f, 0.0f), new
Vector3(1.0f, 1.0f, 1.0f)),
        new VertexPositionColor(new Vector3(0.0f, -0.05f, 0.0f), new
Vector3(1.0f, 1.0f, 1.0f)),
        new VertexPositionColor(new Vector3(-0.05f, 0.00f, 0.0f), new
Vector3(1.0f, 1.0f, 1.0f))
    };
    _vertexBuffer = ToDispose(Buffer.Create(
        _deviceResources.D3DDevice,
        BindFlags.VertexBuffer,
        cubeVertices));
}
```

As you can see, we create an array of `VertexPositionColor` structures. Each vertex holds the information about the position and the color. We use a local coordinate system here, which means that the center of our object lies at 0,0,0. We have to use three numbers here since we are dealing with a three-dimensional space. We have set the Z factor for all vertices to zero, meaning that we have a square in the Z plane without any debt. All color fields are pure white.

Since we have the origin of our square in the center of it, we can see that the square goes from -0.05 to 0.05, both horizontal and vertical. This means that it will be 10 centimeters times 10 centimeters.

Next, the `BuildIndexBuffer()` method is defined, where we specify how to connect each of the vertices to form triangles:

```
private void BuildIndexBuffer()
{
    ushort[] cubeIndices =
    {
        0, 1, 2,
        0, 2, 3,
        0, 3, 4,
        0, 4, 1
    };

    _indexCount = cubeIndices.Length;

    _indexBuffer = ToDispose(Buffer.Create(
        _deviceResources.D3DDevice,
        BindFlags.IndexBuffer,
        cubeIndices));
}
```

Instead of using an array of arrays, as in the pseudocode before, we continue in one line of numbers. The principle stands though--this works just fine.

We need to specify three more private fields in our class--one for the buffer with all vertex data, one with the number of indexes, and one with the actual indexes:

```
private Buffer _vertexBuffer;
private int _indexCount;
private Buffer _indexBuffer;
```

One final line concludes our initialization:

```
_loadingComplete = true;
```

We need to do some work on our cleaning up code--we have done a lot of initialization, and we need to ensure that this gets removed when we do not need it anymore. The full method looks like this:

```
public void ReleaseDeviceDependentResources()
{
    _loadingComplete = false;
    _usingVprtShaders = false;

    RemoveAndDispose(ref _vertexShader);
    RemoveAndDispose(ref _inputLayout);
    RemoveAndDispose(ref _pixelShader);
    RemoveAndDispose(ref _geometryShader);
```

```
        RemoveAndDispose(ref _modelConstantBuffer);
        RemoveAndDispose(ref _vertexBuffer);
        RemoveAndDispose(ref _indexBuffer);
    }
```

That takes care of that!

Rendering and updating

We have told the system what our cursor looks like--a small diamond shape of about ten times 10 cm large, colored completely white.

Telling it what the image looks like is not enough, we also need to instruct the GPU to draw the image when it is time to draw it. Next, we need to make sure that the image gets updated when it needs to be updated and we need that more often than you might think now.

Remember, we are working in a HoloLens app, which means the user will wear the display instead of it being on a desk. If the user moves his head, the image needs to move in the opposite direction to maintain the illusion of it being stationary in space.

The good news is that the platform takes care of that. Once you have drawn an image somewhere in the 3D space, it will remain there. The bad news is that we do not want that in our case -- we are drawing a cursor that should move whenever the user moves his head. So we need to update our drawing every single frame.

Let's begin by giving our class a property that tells the user what the actual location of the cursor is. We defined our coordinates to be centered around the (0,0,0) position, but that was a local coordinate system for the cursor itself. The holographic world has another coordinate system that might have a different point of origin, a different scale, or even a different direction for the axis. So we need to translate our coordinates into world-based coordinates.

We will add a property first:

```
    public Vector3 Position { get; set; } = new Vector3(0.0f, 0.0f, -1.0f);
```

We tell the system that we want our cursors origin to appear at the location (0,0f, 0.0f, -1.0f), or precisely in the center of the view of the user, one meter in front of them.

We can use this property to determine where we want to place the cursor. Of course, a cursor should be in front of the user at all times, no matter where the user moves his head. However, we need to start somewhere, so we will just draw it on the screen in the default position first.

The Render() method

We will add the `Render()` method next. This is the one that will take care of calling the GPU and instruct it to take all the vertex data and transform it into pixels to be put on our display. It looks like this:

```
public void Render()
{
    if (!_loadingComplete)
        return;

    var context = _deviceResources.D3DDeviceContext;
    var stride = Utilities.SizeOf<VertexPositionColor>();
    var offset = 0;

    var bufferBinding = new VertexBufferBinding(_vertexBuffer, stride,
offset);
    context.InputAssembler.SetVertexBuffers(0, bufferBinding);
    context.InputAssembler.SetIndexBuffer(_indexBuffer, Format.R16_UInt,
0);

    context.InputAssembler.PrimitiveTopology =
PrimitiveTopology.TriangleList;
    context.InputAssembler.InputLayout = _inputLayout;

    context.VertexShader.SetShader(_vertexShader, null, 0);
    context.VertexShader.SetConstantBuffers(0, _modelConstantBuffer);
    if (!_usingVprtShaders)
    {
        context.GeometryShader.SetShader(_geometryShader, null, 0);
    }

    context.PixelShader.SetShader(_pixelShader, null, 0);
    context.DrawIndexedInstanced(_indexCount, 2, 0, 0, 0);
}
```

We need to ensure that we have finished loading first. Due to the asynchronous nature of our code, `Render()` could be called to early, resulting in errors. So we check the `_loadingComplete` flag first.

Next, we get our context. This is our gateway to the DirectX device. We also get the size of each datapair and store that in the variable `stride`.

After that, we need to create the variable `VertexBufferBinding`. This is the way to instruct the pipeline what the data looks like and how to treat it when it is being fed to the pipeline. We use this to inform the Input Assembler stage in the pipeline where to get the data and where in the buffer the indexes for the triangles are. You see this in the calls to `SetVertexBuffers()` and `SetIndexBuffer()`.

Now, we need to tell the system how our data is structured. We use a triangle list, meaning that our indexes are a list of connected triangles. There are other topologies available--we could have single triangles, non-connected triangles, and so on. However, the triangle list is the most common and most efficient for our cause.

We also have to give it our `InputLayout` where we describe the structure of our data and the compiled `VertexShader`. We defined this earlier in our initialization code.

After setting the `VertexShader`, the buffers, optionally the `GeometryShader`, and finally the `PixelShader`, we can instruct the GPU to draw our image. This is done by calling the `DrawInstanceIndexed` method. As the name suggests, we can use an index to specify where in the buffer the relevant data is. This means that we can have multiple geometries defined in our buffers and index data, and call this method to define an offset and just draw that small part of our image. Doing this means we only have to transport one buffer of data and one set of shaders to the GPU, resulting in very efficient code. We only have one image in our buffer, so we set all the values to their defaults and draw everything we have defined.

Updating after changes

The world is changing all the time. People move their heads, and that means we have to redraw the scene. This is done in a new method we call `Update()`. Let's create that one now:

```
public void Update()
{
    if (!_loadingComplete)
        return;

    var modelTranslation = Matrix4x4.CreateTranslation(Position);
    _modelConstantBufferData.model = Matrix4x4.Transpose(modelTranslation);

    var context = _deviceResources.D3DDeviceContext;
    context.UpdateSubresource(ref _modelConstantBufferData,
_modelConstantBuffer);
}
```

You might be surprised by how simple this is. However, this is all that it takes to make sure that we see the cursor in the right position. If you look back at the initialization code, you will see we created the vertices in such a way that they were centered around the point (0,0,0), but this was for the local coordinate system; the coordinates only applied to our object. In the `Update()` method, we translate that into the world coordinate system. We take the `Position` property we declared earlier and make a translation out of that. Translation in this case means moving it along another coordinate system, so we can place our object in the real holographic world. The call to `Transpose()` switches columns and rows in the matrix, which is needed to draw things correctly. After that, all we need to do is set the transposed data in our model data we defined earlier in `_modelConstantBufferData` and feed that to the context.

Using our new class

We leave our `HoloCursor` class alone for a while now. We have created the class; it is about time we used it.

If you have a look at the `GazeSampleDirectxMain` class, if you have used the same name as I did, you will find a lot of references to the `SpinningCubeRenderer` class. We will have a closer look at what is going on this class, but for now we will simply duplicate most of the calls to the `SpinningCubeRenderer` class and rename that to our `HoloCursor` class. I have included the original calls to `SpinningCubeRenderer` in the code samples below, so you can easily find where I am adding the new code.

We will add a new private field:

```
private SpinningCubeRenderer spinningCubeRenderer;
private HoloCursor _holoCursor;
```

In the `SetHolographicSpace`, method we add

// Initialize the sample hologram:

```
spinningCubeRenderer = new SpinningCubeRenderer(deviceResources);
_holoCursor = new HoloCursor(deviceResources);
```

In the `Dispose()` method, we add the call to do the cleaning up. This is extremely important--if you forget this step, you will have a memory leak in the GPU and possibly a lock in that device, resulting in a frozen GPU (at least for your app):

```
if (spinningCubeRenderer != null)
{
    spinningCubeRenderer.Dispose();
    spinningCubeRenderer = null;
```

```
    }
    if (_holoCursor != null)
    {
        _holoCursor.Dispose();
        _holoCursor = null;
    }
```

In the Update() method, we add the following line:

```
spinningCubeRenderer.Update(timer);
_holoCursor.Update();
```

This will call our Update() method, which does the translation and transposing of the data and moves that data to our buffer.

One final thing needs to be done; we need to call Render. Not surprisingly, we do this in the Render() method:

```
spinningCubeRenderer.Render();
_holoCursor.Render();
```

That is it. If you run the application now, you will see the default colorful spinning cube as you would expect, but in front of it, you will also see our new object.

Our new cursor object

Positioning

This is all great and fine, but we need to do a bit more before we can move on. The cursor right now is stationary, and it needs to move. After all, the cursor is a helper object that shows the user where they are looking it. That means that if the user is moving their head, the cursor should move also. I have said before that the system makes sure that all objects are locked in the world coordinates, resulting in them being in a fixed place no matter where the user moves to, but we do not want that here. So we need to make some changes. Do not worry--the hard part is done, the changes are not that difficult.

First, we need to go to the `GazeSampleDirectMain` class. In the `Update()` method, we called the `Update()` for the `_holoCursor` instance. We need to extend that a bit:

```
var perceptionTimestamp =
PerceptionTimestampHelper.FromHistoricalTargetTime(DateTimeOffset.Now);
var spatialPointerPose =
SpatialPointerPose.TryGetAtTimestamp(currentCoordinateSystem,
perceptionTimestamp);
_holoCursor.PositionHologram(spatialPointerPose);
_holoCursor.Update();
```

So instead of just calling `Update()`, we also do some other things here. First, we get a variable `PerceptionTimestamp`. This is a timestamp from a moment in the past, right now, or a moment in the future. We will encounter this again later on, but for now just assume it is a normal timestamp. After that, we retrieve the variable `SpatialPointerPose`. This class gives us information about where the user is looking and at what time this is happening. In other words, this gives us information about the position of the virtual camera in HoloLens. We use this information to move our object, something we do in the `PositionHologram()` method. We will write this now:

```
public void PositionHologram(SpatialPointerPose pointerPose)
{
    if (pointerPose == null) return;

    var headPosition = pointerPose.Head.Position;
    var headDirection = pointerPose.Head.ForwardDirection;

    var distanceFromUser = 1.0f;
    Position = headPosition + distanceFromUser*headDirection;
}
```

This method, part of our `HoloCursor` class, will take the position of the camera and move the cursor so that it is right in front of the user. Whenever the user moves his head, the cursor will follow along.

Rotating

If you run this code, you will notice two things:

- The cursor stays nicely in front of the user, just like we want it to do
- As soon as you turn your head more than 90°C to the left or right, you lose sight of the object

This last part is a problem. The cursor moves with the head, but it does not rotate. The orientation stays the same. So when you move it enough, you will look at it from the back. Remember the normal vectors we discussed? I told you that the order in which we specify the indices for the vector is important because that defines the normal for the surfaces. Since the normal is pointing toward the user, this means the front of our cursor is also facing the user. However, when we move it around the user's head without rotating it, at some point they will look at the back of the cursor and that part is never drawn.

We need to rotate the cursor so that it always faces the user.

In `GazeSampleDirectXMain`, replace the call to `Update()`, just below the line where we call `PositionHologram`, with the following line:

```
_holoCursor.Update(spatialPointerPose);
```

We give it the same variable `spatialPointerPose` as we passed to `PositionHologram`. We need to change the signature of the `Update()` method to accept this new parameter as well. The `HoloCursor.Update` method now looks like this:

```
public void Update(SpatialPointerPose spatialPointerPose)
{
    if (!_loadingComplete)
        return;
    var cam = spatialPointerPose.Head;

    var modelTranslation = Matrix4x4.CreateTranslation(Position);
    var modelRotation = RotateCursor(spatialPointerPose);

    var modelTransform = modelRotation * modelTranslation;

    _modelConstantBufferData.model = Matrix4x4.Transpose(modelTransform);
```

```
    var context = _deviceResources.D3DDeviceContext;
    context.UpdateSubresource(ref _modelConstantBufferData,
_modelConstantBuffer);
}
```

We get the new field `cam` from `spatialPointerPose.Head`. This contains the location and rotation of the cam, so we can use this to rotate our cursor. We introduce a new field called `modelRotation` that we get from a call to the method `RotateCursor()`. We will define that method very soon, but for now just accept that this is the magic code that rotates the cursor so that it faces the user.

The rotation and translation are multiplied. This gives us the transformation we need. Remember, we need to rotate and move the cursor all the time. The rest of the method should look familiar now. Do not forget to set the parameter in the `Transpose()` method to `modelTransform` instead of the old `modelTranslation`.

We are almost done. All that is left is to define the `RotateCursor()` method. Here we go:

```
private Matrix4x4 RotateCursor(SpatialPointerPose pose)
{
    var facingNormal = Vector3.Normalize(-Position);

    var xAxisRotation = Vector3.Normalize(new Vector3(facingNormal.Z, 0.0f,
-facingNormal.X));
    var yAxisRotation = Vector3.Normalize(Vector3.Cross(facingNormal,
xAxisRotation));
    var rotationMatrix = new Matrix4x4(
        xAxisRotation.X, xAxisRotation.Y, xAxisRotation.Z, 1.0f,
        yAxisRotation.X, yAxisRotation.Y, yAxisRotation.Z, 1.0f,
        facingNormal.X, facingNormal.Y, facingNormal.Z, 1.0f,
        0.0f, 0.0f, 0.0f, 1.0f
        );

    return rotationMatrix;
}
```

There is a lot of trigonometry going on here. I will not explain how this works; if you want more in-depth knowledge, I suggest that you go online and find some information on how to do transformations and rotations using matrix calculations. This is pretty advanced mathematics and well beyond the scope of this book. If you do not get what is happening here, just accept that it works and use the code as is.

Now, we can run our app and see the cursor is moving the way we expect a cursor to move.

Next steps

We are not really done with our cursor. We want it to do so much more. We want it to be smaller but react when we hover over other objects.

That means we have to do a raycast-- each time the `Update()` is called, we need to check whether there are any objects that the cursor covers. We also need to position the cursor on top of surfaces of other objects; it needs to hug them, so to speak. This gives the user the feeling the cursor really is touching the object they want to interact with.

For now, we will not implement this; we will leave the cursor as it is and just use it to look at things.

Gaze in Unity

It is about time we added the cursor to our project. Before we start Unity, we need to create an object that will represent our cursor. In the DirectX sample, we used a simple two-dimensional tilted square, mainly because creating a nice rounded object with three dimensions takes up an enormous amount of time, vertices, and indices. In Unity, life is much simpler, so we will make a much better-looking cursor here.

The cursor

I have used SketchUp, a tool formerly from Google but now owned by Trimble, to draw a nice looking cursor. You can choose whatever software you want and feel comfortable using, but this is my choice for now. My cursor looks like this:

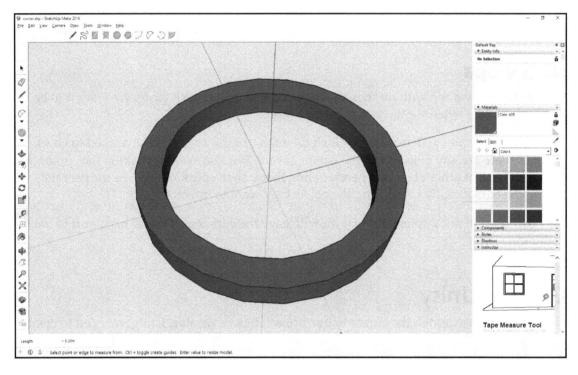

The cursor created in SketchUp

SketchUp is a very nice tool to quickly create three dimensional images. Unity understands the SketchUp format, so it can import these assets without any problem. Just save your SketchUp image under the `Assets /Prefabs` folder in our project under the name `cursor.skp`, and Unity will pick it up.

Creating the assets

We will need to create a new folder in the `Assets` folder named `Scripts`. It is a good idea to have all your assets organized--Unity is file-and-folder-based, and thus it can be hard to find your items again.

Just create a folder by right-clicking on the `Assets` tab, and selecting Folder. Name this `Scripts`.

Inside Scripts, we will add the script, called cursor. Unity will add the extension `.cs` to the file, so do not worry about that.

If you have done that, you can drag the newly created script and drop it on top of the main camera in the hierarchy. While we are dragging items, drag the cursor asset to the scene as well. Do not worry about the location; we will change the location at every frame anyway, so it does not matter where we put it in the scene initially.

Editing the script in Visual Studio

Now that we have everything set up, it is time we wrote some code. Build the *Unity* project and then open the generated `RockOn.sln` in Visual Studio. Again, ensure that you pick the generated `RockOn.sln` and not the one in the parent folder.

If you look at the project named Assembly-CSharp, you will see the folder Scripts we just created, with the `Cursor.cs` file inside it and the `Cursor` class. Open this file, and let's take a look at what we have:

```
using UnityEngine;
using System.Collections;

public class Cursor : MonoBehaviour {

    // Use this for initialization
    void Start () {
    }
    // Update is called once per frame
    void Update () {
    }
}
```

This is what each class looks like when you first create it in Unity. All classes derived from `MonoBehaviour` have a `Start()` and an `Update()` method. `Start()` gets called as soon as an instance of this class is being made. Since we dragged the script from the folder in Unity and dropped it onto the camera object, this means that as soon as the camera gets created, all of its components, including this class, get created as well. So the moment the engine creates an instance of the camera, it will also call the `Start()` method.

The `Update()` method is called for each frame. This is similar to the DirectX code we looked at earlier.

We need to tell the script what the cursor object that we are going to manipulate. To do this, we add a public field to the class, as follows:

```
[Tooltip("The gameobject to be used as cursor.")]
public Transform cursor;
```

I can almost hear you complain--you should never expose fields like this in a C# application. Besides that, the capitalization is all wrong--cursor should be with a capital C. Well, you would be right if we were dealing with a standard C# application here, but we are not--this is the convention Unity developers use.

Using the script in Unity

Save this script, but do not compile it just yet. Go back to Unity, click on the camera, and observe the Inspector:

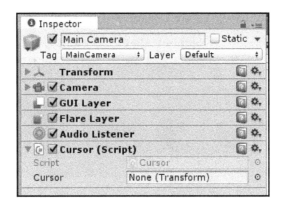

The inspector window for the camera

As you can see, Unity has picked up the change. It saw the public field and made it into a property in the Inspector. It even fixed the case here.

Go back to Visual Studio, and add another field in this class:

```
[Tooltip("The position the cursor is placed at when nothing is hit.")]
public float maxDistance = 5.0f;
```

This will also be visible in Unity. We will use this to position the cursor far away when nothing is underneath it. So if we have no objects we can interact within our view, the cursor will be five meters away from the user.

In Unity, drag the cursor object from the hierarchy to the Cursor field in the Inspector for the camera. The result will look like this:

The Inspector after setting the cursor

As you can see, we also have the tooltip working here, helping the user of the script and telling him what to expect.

Implementing the cursor code

Do a build in Unity and move it to Visual Studio. It is time to write some code again. We need to move the cursor object in the Update() method. This is the code:

```
private void Update()
{
    if (cursor == null)
        return;
    var camTrans = Camera.main.transform;
    cursor.position = camTrans.position + camTrans.forward*maxDistance;
    cursor.up = camTrans.up;
}
```

First, we check whether we actually have a cursor. It would be pointless to do anything when we have no object to draw.

Then, we take the position of the main camera. To do this, we can use the static property main in the Camera class--this will return the camera. This has a transform property that tells us all about the position and rotation. We take this position and add the maxDistance to it in the direction the user is looking--this we give to the Cursor.

The cursor.up part makes sure that we are facing the right way.

I think you will agree with me that this is a lot easier than the code we used for the DirectX sample.

Testing for touch

In the DirectX sample, we skipped the part where we test for interaction with other objects. We will, however, do this in our Unity code.

To do this, we have to use ray casting. Ray casting is a technique that allows us to examine whether the cursor hits an object or not. Imagine a ray of light coming out of the HoloLens, right from between your eyes. It will move straight into the distance. The moment it hits something, it will return and then you know that there is something out there that might be of interest. This is exactly how this works.

We will update our `Update()` code in Visual Studio:

```
private void Update()
{
    if (cursor == null)
        return;

    var camTrans = Camera.main.transform;

    RaycastHit raycastHit;

    if (Physics.Raycast(new Ray(camTrans.position, camTrans.forward), out
raycastHit))
    {
        cursor.position = raycastHit.point;
    }
    else
    {
        cursor.position = camTrans.position + camTrans.forward*maxDistance;
        cursor.up = camTrans.forward;
    }
}
```

The first part has not changed. We check for the presence of the cursor and copy the transform of the camera.

Next, we do a call to `Physics.Raycast()`. This does exactly what I described earlier-- it looks forward, straight from the point we give it in the direction we give it . In our case, we use `camTrans.position` and `camTrans.forward` for these. The result can be false, in which case nothing is hit and we run the previous code. If it is true, we have hit something and then we set the position of our cursor on top of the item we have hit. This is stored in `raycastHit.point`, so we can use that.

Run this code and observe--this does not work.

You might wonder why it does not work. The reason for this is a matter of optimization. In a complex world, such as the ones Unity can create, checking each item can be a resource-intensive and time-consuming operation. To speed things up, Unity ignores all objects during a ray cast, except for those that are marked to be included for this.

We do this by adding another component to our guitar object in Unity. Go to Unity, select the guitar in the hierarchy, and click on Add Component in the Inspector. You get a menu asking you what you want to add. Here, you select Box Collider.

A collider is a component that reacts when the object collides with other objects. There are several kinds of collider available, each with its own shape. Try to find one that matches the shape of the object you are attaching it to. You can have a mesh collider as well--this one fits your object like a glove. The downside is that it is very computing intensive to use this. If you want this, we suggest you use a mesh that is simpler in geometry but still more or less fits your object and then use that in your collider. For now, a box collider will be fine.

Build the project in Unity, go to Visual Studio, do a rebuild, and run it. You will see the cursor will be far in the back as you stare at nothing, but it will be on top of the guitar when you look at that. Since we use a box collider, you will note that the system registers a hit when you look just past the neck of the guitar. However, I guess most users will not notice it--it looks close enough.

Events

Looking at things is pretty nice, showing the cursor when the user looks at something they can use even better. However, the system would be quite useless if we could not command the app to do something with objects. We need to use gestures.

The HoloLens currently only supports one gesture. It recognizes the tap gesture. In chapter 6, *Take a Look Around You*, we will delve into this more and use the different gestures to move our instruments across the stage, but we need to set things up here to delay some groundwork.

Gestures in DirectX

Take a look at our *GazeSampleDirectX* project and the main class `GazeSampleDirectXMain`. In here, you will find the `spatialInputHandler` field of the `SpatialInputHandler` type. This class is part of the template and thus not a part of the framework. Open this file and take a look at it:

```
public class SpatialInputHandler
{
    private SpatialInteractionManager interactionManager;
    private SpatialInteractionSourceState sourceState;
    public SpatialInputHandler()
    {
        interactionManager = SpatialInteractionManager.GetForCurrentView();
        interactionManager.SourcePressed += this.OnSourcePressed;
    }
    public SpatialInteractionSourceState CheckForInput()
    {
        SpatialInteractionSourceState sourceState = this.sourceState;
        this.sourceState = null;
        return sourceState;
    }

    public void OnSourcePressed(SpatialInteractionManager sender,
SpatialInteractionSourceEventArgs args)
    {
        sourceState = args.State;
    }
}
```

The InteractionManager class

The `InteractionManager` class used here is the one that handles all interaction. You need to get one for each view--it is possible to have multiple views in DirectX applications. This does not apply to our HoloLens applications, but we need to call this anyway.

The `InteractionManager` generates events whenever something of interest happens. Next, you can ask it for any events that have happened in a certain timeframe. This means that, when your app is busy doing something else, you can always go back and not lose any gesture your user has made.

The `InteractionManager` supports the following events:

- SourceDetected
- SourceLost
- SourcePressed
- SourceReleased
- SourceUpdated
- InteractionDetected

The first five events are generic events. They tell you what happened, but not what they mean. In the given arguments, you can ask what the source of the event was. Currently, the following source types are recognized:

- Hand
- Voice
- Controller
- Other

The `SourceState` property you see being used tells us if the state is Pressed or not, the time and the location this happened in the space in front of the device. An interesting field here is `SourceLossRisk`--this tells us whether it is likely the device will lose track of the source or not. This might happen if, for instance, the hand is detected on the edge of the view of the cameras or if it moves fast in the view area.

The SpatialGestureRecognizer

Using this class in our code, we can detect if a source is pressed. It does not matter how the event is raised--this could be an air-tap, a voice command, or by using the clicker. However, if we want to know more about what is going on, we can use another class in the `Windows.UI.Input.Spatial` namespace--the `SpatialGestureRecognizer` class.

This class takes the data from the `InteractionManager` and turns that into more meaningful data. This class can generate events depending on the kind of gesture the user uses. For most gestures, it recognizes the `Started`, `Completed`, `Updated`, and `Cancelled` states. These are those gestures:

- Hold
- Manipulation
- Navigation

Next to these, it also has the `RecognitionStarted`, `RecognitionEnded`, and `Tapped` events.

If you need to have control over the kinds of gestures you want to recognize, I suggest that you use the `SpatialGestureRecognizer` class. However, this is a pretty slow way of dealing with gestures. If you just want to know if the user did a tap, or used the voice command for select or the clicker, but you do not really care which one it was, use `InteractionManager`.

The `SpinningCubeRenderer` class uses this to handle a tapped event--if you air-tap, the cube will be repositioned. You could do the same with our cursor.

Gestures in Unity

On the Unity side of things, it works in an identical manner. We can interact with objects using gestures. To do this, we need to create another script.

As I have said, scripts are components that are attached to objects in the hierarchy. For a general event handler to recognize gestures, it does not really matter which object owns the script but I would suggest that you use the camera. After all, it is always there, so we can ensure that our scripts get called.

Let's take a look at how this is done.

In Unity, create a new script in the `Scripts` folder and name it `GestureHandler`. Again, do not bother with the `.cs` extension--Unity will take care of this.

You do not have to build the project--the moment you open Visual Studio, you will see the file there as well. If you had Visual Studio open, you might have to reload the *Assembly-CSharp* project to see the file appear.

This is what the code looks like:

```
using System;
using UnityEngine;
using UnityEngine.VR.WSA.Input;

public class GestureHandler : MonoBehaviour
{
    private GestureRecognizer _gestureRecognizer;
    void Start () {
        _gestureRecognizer = new GestureRecognizer();
        _gestureRecognizer.TappedEvent += GestureRecognizerOnTappedEvent;
        _gestureRecognizer.StartCapturingGestures();
```

```
    }

    private void GestureRecognizerOnTappedEvent(InteractionSourceKind
source, int tapCount, Ray headRay)
    {
        // Here we handle the events
    }
}
```

The code is pretty straightforward. We create an instance of `GestureRecognizer` and tell it what event to fire if the `Tapped` event occurs. Like the DirectX solution, we could also have written handlers for the other events such as Hold, Manipulation, and Navigation. We finish the `Start()` with the `StartCapturingGestures()` method.

The `GestureRecognizerOnTappedEvent()` method gets called whenever the user performs an air-tap. You can test this by running the app and placing a breakpoint there. You can take a look at the source parameter to see what caused the event. Similar to the DirectX code, this can be one of the following:

- Hand
- Controller
- Voice
- Other

We will use this event in later chapters, but for now let's finish this off with something interesting to start with. We want to place more guitars wherever we look and tap.

Creating a prefab

To do so, we must make a prefab out of our guitar. A prefab in Unity is analogous to a class in C#. It is a template for objects we can use later on.

First, we will tell our script which prefab we will recreate by tapping on it. Add the following field in our `GestureManager` script :

```
public GameObject objectToPlace;
```

To create a prefab, we first need to create an object in Unity and then move it to the Assets pane. Later, we can use this to create instances of this prefab. Like C# instances, they will be live objects based on the template.

So, grab the guitar from the hierarchy tab and move it to the `Prefabs` folder in the assets pane. Once you have done that, delete the guitar from the hierarchy.

Since we already had a guitar in our assets, namely the one we imported from the store, we will have a guitar 1. We can rename this by going to the Inspector and giving it a different name in the top edit box. We will call this **GuitarPrefab**. You can also select the object in the Assets pane and press *F2* to rename it; the result is the same:

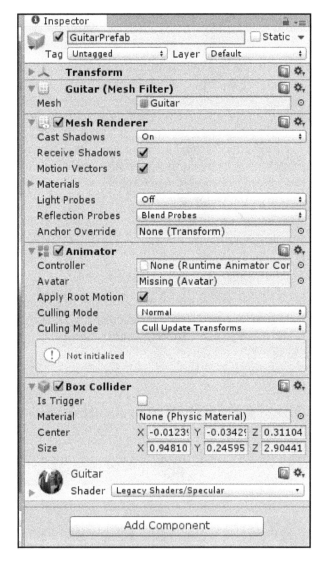

The Inspector pane for our guitar prefab

Once we have done this, we should tell the script that this is the prefab we want to use. To do so, you should select the camera, look at the script we have added there, and drag the prefab from the assets pane to the new slot saying Object To Place:

The new Object To Place parameter in action

Creating the creation code

Build the *Unity* project and open our `GestureHandler.cs` file in Visual Studio.

Change the event to look like this:

```
private void GestureRecognizerOnTappedEvent(
    InteractionSourceKind source,
    int tapCount,
    Ray headRay)
{
    if (objectToPlace == null)
        return;
    var distance = new Random().Next(2, 10);
    var location =
        transform.position +
        transform.forward*distance;

    Instantiate(
        objectToPlace,
        location,
        Quaternion.LookRotation(transform.up, transform.forward));
}
```

First, we check whether the user of our script has actually attached a prefab. If so, we generate a random distance from the user. Then, we create a location by looking at the transform.position of the object that contains this script, which in our case is the camera.

We call the Instantiate() method that creates an instance of the object and place it at the location. The Quaternion defines the rotation of the object. Here, we want the object to face the user.

Run this. You will see that the space is empty besides our cursor; now, tap and see the guitars appearing. Tap again and again until you think you have got enough guitars to form a solid rock and roll band.

A whole lot of guitars

However... what is a band without sound? That is what we will look at in the next chapter.

Summary

In this chapter, we have taken a look at gaze and gestures, the two most important ways of communicating with HoloLens apps. We examined what a NUI is and where it came from. We started developing in DirectX and have taken a look at the different parts we need to tell the GPU to draw those images on the screen. That also included shaders and the way we break down images into triangles. After that, we moved to Unity3D and gave our users the power to place objects everywhere around them, using nothing else besides gaze and gestures.

Make Some Noise - Sounds

Most developers that I know ignore sounds in their applications. Let's be honest: most applications do not need sounds. If you were working on the next great word processor, you would not think about using a ping sound every time the user presses the *Enter* key. That would get quite tedious and tiring pretty soon.

However, we are not writing a word processor. We are writing immersive software-- software that mimics the real world. In the real world, everything we do is accompanied by sound, so we should do the same.

Sounds can be very powerful. They can give a sense of realism to the virtual world we are building. Not only that, they also can act as part of the user interface. We can use sounds to give the user information about what is going on in our virtual world.

Holograms we draw in our apps are only visible when the user looks at them. Since the field of view can be somewhat limiting, it is not always obvious where the user should look to find things of interest. Sounds, however, can be played at all times. Sounds can be heard no matter where the user is looking, providing a true 360 degree experience.

When developing for HoloLens, sounds are extremely important. We want the user to feel as if the objects they work with are as real as possible. Everything we do in real life generates some sort of noise. As I am typing this text, I can hear the clicking sounds the keys on my keyboard make. They are not noticeable; most of the time I do not even hear them, but if they were to suddenly disappear, I would notice that.

Pressing buttons in applications usually does not generate sounds. In HoloLens apps, they should; we want to give the user feedback.

Be warned though that too many sounds can be distracting and would take away the effect we want to achieve.

Let's take a look at good sound design in holographic applications.

How our bodies work when it comes to sound

Stereo sound is something most people are familiar with. Back in the 60s and 70s, you could buy albums that contained nothing but stereophonic sound effects. You hear a car coming from the left, then going to the right. Then, there was an airplane coming from the right flying to the left. Next to that, there is the Doppler effect. The Doppler effect is the way sound changes as it moves toward or away from the listener. There is a shift in the frequency that we, as people, can use to identify whether something is moving toward us or away from us. Think of the sound of a train passing by; if it is coming toward us, the sound will be slightly higher in tone than when it is moving away from us. Together with varying in volume, we could use this to simulate the placement of sounds in music and computer programs.

Although, at that time we, were quite impressed with this, it always turned out to be something moving from one side to the other. In HoloLens, we do not use this. The reason for this is that in real life, this almost never happens. You might experience this if you are standing by a road and stare right ahead across that road, listening to the cars. However, in reality, you would probably look in the direction the car comes from and turn your head as the car passes by to see it go. You would have a completely different experience that way.

This is what spatial sound does. It takes that experience and replicates it in HoloLens.

Head Related Transfer Function

As you know, the HoloLens has two rather small, red colored built-in speakers. These speakers, however small, are capable of delivering very realistic spatial sound. To do this, they use a so-called **Head Related Transfer Function** (**HRTF**) filter.

Before we can discuss how this technique works, we need to take a look at how determining the source and direction of sounds works in a typical person.

Left and right

We use our ears in two different ways when determining the direction of sounds we hear. First, we have something called **interaural time difference** (**ITD**). When we hear a sound, it reaches both ears. However, it does not reach both ears at the same time. If the source of the sound is to the left of the person, the sound will reach the left ear first and then the right ear. This way, we can tell the sound is coming from the left.

Next, we have **interaural level difference** (**ILD**). Again, if we have a sound source to the left, the volume of the sound will be larger when it reaches the left ear than when it reaches the right ear. After all, the volume of sounds will be decreased by the additional distance squared. So, the overall level of the sound will be less when it finally reaches the ear on the right-hand side.

We use both techniques at the same time. However, some physics applies here as well. Sounds below 800 hertz are very hard to hear with human ears. We can hear them, but we are not very good at hearing the volume differences. Thus, the interaural-level difference does not work very well in this scenario. For these sounds, we rely mostly on the interaural time difference, or the difference in timing when we hear sounds in each ear.

A funny thing happens when we hear sounds above approximately 1500 hertz. Sounds at this level have wavelengths which are shorter than the size of an average human head. This means the sounds are blocked by our own body; not every soundwave will reach the ear on the shadow side of the head. When this happens, we use the interaural level difference--the difference in the volume of these sounds is big enough to make it easy to distinguish where the sound is coming from. Of course, all this is dependent on age--younger people will hear sounds in a broader spectrum than people who are older.

In all other frequencies--between 800 Hertz and 1500 Hertz--for the average person, we use both techniques at the same time.

Front and back

What we have just discussed is very helpful in determining which side the sound is coming from. We use this to check whether the noise we hear is coming from the right or from the left. However, you may ask, what about the front and back? Almost everybody is able to tell whether someone who calls out their name is in front of or behind them. Since we have no ears on the back of our heads, we have to use something else to help us find the source.

The trick used here is due to the shape of our bodies, and especially the shape of our ears. Sounds coming from the front have different properties than the same sound coming from the back. For instance, sounds reaching our ear from the front will enter the aural cavity directly and even be enhanced slightly by the outer ear. If, however, sounds originate from behind us, a large portion of the sounds will be blocked by our outer ear, and the sounds have to go around this before they can enter our ears. We notice this difference, and this tells us where the source is. The same goes for the rest of our body, such as sounds being deflected by our torsos and shoulders.

Up and down

So far, we have taken a look at audio sources that are in a horizontal plane around us. However, we also have the vertical plane. How does that work?

In general, we use head movement somewhat to listen to the direction when it comes to sounds coming from above or below us. We also tend to notice if sounds are echoed from our shoulders--this would indicate a sound source above us; or sounds tend to be muffled slightly by our bodies, leading us to understand the sounds we hear are coming from below.

To be honest, we are not very good at determining the direction of a sound on the vertical plane. We can to some extent, but nowhere near as good as on the horizontal plane.

Head Related Transfer Functions

Next to the ILD and ITD, we have the HRTF. These are ways our body helps us to determine the direction sounds are coming from. You could see this as mathematical equations our body uses to determine the source of sounds. As we described before, we as humans use all sorts of tricks to find out where a sound is coming from; we could translate these into mathematical functions. That is what we are talking about here.

Moving our heads

If we are not capable of determining the source of a sound, we tend to move our heads. Turning our heads left and right, or up and down a bit, will have different effects. Say a sound origin is located directly to our right. If we hear this, then the sound entering our right ear will be, for instance, twice as loud as the sound entering our left ear. If we, however, turn our heads a bit, this difference will be something like 1.5 times as loud. By constantly moving our head a little bit, we can use this information to calculate the direction of the source of the sound.

Echo

Another thing that helps us to locate the source and direction of sounds is the echo that sounds have. When a sound comes from the left, we hear that in our left ear first, then the right ear, but then we also get to hear the echo as the sound bounces off the wall and returns to our ears. The ear that will be hit first is dependent, of course, on the distance we are from walls and other objects, but we can use this to find the source as well.

Spatial sound in computer programs

When we need spatial sound in a computer program, we are faced with one technical limitation. We only have two speakers. One for the left ear, and one for the right ear; that's it. For years, this has been considered enough-- with two speakers, we can create stereo sounds by changing the volume of the sounds for each ear. Along with using the Doppler effect, we can use this to simulate the effect of a passing car. However, as you understand by now, this is not enough. We do not live in a two-dimensional world, so we should not use two-dimensional sounds.

Using spatial sound in a computer program is hard. It requires special hardware and sophisticated algorithms to simulate all the effects we have discussed above. The good news is that with HoloLens, we have those at our disposal.

In a perfect world, we would work like this. We would take our user, place them in a room, and place some microphones in their ears. Then, we would play sounds from all over the room and record how they reach the microphones. After all, we just learned that the way our bodies are shaped effects the way we hear sounds and how we interpret the direction they are coming from. By recording sounds from all possible locations and noting how sounds in the ear differ from the actual sounds we played, we can generate the HRTFs for that person.

This is, of course, not very practical. We cannot have the user in the room to do this before we have deployed our app to the user. Luckily for us, most people are more or less built the same way. The method I have just described is exactly what some research laboratories have done, and they have published their findings. All the HRTFs are documented and available for use. The people at Microsoft have taken some of these libraries and implemented them in the audio SDK we are going to use. So, we can just specify a location, and the HRTFs will be used to simulate all of the effects we have just described.

The reason this works in HoloLens and not in older systems, such as traditional applications, is that with HoloLens and other virtual reality devices, we can accurately track the position of each ear. This also works if the user moves their head. This way, we can change the characteristics of sounds to mimic real-life scenarios.

Most of this is of no concern to us; we can just use it. Sometimes, however, you need to be aware of this in order to solve bugs or to get a better experience. Now that you know all this, you can use it much better in your apps and make them a truly immersive experience.

Sound design

You need to plan your sounds. Just like graphics, sounds are an important part of the experience for the user. As I have stated before, you need a good modeler and visual artist in your team if you want to create compelling experiences. The same goes for sound; you need to have effects that are used well. Now, it is hard to find people who can advise you on that. The gaming industry figured this out long ago, but for most developers, this is all new. Add to that the capabilities of HoloLens, and you will understand why we need to spend some serious time on this topic.

The design principles for spatial sound

We need to discuss some general principles that come into play when we want to use spatial sound in our applications. These design principles should be firmly locked in your brain, as they apply all the time, in every single app you will write for this platform.

The benefits of spatial sound

By using the spatial sound capabilities of HoloLens, we can have a great experience. After all, we all use sounds in our everyday life. Have you ever lost your phone and then called it from another phone just to find it? Have you ever had one of those key rings that whistle when you whistle so that you can locate your keys? These are the things spatial sound can do for you.

There are four key things spatial sound provides you as a developer. The boundaries between these are not as clear as they appear to be; most sound effects have more than one benefit.

Grounding

We can use spatial sound to help the user find objects. We are used to having our holograms fixed in the world by giving them coordinates, but we can do more. By giving objects a sound, coming from that actual object, we ground those objects in the real world around the user. We are so used to finding objects by listening to them that it is very natural to do this in HoloLens apps as well.

User attention

Sometimes, we want the user to act upon a hologram. We can give visual cues when we want the user to do something with a hologram, but that only works if they see the item we want them to work on. By having a sound coming from the hologram, the user's attention will be drawn to the object and, thus, notify them of an expected action. Of course, this works best if you combine visual and auditory notifications.

Immersion

We want the user to believe all holograms are real. Although the user will know it is all fake, we want to have as much of an immersive experience as we can get. We do this by having objects behave in the same way they do in real life. One of the things objects do in the real world is make noise. So, if we move a hologram from one side of the room to the other, but somewhere along the path it hits another item (real or not), the user expects a sound to be heard. After all, that is what happens in the real world. By providing this kind of auditory feedback, the user will feel more immersed.

Interaction design

When dealing with user interface items, such as buttons and checkboxes, we want to give the user feedback whenever they are used. If the user air taps on a button, it would be good design to have a click sound played. We can do the same for other UI-related effects, such as zooming, swiping, and so on. This is something that people have been doing in regular screen-based applications as well, but because everything in HoloLens has a three-dimensional, world-oriented location in the area around the user, we can use this to have the sound coming from the object itself.

Best practices in sound design

Just as with graphics, using sounds in your app requires design. There are people who have studied this field for years and have years of experience designing the best possible use of sounds in games and movies. Chances are, you are not one of them. Luckily, there are some best practices you can follow to have a great experience in your app.

In no particular order, these are best practices you can think of when using sounds in your holographic app:

- **Use spatial sound as much as possible**: In the real world, sounds come from a source; there is no reason not to do this when building your holographic app. You might be tempted to think you only need spatial sounds when you want to draw attention to items, but this is not the case. Even ambient background music can be spatialized. Although it is true that generating spatial sound costs in terms of CPU usage, the difference is not big enough to justify not using it. So, use spatial sound as much as possible.

- **Make it clear where sounds come from**: Sounds have a source. They do not come out of thin air. People tend to like to know where sounds come from, so make sure that you have that covered in your app. When items make a noise, make sure that it is clear to the user where that noise comes from. Your user will look for the source, so it is up to you to give them a clue as to what the source is. Do not use invisible sources. Of course, the exception here is when you use ambient background sounds; they do not need to have such a source.

- **Make sure that your ambient sounds do not mask other sounds**: If you have fairly loud rock music in your app to create that rocking atmosphere, you might run the risk of this music drowning out the subtle sound a button makes when the user clicks on it. Or worse, you might have a piece of your world generate a sound to attract the attention of the user, but they do not hear it because of your loud ambient music. If you use ambient sounds, make sure that the volume level is low enough for other sounds to be heard.

- **Place your sounds in a logical place**: People are used to sounds coming from certain directions, for example, the sounds of your footsteps comes from below-- not from above, a passing airplane will be heard coming from above, and so on. People are so used to this that they will look up to the sky if they hear an airplane, even if you place the source of the sound on the floor. This will, of course, confuse people; they expect something, but something else happens. Try to avoid this confusion and place sounds where a user might expect them.

- **Use real sounds**: People are very good at interpreting sounds. We can distinguish between all sorts of sounds and identify what makes those sounds without too much trouble. In order to have the best experience, you should use that ability. Use real sounds, sounds that people can relate to. Try to avoid computer-generated sounds as much as possible. Of course, when I say *real sounds* I mean sounds that occur in the real world. They will still be generated by the computer, since that is what the source of the sound is, but your user will recognize it as real sound. One particular example is using the human voice. Voices are so native to use that we tend to treat them with more attention. Use this and try to have human voices in your app wherever you can.

These best practices should be observed as much as possible, but not more than that. I always say:

> "*You have to follow these rules, always and no matter what, except, of course, if you have a good reason not to.*"

Use your own judgement.

Applying these principles

If you want to use sounds in your app, and I assume that I have convinced you that you do, you need to have source files for these. In the world of gaming and movie pictures, there are people responsible for making these sounds. This process, named **Foley**, takes place in studios, where sound engineers record the sounds they need, sometimes recording the real thing, but more often simulating the sounds using other means. You can imagine a recording engineer standing next to a door with his recording devices to capture the sound of a closing door. The recording of other sounds is often done using other means. One of the most famous examples of this is the use of two coconut halves to mimic the sound horse hoofs make. This last example is brilliantly used in the Monty Python movie, *Monty Python and the Holy Grail*.

Licensing

You can do this yourself, but you do not have to. There are a lot of resources that can help you get access to stock sounds. Do a search on the internet and you will find dozens of sites that offer free or almost free sounds you can use in your app. Do pay attention to the licenses though; free does not always mean you can reuse the sounds in your app and make money out of it. I will not go into the different licensing models, but you have to be careful not to do something that goes against the will of the original owner of the sounds.

Most of the sources for free online sounds have some form of the available **Creative Commons** licenses. These licenses tell you what you can do with the sounds. The same applies to sites that contain 3D models and those that have other artwork, such as textures and images. It is worth the time to investigate the different licensing models there are and what model the copyright owner of the asset you want to employ uses.

I suggest that you do some research on the different licensing models. However, most models allow you to use the work without paying for it. All you need to do is mention the original author of the work you are using. Some models allow you to make money on your product containing their artwork; others do not. Take a look at the different websites that deal with this sort of work before using artwork in your app.

Background music

Background music is a great way to create atmosphere in a virtual environment. There are different movie clips to be seen on YouTube, where you can see and hear the difference when they change the background music to a certain scene. If you watch these, you will notice the effect the background music has on the overall atmosphere of the scene.

You can achieve a similar goal in your app. However, keep in mind that background music is named that way for a reason; it should remain in the background. As we discussed earlier, it should never mask the sounds holograms might make in your application.

Not every app needs background music all the time. Some apps can benefit from background music in all scenes, such as in games. However, other apps only need it during start up, during transitional screens, and other such places--do not over use it. Silence can truly be golden sometimes.

Background music, if long enough, might take a up lot of room in your app's package. It might be useful to stream that data instead of packaging it all up in your app. We will not discuss how to do this here; this is a basic UWP programming for streaming audio. In our examples, we will include the source sounds in our app. I just wanted to let you know about the alternative, if file size is of concern to you.

DirectX

Before we begin coding in DirectX, there is something that I need to tell you. It seems the authors of the templates we use in Visual Studio forgot about sounds. I have said this before; sounds are something most developers tend to forget about, and apparently, this is also true for the people writing the templates.

Getting the right NuGet packages

The templates we have used so far all have the correct references and NuGet packages preinstalled, with the exception of the libraries for XAudio, the sound engine used in DirectX, so you have to import that yourself.

Use the Package Manager Console to install the `SharpDX.XAudio2` library, or go to **Manage Packages** and install it from there:

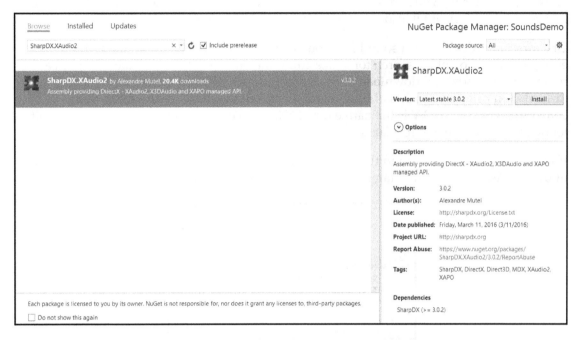

The NuGet Package SharpDX.XAudio2

If you have installed this, you will probably notice that the version you installed does not match the versions of the base libraries for `SharpDX` that come preinstalled with the template. You have to update those libraries as well. Just go to the **Updates** panel in the NuGet Package Manager and click on U**pdate all**. This might take some time, but at least you end up with the latest packages that actually work with the XAudio parts.

You need to do this for every holographic application that you will write that contains audio. I hope that by now you understand how important sounds are, so I am sure that you will do this for every single application you write for HoloLens; they should all contain audio.

Once you have done this, you are ready to go!

Let's begin by creating a new application. By now, you know the drill--just create a new blank app by starting Visual Studio and creating a new **Universal Holographic app**. Now, add the XAudio package, as described above.

It is time to do some audio coding. I want the app to behave slightly different. The default sample app shows us a multi-colored cube that spins around. If you air tap somewhere around you, the cube will suddenly appear at the position you are looking at. We have seen this before. Now, I want it also to make a nice sound when you do this.

Of course, in order to play a sound file, you need to have a sound file. Sounds simple enough, right? Go online, search for a nice audio file on one of the many sites that have royalty free sounds, and download them. Do not use an MP3 file, choose a .WAV file instead. You can play all sorts of files in HoloLens, but you have to do a lot of the converting yourself. WAV is the native format XAudio understands, so you save yourself a lot of time if you use that format.

If you have found a nice sound that might accompany the moving cube, create a new folder under the **Assets** folder and name it **Sounds**; place your file there:

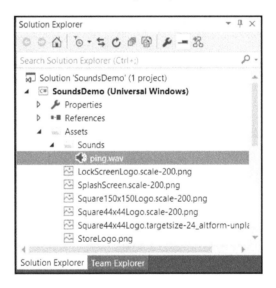

The location of our sounds

It is time to write some code.

Create a new class in the same location as the `SpinningCubeRenderer.cs` file. Let's call it `SoundPlayer`, which will be placed in the `SoundPlayer.cs` file. The class implements `IDisposable`, or is a subclass of the `Disposer` class, which is part of the template--I'll leave that up to you. The `Disposer` class is a nice helper, but to me it feels like it is a bit overkill. I just want to make sure that our resources are disposed, and I can do that perfectly myself using the `IDisposable` pattern.

Loading and preparing the sound we want to play

Our class will have two parts: one to load in the sound data so that it is ready to play whenever we want it to, and one to actually play the sounds.

It is best to load the sounds beforehand--loading data from the assets might take time, and we want the sounds to be available when we need them. Any delay caused by loading will distract from the experience the user has.

That being said, when you have a large sound file, or you only need to play it once or very sparingly, you might want to load the file at the time you need it. After all, it is doesn't do us much good to have a large chunk of data in memory when we never need it.

In this case, however, we need the sound to be ready at all times. As soon as the user air taps, we need to play it, so it had better be ready!

Our class has two methods and four private fields. Let me show you the first method first, then I will explain what is going on:

```
public void LoadSounds(string soundFileAssetName)
{
    _xaudio = new XAudio2();
    var masteringVoice = new MasteringVoice(_xaudio);
    var nativeStream = new NativeFileStream(soundFileAssetName,
        NativeFileMode.Open,
        NativeFileAccess.Read,
        NativeFileShare.Read);
    _soundStream = new SoundStream(nativeStream);
    _waveFormat = _soundStream.Format;

    _audioBuffer = new AudioBuffer()
    {
        Stream = _soundStream.ToDataStream(),
        AudioBytes = (int)_soundStream.Length,
        Flags = BufferFlags.EndOfStream
    };
}
```

This is the method we will use to load the data. First, we create an instance of the XAudio2 class. This is the entry point for all DirectX Audio calls. Think of this as our main sound engine.

The DirectX Audio framework works with voices. To be more precise, the audio framework is a pipeline that uses voices. You can think of the voices as the parts that actually make the sounds. We always have a master voice. This is the thing we will give to the sound engine to produce the audio we want. The master voice is responsible for taking all processed data and feeding it to the actual sound device. This is at the end of the pipeline. The data inside our pipeline has to come from other sources--these are either mixers or actual sources. We will not deal with mixers, but we will deal with sources. These are called the `SourceVoice`, and we will encounter them shortly.

We have our mastervoice; next, we will create a native Stream. This class takes care of loading the data from the file we have specified. We cannot use the normal file IO we use in Store apps, since they use a different format. Remember, in DirectX, we are dealing with a much lowerlevel system than you might be accustomed to. So, we need a nativestream and tell it to open the file to access it, to read and set the share flag to read as well. This means that we can open the file, but we will not have exclusive access to it. That is fine of course; we just want to get to the bits.

When this is done, we can create a new `SoundStream` class and give it our newly created `NativeStream`. The `NativeStream` class does not care about the type of data, it could be anything, whereas `SoundStream`, on the other hand, will only have sounds in it. We can interrogate `SoundStream` and ask it what the WAVE format of the audio file is. This WAVE format describes the internal structure of our audio file. It tells us the bits per seconds, the bits per sample, the sample size, and so on. There are a lot of properties that are important to the audio engine. We do not really care about them at this point, so we just store the WAVE format we get from `SoundStream`.

We are almost done. We have the native stream, we have the sound stream, and we have the format. Now, we need to have the actual data coming out of those streams. The data will be stored in a buffer. More accurately, all data needed to produce audio will be buffered as it comes out of the stream. The buffer can be thought of as a bucket underneath a water hose that fills up until you have enough water to do what you want to do with it. In this analogy, the hose is the stream, the bucket is the buffer.

So, create an audio buffer, give it the data stream coming out of the sound stream, tell it how big it is, and make sure that the buffer closes whenever the stream runs out of data. You see all that in the constructor of the buffer.

That is it. The sound is ready to be loaded in, the buffer is ready to be used, and we are almost ready to play the sounds.

Playing the sound

It is time to write the part that actually plays the sounds. Let's create a new method in our class. We will call it `PlaySound` because, well, that is what it does:

```
public void PlaySound()
{
    var sourceVoice = new SourceVoice(
        _xaudio,
        _waveFormat,
        false);

    sourceVoice.SubmitSourceBuffer(
        _audioBuffer,
        _soundStream.DecodedPacketsInfo);

    sourceVoice.Start();
}
```

This looks simple enough. We create a `SourceVoice` object. This will be the actual voice making the noise. We give it our `XAudio2` instance, tell it what format the data will be in, and say that we do not want to use callbacks when the sounds have finished playing. That last part is indicated by the `false` in the constructor.

When we have created this voice, we can give it the buffer we created in the previous part. To do this, it needs `_audioBuffer`, obviously, and it needs some information about the structure of that data. That last part is stored in `_soundStream`, so we can use that as well.

Now, all that is left to do is just call `Start()` and it will start. Easy enough, right?

Actually play the sounds

We have our code ready. Now, we should place it in the right spots to make use of it. I have called my project `SoundsDemo`, so I have a class called `SoundsDemoMain`. You might have another name, but it will end in `Main`. This is where the `SpinningCubeRenderer` instance is created, so you will have seen this before.

Speaking of which, the place where we create our `SpinningCubeRenderer` is also a great place to create an instance of our new `SoundPlayer` and load the data we need. Find the bit in the `SetHolographicSpace()` method where the `SpinningCubeRenderer` is called and change it to look more like this:

```
#if DRAW_SAMPLE_CONTENT
    // Initialize the sample hologram.
    spinningCubeRenderer = new SpinningCubeRenderer(deviceResources);
    _soundPlayer = new SoundPlayer();
    _soundPlayer.LoadSounds(@"Assets/Sounds/ping.wav");

    spatialInputHandler = new SpatialInputHandler();
#endif
```

We added the `_soundPlayer = new SoundPlayer()` line and called our `LoadSounds()` method. Make sure that you use the right folder name; if you placed your files somewhere else, you obviously have to use that here as well.

I have also added a private field `_soundPlayer` of the `SoundPlayer` type to this class, so we can call this later on.

I told you I want to call the sound whenever the user places the cube in a different position. This is done in the public HolographicFrame Update() method which is the same class you are in right now. If you go there, you might find the code that positions the cube. It is between the `#if DRAW_SAMPLE_CONTENT` / `#endif` parts. Change that part to make it look like this:

```
#if DRAW_SAMPLE_CONTENT
// Check for new input state since the last frame.
var pointerState = spatialInputHandler.CheckForInput();
if (null != pointerState)
{
    // When a Pressed gesture is detected, the sample hologram will be
repositioned
    // two meters in front of the user.
    spinningCubeRenderer.PositionHologram(
        pointerState.TryGetPointerPose(currentCoordinateSystem)
        );

    // Also, play the sound!
    _soundPlayer.PlaySound();
}
#endif
```

As you can see, all I did was add the `_soundPlayer.PlaySound()` line.

What I did not show you was the part where we dispose of our stuff. I'll leave that to you--just dispose of the `XAudio` instance and the `SoundStream` instance.

That is it. You just added sounds to your application. Granted, it is not spatial sound yet, but we will get to that. We have to learn to crawl before we can walk, let alone run.

Unity

In Unity, things are a little different. The system takes care of all the things we have talked about and we only have to worry about the actual sounds and when to play them. Since you have already been working with Unity for a while now, you have probably guessed that the world for a Unity developer is a lot less complicated than the same world for a DirectX developer. This is true for the sounds in your app as well.

In the previous part, we added a sound to our scene that will play whenever the user taps in the air to relocate the cube. Of course, it would be better to not only have an ambient sounds but to have that sound come from the cube. As we have discussed, spatial sound adds to the realism, so we should do that as often as we can. Unfortunately, this is not easily done in DirectX. There are some extra hoops to go through in order to achieve those kinds of sounds. In Unity, however, this is a matter of just setting a couple of extra properties, and you are ready to go.

So, for now, I am skipping this part. I will not show you how to create ambient sounds in Unity. I will show you this when we get to the part that deals with spatial sound. It would be silly to have you do the work twice, but with just two settings and three options turned on. We will move on to spatial sounds right away.

Spatial sound

Spatial sound is a very important item in Holographic apps. Everything we do in life makes a sound. Every sound we hear has a source. There is no such thing as ambient sound in the real world.

This is kind of strange if you think about it. For decades, we have been trained by television and movies to expect music and ambient noises to be around us. However, in reality, this is never the case. Every noise comes from somewhere; every noise has a source you can point at. These sources might be hidden, so they are not obvious. They might be distributed across a room, so you are tempted to believe the sound is ambient, or they might be so loud that it seems the sound is coming from all directions, but you know as well as I do that this is not true. There is a source, always. So, why did we invent this crazy notion of ambient sound?

The answer to that question is, of course, lack of technology. When we talked about HRTF in previous parts of this chapter, you learned that you cannot achieve this with just two speakers. You also cannot achieve it with some fancy 8.1 surround system. That might feel a bit more realistic, but in reality, it is not. Only with the advent of wearable devices, such as the HoloLens, can we realistically mimic nature when producing synthesized sounds.

I think it is time to try it out. Let's see how we can achieve a higher level of realism by creating spatial sound in our apps.

DirectX

There is one thing that I did not tell you. We have a problem. The problem is this: in our C# / DirectX samples, we are not directly dealing with DirectX. If you want to do that, you would have to go deep into the bowels of Windows, learn COM, and do all that in C++. The reason we can use these techniques in our apps is that there are some friendly people out there who have written wrappers for us. These wrappers, in our case SharpDX, take care of all the low-level C++ stuff and give us access to the things we need.

The downside of all this is that SharpDX is an open source project, driven by enthusiastic people, but people who do not always have time to implement the latest features. This means that the HRTF functionality and spatial sound capabilities in DirectX and DirectAudio are not available to us. So, we need to write this ourselves, and yes, we need to go into C++ and write this code.

The SpatialSound library

Before you start to panic, I can assure you that I have already done all the hard work. I written a simple component that you can use to have the required capabilities in your app. You can find them at `https://github.com/dvroegop/HoloSounds`.

Let me break it all down for you.

The heart of what I have done is in the C++ project `SpatialSoundPlayer`. This contains the `SpatialSound` class. This class is a `WinRT` type class, meaning that it can be used in any C# project. The header looks like this. Do not worry if you do not know much, or anything, about C++, the code is pretty self-explanatory.

```
#pragma once
using namespace std;
namespace SpatialSoundPlayer {
  public ref class SpatialSound sealed
  {
    public:
    SpatialSound();
    void Initialize(Platform::String^ fileName);
    void SetPosition(float x, float y, float z);
    void SetRoomType(RoomType roomType);
    void Cleanup();
    void Play();
    void Stop();
    private:
    bool _isPlaying = false;
    std::shared_ptr<OmnidirectionalSound> _internalPlayer;
    HrtfEnvironment TranslateRoomType(RoomType sourceType);
  };
}
```

As you can see, we have a bunch of public methods which allow the user to specify which file to use, how to play it, and when to play it.

Let's break this down.

We have a constructor, but there is nothing special about this. We have the Initialize method, which takes a normal .NET string containing the filename of the sound we want to play.

Now, this is very important--the audio files you provide have to be a `.wav` file with a 48k sample rate. If it does not fit this sample rate, the HRTF parts will probably crash, and you will have a hard time figuring out why this happened.

You could, of course, use other formats, such as MP3, but you would have to write a converter for this or find a third-party library that helps you. You need access to the bytes that describe the actual wave forms, so you must be able to get to that data--most libraries allow you to do this.

We have the `SetPosition` method. This takes three parameters: an *X*, a *Y*, and a *Z* coordinate in the 3D space. Remember, we are working with spatial data, so we need to give it a location.

Then, you see the `SetRoomType` method. This is a method that tells the HRTF code to behave in a certain way, matching the kind of room you are in. You can imagine sounds behaving differently in a small room than in a large hall--in the former situation, you would have much more echo. The HRTF system needs to know what kind of room you are in order to mimic this behavior. The room could be small, medium, large, or outdoors.

The `Cleanup` method is used for cleaning up the resources. The `Play` and `Stop` methods are self-explanatory.

This API is not that hard to use. I will show you how to use it later on, but first I want to show you a bit of the inner workings of our component.

This class is a wrapper around another class:

```
namespace SpatialSoundPlayer
{
  class OmnidirectionalSound
  {
    public:
    virtual ~OmnidirectionalSound();
    HRESULT Initialize(_In_ LPCWSTR filename);
    HRESULT Start();
    HRESULT Stop();
    HRESULT SetEnvironment(_In_ HrtfEnvironment environment);
    HRESULT SetPosition(_In_ float x, _In_ float y, _In_ float z);
    HrtfEnvironment GetEnvironment() { return _environment; }
    private:
    AudioFileReader _audioFile;
    ComPtr<IXAudio2> _xaudio2;
    IXAudio2SourceVoice* _sourceVoice = nullptr;
    ComPtr<IXAPOHrtfParameters> _hrtfParams;
    HrtfEnvironment _environment = HrtfEnvironment::Outdoors;
    ULONGLONG _lastTick = 0;
    float _angle = 0;
  };
}
```

As you can see, this looks very similar to the `SpatialSoundPlayer` class, but with different types. The types we use here are the real, DirectX types. We cannot use those in the `SpatialSoundPlayer` because they cannot be passed on to a Windows Store app. This is why we have this intermediate class, translating all the types for us.

The rest of the code is quite complex, and you should have a thorough understanding of COM, C++, and DirectX to figure out what is going on here. I will leave that alone; it is way beyond the scope of this book. You can use the component `SpatialSoundPlayer` as it is. All you need to know is how to use it, which is what we will discuss now.

Using the library

The Git repository that contains the `SpatialSoundPlayer` also contains a sample project. This is just the standard spinning cube sample; however, now, when you tap to position the cube, it will also make a noise, coming from that cube.

Let's investigate how this works.

Open the `HoloSoundsMain.cs` file. I have a new private member here:

```
private SpatialSound _spatialSound;
```

This is our component. In the `SetHolographicSpace` method, you see how I initialize it. I give it `RoomType` and a file it can process. Of course, the `ping.wav` file is part of the app as well:

```
_spatialSound = new SpatialSound();
_spatialSound.SetRoomType(RoomType.Medium);
_spatialSound.Initialize(@"Assets/Sounds/ping.wav");
In the Dispose we clean up after ourselves:
if (_spatialSound != null)
{
  _spatialSound.Cleanup();
  _spatialSound = null;
}
```

This is all pretty straightforward. The interesting part is to be found in the `Update()` method. The part of the code that is called when you do an air tap (to position the cube) has been altered; we also call the `Play()` method of our sound:

```
_spatialSound.Play();
```

However, this is not enough. We need to take the new position of the cube and pass that on to the sound. After all, we are dealing with spatial sound here, and we need to give it a position. Remember the API definition we created was the `SetPosition` method? Well, we will use that here. In the sample, I have slightly altered `SpinningCubeRenderer` so that it stores the position in a local variable. We will use that here.

First, we store that position in a field so that we can reuse it later. The reason we do this is the following: the position of the sound has to be altered every time. The position changes whenever the user moves her head. We do this so that, to the user, the sound appears to come from one single place, no matter where the user is.

This is also what happens with the rendering of the cube; we have to move it whenever the users moves about, so that it appears to be static in one position. However, this is something that the demo code and the framework are doing for us. With spatial sound, however, we have to do this.

In Chapter 7, *Lets Talk! Communications Between Devices,* we will deal with coordinate systems, so I will not spend too much time on the inner workings here, but let's examine the SetSoundPosition method:

```
private void SetSoundPosition(HolographicFramePrediction prediction,
SpatialCoordinateSystem currentCoordinateSystem)
{
  SpatialPointerPose currentPose =
  SpatialPointerPose.TryGetAtTimestamp(currentCoordinateSystem,
prediction.Timestamp);
  if (currentPose != null)
  {
    Vector3 headPosition = currentPose.Head.Position;
    Vector3 headUp = currentPose.Head.UpDirection;
    Vector3 headDirection = currentPose.Head.ForwardDirection;
    Vector3 negativeZAxis = Vector3.Normalize(headDirection);
    Vector3 positiveYAxisGuess = Vector3.Normalize(headUp);
    Vector3 positiveXAxis = Vector3.Normalize(Vector3.Cross(negativeZAxis,
    positiveYAxisGuess));
    Vector3 positiveYAxis = Vector3.Normalize(Vector3.Cross(negativeZAxis,
positiveXAxis));
    Matrix4x4 rotationTransform = new Matrix4x4(
      positiveXAxis.X, positiveYAxis.X, negativeZAxis.X, 0,
      positiveXAxis.Y, positiveYAxis.Y, negativeZAxis.Y, 0,
      positiveXAxis.Z, positiveYAxis.Z, negativeZAxis.Z, 0,
      0.0f, 0.0f, 0.0f, 1.0f
    );
    Matrix4x4 translationTransform = Matrix4x4.CreateTranslation(-
headPosition);
    Matrix4x4 coordinateSystemTransform = translationTransform *
rotationTransform;
    Vector3 positionRelativeToHoloLens =
Vector3.Transform(spinningCubeRenderer.Position,
    oordinateSystemTransform);
    _spatialSound.SetPosition(positionRelativeToHoloLens.X,
positionRelativeToHoloLens.Y,
    ositionRelativeToHoloLens.Z);
  }
}
```

This is the full method. We pass it the prediction and `currentCoordinateSystem` that we are using. The prediction is a predicted position of the user for the next frame. The framework does this for us. It tells us where the system expects the user to be at the end of the current frame. This is pretty handy; we can have a very good responding system that feels very natural instead of lagging behind.

Again, the coordinate system is something I will explain in a later chapter.

First, we get the position from the prediction I just mentioned. If we do not get one, we just leave it at that. However, if we do, we use this position as the basis for our calculations. What follows is a whole set of transformations that takes the position and direction of the camera (in other words, of the user) and transforms that into the position of the cube. Basically, what we are doing here is calculating how to move and rotate things from our position toward another position, in our case, the position the cube is at. Since we want the sound to come from the cube, this is where we will position the sound--this is what happens at the end of the method.

Do not worry if this all looks complicated. The math involved is quite straightforward if you are proficient at trigonometry. If you are not, take the code for granted and use it whenever you need to move objects from one spot to another in our three-dimensional world--this works.

Unity

That was a lot of work. Even if the people at SharpDX had managed to include the necessary wrappers, we still would have had to do a lot to get a sound to come from a designated place.

Fortunately, this is much easier to do in Unity. We just need to add one component, set a couple of properties, and make some global changes to the settings of the project. I will show you all these steps right now, and I will do that in our **RockOn** app.

We have a bunch of guitars that we can place in our room. I think it would be nice if each one of them makes a guitar sound every time we place it, just as if the user were not careful enough when putting the expensive instrument on the stage.

To begin, we need a sound. Again, there are tons of websites out there that offer free or cheap sounds, so go ahead and find something that suits your taste. It does not matter whether the sound is mono or stereo. Actually, it is better if the sound is mono. After all, we do not care about stereo effects at all; we will generate the spatial effects in our application. Stereo only makes the file bigger, since we have data for both the left and the right channel; something we will not use. So mono is preferred, although stereo does not hurt. It just does not add anything.

I have found a nice one-chord sound that I would like to use, but you can choose whatever you want. If you want to use the sound of a passing spaceship instead, be my guest. After all, we are in virtual reality.

Once you have got the sound, you need to import it into our project. I suggest that you make another folder in the Assets folder in Unity and call it Sounds. Place your downloaded file into that folder.

Once you have done that, you might notice the change in the **Inspector** part of Unity. As you know by now, the **Inspector** works like the property editor in Visual Studio; you can change the properties and behavior of all your components.

There is a difference, however, between the **GameObjects** and the **Assets** in Unity. A GameObject is an item you see in the hierarchy and in the scene; they are actively being used. A GameObject always has a transform, consisting of a position, rotation, and scale. This is true even if the GameObject is not visible, such as an empty GameObject that only acts as a placeholder. They will always have that transform component.

An Asset, however, is something we might use in the game at sometime. It goes without saying it would be of very little use to have Assets without using them, but there is nothing stopping you from doing that--well, besides common sense that is.

The difference between these is very visible the moment you import items from the outside. If you use a model from an outside source, Unity will do the import when you place them in the Assets folder, or a subfolder thereof. Once you copy an item from the Assets folder to the scene or the hierarchy window, they will be instantiated and placed in your game.

The Inspector shows this. When you select an object in the hierarchy, you can see its properties in the Inspector, which tells you how this instance behaves in the game. If you select the item you just imported in the Assets folder, you will see some properties that tell you how it was imported.

This can be very helpful. Sometimes, items you import are not very usable in Unity; they need to be smaller, rotated, animated, or any other thing you may need before you can use it in a scene. The same goes for audio files. I have added my downloaded item to the Assets/Sounds folder, and the **Inspector** shows me the import settings for this file:

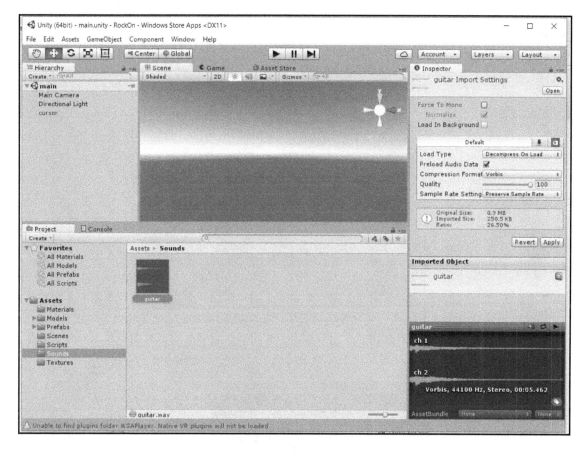

The import settings for a newly imported sound file

I have selected my new file in the Assets folder, and you see the properties belonging to this file in the **Inspector** on the right-hand side.

This is clearly a stereo file. I do not need it, so in the Windows Store tab, I will tick the **Force To Mono** checkbox. I also want **Load In Background** to be checked to make sure that the app runs smoothly even when it is loading my files. The sample rate is very important. By default, it is set to **Preserve Sample Rate**, meaning that it will use the data in the file as it was when imported. This will not work in Holographic apps. You need to set it to **48,000 Hz**. So, change that option to look like this:

Final audio import settings for a Holographic app

Once you have done this, it is time to set the global settings in the way our device wants them to be.

Setting the audio settings in Unity3D

There are a set of settings we need to change in order to have Unity play our sounds correctly. In fact, since we always want to use spatial sound, you should always change these settings at the beginning of the project you are working on. Let me show you what I mean.

When you go to **Edit** | **Project Settings** | **Audio**, you will see your **Inspector** window, showing these options:

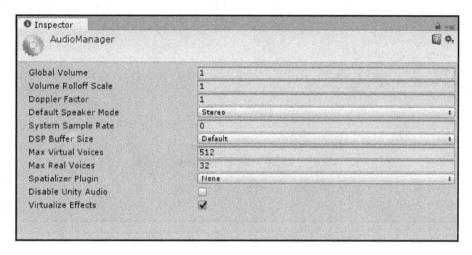

Default audio settings for a Unity3D project

Let's look at what we need to change.

First of all, we need to set the **System Sample Rate**. As I told you earlier, HoloLens works with 48,000 Hz files. Any sound file that has a different sample rate needs to be converted. We have already specified that for our individual sound file, but we can set it here on a project-wide scale. So, the **System Sample Rate** should be set to **48000**.

The other thing we need to set is the **Spatializer Plugin**. This plugin is a separate piece of software that handles all the spatializing intelligence. By default, this is set to **None**, meaning that there is no spatializing going on. We need to change this to **MS HRTF Spatializer**.

It might be tempting to change the **Default Speaker Mode** to something else. By default, it is **Stereo**, but you can change it to **Mono** or one of the several surround sound options--do not do this. Leave it as **Stereo** if you want things to work. The spatializer will take care of everything, so do not try to preoptimize things by changing this option.

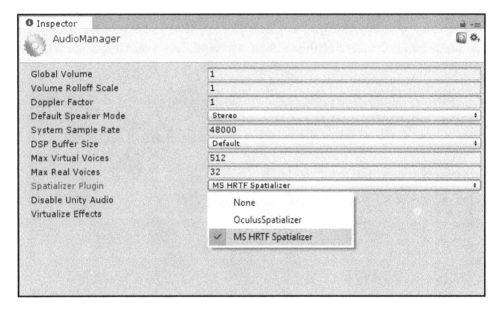

Selecting the Spatializer Plugin

This is the code, made by the HoloLens team, that takes care of all the magic for us.

Once you have done this, we are ready to have some spatial sound in our applications.

Adding spatial sound to GameObjects

We have set the default settings and applied import settings to the sounds we want to use. Now, we will finally make some noise. It is time to allow your objects in your game to be heard.

We have been working on the RockOn app, where we can place guitars in our scenes by looking at a point and making the air tap gesture. You may have chosen another instrument, but the principle remains the same.

We have added the sound we want to play to our assets and set the general audio settings to the correct values.

The `Assets` folder in our project has `GuitarPrefab`. This is the prefab we created earlier, the object that gets instantiated. If you select the prefab in the `Assets` folder, you can choose **Add Component** in the **Inspector** window; do it. If you want, you can start typing `Audio`, and the window will show you all the available components starting with the word `Audio`. This makes life a bit easier; there are dozens of possible components to choose from, all organized in different subsections. **Audio Source** is part of the **Audio** group, which in my opinion makes sense.

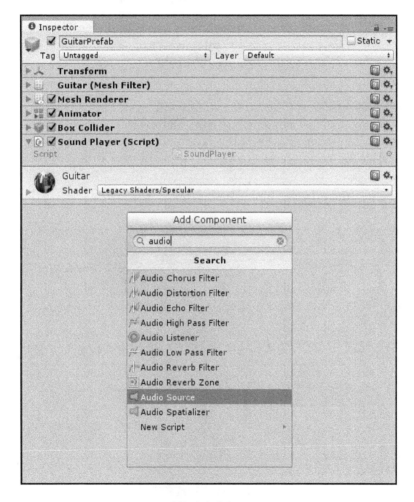

Adding the Audio Source

Once you have done this, you can set the individual properties for the **Audio Source**. Let's examine these.

First of all, we need to select the **Audio Source**. You can drag your audio file from your assets to this slot, or you can click on the little circle next to this field, which will result in a search box showing all available audio files. Either way, select our imported audio file so that we know what to play here.

Next, you need to check the box next to the **Spatialize** text. I think this is pretty obvious, but still, people tend to forget this. We want this audio source to be spatialized, meaning that we want the audio source to be placed as coming from our object.

The **Spatial Blend** is a slider that determines how much 3D effect you want in your sounds--do you want it to be plain stereo, do you want it to be fully 3D, and thus spatialized, or do you want a mix of those? Guess what, we want full 3D, so we need to slide this all the way up to a value of **1**.

I have set the **Play on Awake** setting, so the sound will be audible when you instantiate the instrument. I have also set the **Loop** option, so it will repeat the sound all the time. I will turn this off later on, but for now, I think this is a handy way to test the sounds and all the different settings. If I did not have this loop, then I would have to restart the app every time to hear the effects.

Your **Inspector** should look like this:

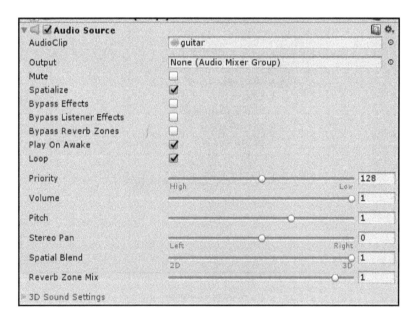

First part of the settings for a spatial audio component

We are almost there! We only have the **3D Sound Settings** part to go through. This is the part that can be found at the bottom of the panel. Here, we specify how sounds behave. As you know, sounds that are further away are quieter than sounds closer to us. However, there are a lot of factors that determine how this works in reality. We need to tell the engine how we want it to control these effects.

There are no hard rules as to how to set them. You can do whatever you want here. I suggest that you try it out, play with the settings and listen to them on the HoloLens to see if this is what you want to achieve. I will show you what I do for this application, but by all means, do whatever you want.

First, we can set the Doppler effect. As you probably know, the Doppler effect is the effect of changing frequencies of moving sounds. We all know this effect; anyone who has heard an ambulance drive by knows that the sirens are a bit higher in pitch when the vehicle is approaching than when it drives away from us. The same goes for cars, planes, trains, and anything else that moves at a reasonable speed. We can animate our objects and have them move about, so we can also have the Doppler effect take place. This is where you determine how strong you want this effect to be. I just leave it to its default of 1.

Another setting you might want to change is the **Volume Rolloff**. This is where you tell Unity how fast the volume should drop if things are further away. By default, this is set to **Logarithmic Rolloff**, but I strongly suggest that you change that to **Custom Rolloff**. If you do not do this, you will find the system is way too aggressive in reducing the volume; you will only hear sounds close to you.

When you set it to **Custom Rolloff**, you can change this. I always leave it to the default for custom, but you can alter this if you feel this works better for you. Again, experiment with it a bit so that you know what all this does.

In the end, my **3D Sound Settings** look like this:

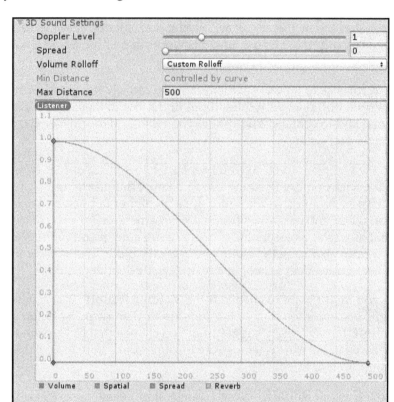

3D Sound Settings for our asset

Play the sound at the right time.

It is time to actually make the sound audible. We want the sound to play as soon as we add a guitar to our scene.

Well, to be honest, we have already done this. Since we have added an audio source to our prefab and set it to play on awake (and loop as well), it will play the moment you instantiate an object.

You will hear the sound immediately, but let's say for the sake of completeness that we want to control this from a script. Let's assume some other piece of code calls Play Sound, and we want our guitar to respond to that.

Let's change our application a bit so that it does just that.

First, we remove the **Play on awake** and **Loop** options in the `AudioSource` component; we want it to play when we ask it to, not automatically.

Let's work on the scripts we already have. The main camera contains the `Cursor` script. This looks like an ideal candidate. After all, here we track the gaze of the user and we know where the user is looking. If the user is looking at an object, we draw the cursor on top of that object, otherwise we draw it somewhere far away. I want our guitar to make a noise whenever we look at it. I only want it to make that noise the first time we look at it after not looking at anything else; if we do not do it like this, we will have that sound 60 times per second, which is a bit much I think.

So, open the `Cursor.cs` file in your code editor and make these changes. We need a new private field, called `_objectBeingHit` of the `GameObject` type:

```
private GameObject _objectBeingHit;
```

This is set to whatever object we are looking at, or null when we are not looking at anything. When we set this, we can track it in the next frame, whether we have already done work on this object or not.

In the `Update` method, we did the `Raycast`. We set the position of the `Cursor` object to the new position when we hit something. Otherwise, we placed the `Cursor` object far away. Change the code to look like this:

```
private void Update()
{
    if (cursor == null)
        return;

    var camTrans = Camera.main.transform;

    RaycastHit raycastHit;

    if (Physics.Raycast(new Ray(camTrans.position, camTrans.forward), out
raycastHit))
    {
        cursor.position = raycastHit.point;
        if (_objectBeingHit != raycastHit.transform.gameObject)
        {
            _objectBeingHit = raycastHit.transform.gameObject;
            _objectBeingHit.SendMessageUpwards("PlaySounds");
        }
    }
    else
```

```
        {
            cursor.position = camTrans.position + camTrans.forward*maxDistance;
            cursor.up = camTrans.forward;
            _objectBeingHit = null;
        }
    }
```

If we hit something, we set the cursor position, but we also get the `raycastHit.transform.gameObject` property. This tells us which object is being hit. We compare this to the previous object being hit, so we can tell whether this is the first time we have hit this object since not hitting anything. If it is, we store `gameObject` and call the `SendMessageUpwards("PlaySounds")` method on it.

If we are not hitting anything, we just set our new field to null.

The `SendMessageUpwards` method goes to the `gameObject` and traverses to its components and all its parent components to check whether there is a script with a method in it that has this particular name. If there is, it invokes it; you could also use `SendMessage`. This will only investigate the `gameObject` itself. The advantage is performance; it does not need to check everything. The downside is that the part being hit might be a part of a larger set of objects combined together. You would miss the method if the script were part of the owning object, instead of this particular item you are hitting.

Now, all we need to do in Unity is add a new script, called `SoundPlayer`, place it in the `Scripts` folder, and add it as a component to our `Guitar` prefab. You can do so by dragging the script from the `Scripts` folder to the **Inspector** for the prefab, or you can go to the **Inspector** for the prefab, click on **Add Component**, and find the script there--either way works.

The code in our new script is extremely simple:

```
using UnityEngine;

public class SoundPlayer : MonoBehaviour
{
    public void PlaySounds()
    {
        var audioSource = GetComponent<AudioSource>();
        if (audioSource == null)
            return;

        audioSource.Play();
    }
}
```

I have removed the `Start()` and `Update()` methods; we do not need them here. I have added a `PlaySounds()` method instead. In this method, I try to get the `AudioSource` component. Since this script is a component of the `Guitar` prefab, `GetComponent` will traverse all other components in the same `GameObject`. There can be at most one `AudioSource`, so if there is one, we will get it. If we have none, we will simply return.

Once we have gotten hold of our `AudioSource`, we call `Play();`.

Rebuild the project, go to Visual Studio, and deploy it.

The app will start and you will see the cursor. Once you air tap, the app will instantiate a new instance of our `Guitar` prefab. Since the cursor will be at that place, it will immediately register a hit, so the sounds will be audible. This is the reason we remove the **Play on awake** option; this will happen anyway. Look away, and then look back at the instrument. You will hear it sound again.

Here is a fun thing you can try: place a dozen guitars in different places around you, close your eyes, and move your head. You will hear the sound the moment the HoloLens is aimed at a guitar. Try to see if you can find them all by just moving your head with your eyes closed. This is the final proof that spatial audio actually works!

Some final thoughts on spatial sound

We have covered a lot in this chapter. Again, most developers seem to forget about sounds in their applications. It is not part of our DNA, it seems. Sounds are not as important as great graphics, is what most developers seem to think. I hope that I have convinced you of the opposite, that is, sounds are important. They are even more important in an immersive experience such as virtual, augmented, and mixed realities scenarios.

Sounds are a part of our world. Everything we do makes a sound. We always hear sounds. As I type this, I hear the clicking of the keys I press. In the background, I hear a dog walking around the house, its claws ticking on the floor. I hear the squeaking of the chair as I move about. I do not notice these sounds, just you do not notice the sounds around you. We only pay attention to sounds if they are out of the ordinary. However, if you remove all these sounds, the world seems flat and uninteresting. Having no sounds, even those that are filtered out by our brains, makes things less realistic. Since the whole idea behind our apps is to make the scenarios we think of as realistic as possible, we need to have a bit of noise, coming from a certain point around us. We need spatial sound.

There are some general concepts you need to be aware of when designing your sounds in your app. These are things you should know about and should apply if you can. These are not hard rules you have to obey they are more on a conceptual level. Read them and take advantage of them.

General concepts when it comes to sounds

The following are general concepts when there is sound involved:

- **Sounds should be spatialized**: In the real world, all sounds come from someplace. There is no such thing as ambient sound in the real world. So, you should not create ambient sounds. Everything makes sounds, so use this in your app as well. To help your user find objects, make use of the spatial nature of these sounds. It helps convey the message that this is a new way of looking at reality.
- **Make objects and user interface elements discoverable**: If you want your user to find their way in the virtual world, make sure that things make a noise. This helps in the discoverability. Your user will find the big robot that is about to shoot at the user more easily (and thus dodge the laser beams) if the robot makes a noise before blasting away. The same goes for more simple things, such as menu items or buttons that need attention. Draw attention with animations, but also by employing spatial sound. People are very good at finding the source of sounds, so use that.
- **Use spatial sound, do not use 3D sound**: 3D sound has been available in software for a long time. All the surround 8.1 settings you find are for this kind of sound. The technology here, however, is different from what we have been using so far. 3D sound is an older technique, depending on the use of multiple speakers surrounding the user. This does not work for us. It does not take into account the fact that the user may walk about, even outside the area covered by the speakers. Spatial sound does take this into account. Although the device will have to work a bit harder, it is definitely worth it.
- **Always have a source for your sounds**: Never have sounds coming out of thin air. Everything in the real world that makes a sound has a source, even though it might not be obvious immediately. Always have your sounds coming from an object. If your objects are rather small, such as our guitar, you could have the audio source in the center of our object. If your object is quite large, you could use multiple audio sources. Imagine that you have a large airplane flying over, consider having each engine make a sound. Again, try to mimic the real world as much as you can.

- **Sound sources can move around**: Most sound sources are static in our world; however, there can be items that move in the world around the user. The sound source should travel with it. Now, when you do this, make sure that you do not vary the location much on the vertical plane. People are very bad at locating sources there. They can find audio sources more easily when they are somewhere on a circle around them. If you have items moving about, try to have them moving from side to side. If you need to have them move from back to front, or vice versa, try to avoid having that source travel directly overhead or underneath (or through!) the user. Have it pass to one side of the user instead.
- **Use attenuation wisely**: Attenuation controls how much sounds gain in volume depending on distance. An object further away will sound quieter than an object closer to the user. Attenuation controls this. It is tempting to turn this off--you want your audio sources to be audible. However, this takes you away from the level of realism. The preferred options for attenuation levels are as follows:
  - **Minimum Gain**: -20 dB
  - **Maximum Gain**: +12 dB
  - **Unity Gain Distance**: 5 meters. This means that at a distance of five meters distance, a sound cannot be heard anymore.
- **Use streaming for large sound files**: Sound files can be rather big, so you might consider using streaming instead of loading them into memory at the start of a scene. Voice-overs are also a good candidate; you need them once, so you might as well stream them from your storage instead of loading them into memory and have them occupy valuable resources.

What is next?

Add sounds to your app. Make those sounds come from someplace. Ensure that you do not use ambient sounds and that the sounds make sense, meaning that they should fit the object they are coming from. Stream when you can, and preload if you have to.

Now, it is time to look at voice. Voice, as in generated voice texts, coming from your app and, the more exciting, other way around--voice commands.

Summary

This was a complicated chapter. We have covered one of the most ignored features of any app, especially HoloLens apps: sounds. We examined the usage and importance of spatial sound. We have seen that the helper library SharpDX does not offer spatial sound, but we discussed a library written in C++ that helps us achieve our goal in DirectX anyway. Along with that, we talked about implementing spatial sound in Unity3D. We dived into the requirements needed to achieve spatial sound, such as limiting the sample rate to 48,000 hertz. Lastly, we discussed some things we need to keep in mind when using spatial sound.

5

Be Heard - Voice Interactions

One of the things that distinguishes humans from other life forms we know of is the ability to have complicated conversations. We use body language, of course, but we mostly use our voice. Voice is extremely important to us as a species; it gives us the ability to exchange ideas in a very concise way.

People are so good at distinguishing voices that even when the sounds are distorted we still can make out the intent of what is being said. A great example of this is the weird phenomenon of people who play music backward to find a hidden message. The fact that they actually do find something there say a little about the recording artists but a lot about our ability to hear meaningful sounds in almost anything. The human mind is a powerful thing. So, it would be great to use that in our apps as well. Fortunately, we can. Which is what this chapter is all about: harnessing the power of the human voice.

Let the HoloLens speak

In the previous chapter, we generated all sorts of sounds. We did this in DirectX and in Unity. We had ambient sounds to start with, sounds that sound like they are all around us. We finally moved on to spatial sounds. All the things we looked at in that chapter also apply to voice. After all, voice is just another source of sounds.

We could, of course, pre-record sentences by having a voice actor stand in some booth with a microphone and record what she has to say. This can be a great way to get good-sounding content. After all, this will sound very natural and very realistic. Again, we want to strive for an experience that is as realistic as we can get it. This is your best option.

When you do this, you have to think of all the things you want your app to say to the user. When you have this list, have someone read those items into a high-quality microphone and record that. Then you can import those sounds into your app, preferably at 48,000 Hz, and play that back whenever you need to.

However, this is not always the best solution. If you have a complicated scenario with lots of random text, you might not be able to get away with this way of working. Not every phrase can be predicted. Or sometimes you have too many options to have someone record those phrases. Sometimes you just do not want to go through the hassle of recording a human voice simply to have some nice sounding voices in your app.

Luckily, computers these days can generate a pretty convincing human voice. The days of computerized voices as we have seen in motion pictures from the eighties are gone. We no longer have a clearly synthesized voice like we had in movies such as WarGames. We can have voices in our app that sound just like a human. If we want this, we have got some work to do. So, let's get started.

General principles behind voice generation

All the things we talked about when we discussed sounds apply to this chapter as well. In the code samples I will show you we will only use ambient sounds. I know, we said you should avoid this, but by doing so we will avoid all the hard work we need to do to get sounds coming from a spatial point. Of course, when we look at the Unity side of things, we will use spatial sound. After all, this is hardly more work than using ambient sound so why not do it correctly?

I will show you the way to make a voice come from a spatial point in one sample. The reason for this is that this uses streaming. Since I said in the previous chapter you should use streaming for occasional sounds, I decided to show you how to do that here. Especially since voice generation will give us a sound stream, so for voice this is the only way to do it.

There are basically two ways to generate a voice in Windows 10:

1. **Use text-to-speech**: This method is straightforward. You give the system a string containing the things you want it to say and the computer will say those things out loud. It could not be simpler than that. However, this will give you a clearly computer-generated feeling to the voice. This can be all right if it fits your scenario or if you only want your app to say one or two words. But if you have a sentence you want to be heard and you want it to be more lifelike, we should use the other method.

2. **Use SSML: Speech Synthesis Markup Language (SSML)** is a standard for representing speech in an XML file. This way, we also give it a string, but this string is augmented with commands on how to say parts of the string.

SSML is the preferred method, but of course it takes a bit more work. Do not worry though: the actual code to render the voice is the same for both methods except for one line. The big difference is in the way you deliver the text you want to be spoken out loud.

Voice generation in DirectX

As you are no doubt used to by now, we begin with the DirectX way of doing things. Let us start up a new project from the well-known template **Holographic DirectX 11 app**.

Creating the base of the VoicePlayer class

In the `Content` folder, next to `SpinningCubeRenderer`, we will add our `VoicePlayer` class:

```
using System;

namespace VoiceInHolographicDirectX.Content
{
    internal class VoicePlayer : IDisposable
    {
        public void Dispose()
        {
            Dispose(true);
            GC.SuppressFinalize(this);
        }

        ~VoicePlayer()
        {
            Dispose(false);
        }

        protected virtual void Dispose(bool isDisposing)
        {
            if (isDisposing)
            {
                // Here we will dispose our voice parts
            }
        }
    }
}
```

As you can see, I have added the `IDispose` interface and implemented the dispose pattern. Since we will be using many resources that need to be cleaned up, I thought I would show you how this is done just the once.

Because the code in our `VoicePlayer` will be an almost exact copy of the `SoundPlayer` we created before, you need to update the NuGet packages and import the NuGet package for `SharpDX.XAudio2`. This is the same thing you did before, so I am sure you can do this by yourself by now.

We will add an `Initialize` method to our class, but first we will declare the fields we need:

```
private XAudio2 _xaudio;
private MasteringVoice _masteringVoice;
private SoundStream _soundStream;
private WaveFormat _waveFormat;
private AudioBuffer _audioBuffer;
```

Of course, you also need the correct namespaces for this to work:

```
using System;
using System.IO;
using SharpDX.Multimedia;
using SharpDX.XAudio2;
```

Initializing the sound system for streaming

The `Initialize` method is almost identical to the `LoadSounds` method we used before. However, this time we give it a stream, which we will use as the source for our audio. If you want, you can change the code from the previous chapter to look like this if you want to use streams instead. Sounds are, after all, still sounds: it does not matter if it is a humble ping noise or a complicated computer-generated voice:

```
public void Initialize(Stream stream)
{
    _xaudio = new XAudio2();
    _masteringVoice = new MasteringVoice(_xaudio);

    _soundStream = new SoundStream(stream);
    _waveFormat = _soundStream.Format;
    _audioBuffer = new AudioBuffer
    {
        Stream = _soundStream,
        AudioBytes = (int) _soundStream.Length,
        Flags = BufferFlags.EndOfStream
```

```
        };
    }
```

As you can see, the code looks familiar. We do not load the audio file here but we give the stream as a parameter to the method. It just makes life a bit simpler.

Implementing IDispose the right way

We need to be sure we are cleaning up after ourselves. The Dispose method should look as follows:

```
protected void Dispose(bool isDisposing)
{
    if (isDisposing)
    {
        _audioBuffer = null;
        _waveFormat = null;
        _soundStream.Dispose();
        _soundStream = null;
        _masteringVoice.Dispose();
        _masteringVoice = null;
        _xaudio.Dispose();
        _xaudio = null;
    }
}
```

Playing the sound

Let us have a look at the actual playing of the sounds:

```
public void Play()
{
    var sourceVoice = new SourceVoice(
    _xaudio,
    _waveFormat,
    false);
    sourceVoice.SubmitSourceBuffer(
      _audioBuffer,
      _soundStream.DecodedPacketsInfo);
    sourceVoice.Start();
}
```

Synthesizing voice

Guess what: this is exactly the same code as we have seen before. Surely, there must be something different in this class? Well, there is, and this is it:

```
public async Task<Stream> GenerateVoiceAsync(string textToSay)
{
    var synth = new Windows.Media.SpeechSynthesis.SpeechSynthesizer();
    var speechVoice = Windows.Media.SpeechSynthesis
      .SpeechSynthesizer.AllVoices[0];
    synth.Voice = speechVoice;
    var voiceStream = await synth.SynthesizeTextToStreamAsync(textToSay);
    return voiceStream.AsStreamForRead();
}
```

There you have it: the sample to load audio data asynchronously from a stream. But of course, the important part is the voice-generation component.

I used the `SpeechSynthesizer` class from the `Windows.Media.SpeechSynthesis` namespace. This namespace contains all the code you need to generate speech. As you can see, there is no specific DirectX code here: all this is done in standard UWP code. You can use this in all your managed C# UWP Windows 10 apps - they all work the same. The difference is the way we use the stream coming out of this code: this is fed to the XAudio library so we can use it in our DirectX application. But you could just as well use a `MediaElement` in a normal XAML UWP app and set the source of that element to this stream. That will work just fine.

Let us have a look at the code line by line.

First, we create an instance of the `SpeechSynthesizer`. The constructor of this class has no parameters, so this is rather straightforward.

This class has a static property called `AllVoices`. This list contains all the voices the system currently has. The number of voices available differs per machine: if a user decides to add more languages to his Windows installation then there will be more `VoiceInformation` instances in this list. However, by default on HoloLens, there are three, as follows:

ID	Name	Gender	Language
0	David	Male	en-US
1	Zira	Female	en-US
2	Mark	Male	en-US

You can install additional languages and voices on a normal Windows 10 device but on HoloLens this is currently not possible; the device is en-US only at the time of writing.

In our code, we get the first voice and set that to the voice of our instance of synth. This is a bit redundant: this is the default choice anyway, but I just wanted to show you how it is done.

Now the magic happens: we call the asynchronous method, SynthesizeTextToStreamAsync, and give it the string we want it to say. This returns a SpeechSynthesisStream instance, which we convert to a normal stream that we can read. That final stream is the result of our method, and we return that.

Setting things up

It looks like we have all our things in place to get going. However, there are some caveats here: the method SynthesizeTextToStreamAsync is an asynchronous method, hence the name. That means our GenerateVoiceAsync is also asynchronous, a method that should waited for. Every caller in the call tree needs to be aware of this.

The result of all this is that we cannot really use this in the Update() method in the main class like we did before: this is being called 60 times per second. We do not want to instantiate an asynchronous stream 60 times per second. We need to do this earlier.

We can fix this as follows. In our main class (in my application it is called VoiceInHolographicDirectXMain), I add a private field for our VoicePlayer:

```
private VoicePlayer voicePlayer;
```

In our previous samples, we created instances of our new classes in the SetHolographicSpace method. This is also where SpinningCubeRenderer is made and where we added the construction of our SoundPlayer class. We will not do that here this time. Since we need to have an asynchronous method call, we will put this in a separate method we create in VoiceInHolographicDirectXMain:

```
public async Task InitializeVoiceAsync()
{
    voicePlayer = new VoicePlayer();
    var voiceStream = await voicePlayer.GenerateVoiceAsync("Hello
HoloLens");
    voicePlayer.Initialize(voiceStream);
}
```

This method is responsible for setting up the `VoicePlayer`, loading the stream, and giving that stream to our `Player`. We create the instance, await the generation of the voice stream, and give the result of that to the `VoicePlayer` in the initialize method.

We need to call this method, of course. We will do so in `AppView.cs`. Find the `SetWindow` method and, at the end of the method, add the following line:

```
await main.InitializeVoiceAsync();
```

Change the signature of `SetWindow` as follows:

```
public async void SetWindow(CoreWindow window){...}
```

It needs to be marked as `async`, otherwise the compiler will complain.

Calling Play to hear the voice

There is one final thing we need to do. We need to call `Play()` so we can actually hear it.

For this app, I decided to abuse our old friend the `Update` method again. You know, the code that makes the cube you see reappear at the place you air-tap.

So, in the main class, which in my case is still `VoiceInHolographicDirectXMain`, find the `Update` method and look for that part in the compiler directives `#if DRAW_SAMPLE_CONTENT`. We will add the code here:

```
#if DRAW_SAMPLE_CONTENT
    // Check for new input state since the last frame.
    var pointerState = spatialInputHandler.CheckForInput();
if (null != pointerState)
{
    // When a Pressed gesture is detected,
    //the sample hologram will be repositioned
    // two meters in front of the user.
    spinningCubeRenderer.PositionHologram(
    pointerState.TryGetPointerPose(currentCoordinateSystem)
    );
    voicePlayer.Play();
}
#endif
```

That is all there is to it. Run your app and, as soon as you see the multi-colored cube, air tap somewhere. You see the cube change position, but you also hear the voice say, *Hello HoloLens*.

Making the voice spatial

This should be extremely easy by now: all we need to do is make sure we call the code presented in the previous chapter.

I have not made it a part of the `VoicePlayer`; instead I just called the code that generates the data stream and passed it to the class we created in the previous chapter. I created an overload that, instead of taking a filename, takes a stream of bytes. Coincidentally, this is exactly what `GenerateVoiceAsync` gives us. So, let us use that.

This is what it looks like:

```
async void PlayGeneratedVoice()
{
    Stream buffer = await GenerateVoiceAsync("Hello from Direct X");
    _spatialSound.Initialize(buffer.AsRandomAccessStream());
    _spatialSound.SetRoomType(RoomType.Medium);
    _spatialSound.Play();
}
async Task<Stream> GenerateVoiceAsync(string textToSay)
{
    var synth = new Windows.Media.SpeechSynthesis.SpeechSynthesizer();
    var speechVoice = Windows.Media.SpeechSynthesis
      .SpeechSynthesizer.AllVoices[0];
    synth.Voice = speechVoice;
    var voiceStream = await synth.SynthesizeTextToStreamAsync(textToSay);
    return voiceStream.AsStreamForRead();
}
```

We have seen this code before, so I will not talk you through it, with one tiny exception: we have the `_spatialSound` class that has an `Initialize` method. This is the class I introduced in the previous chapter - the one that enables spatial sounds in the DirectX environment. In the previous chapter, we gave it a filename; here, we give it a stream. This makes sense: our generator generates this stream. This stream contains the file in memory, so we can bypass the reading of the file. For more details on this `SpatialSound` component, I refer you to the previous chapter; for now, all you need to know is that you can give it a stream and the component will generate the sound for it.

Before I forget: we also need to set the position. I have reused the code from the previous chapter, where I introduced the method `SetSoundPosition`. This is what I use here as well.

You can find all of the code in the solution called HoloSounds in the code samples for this chapter, so you can play with it yourself.

Voice generation in Unity3D

This was again quite a lot of work, but I do hope you understand the way it works now. On the Unity side of things, it works more or less the same. We need to write the same sort of code to generate the voice stream and play it.

We will use a different scenario this time. In our RockOn app, I want things to behave a little differently. We will create a reusable asset so we can have voice in all our Unity apps without having to rewrite everything.

It is best to start a new project in Unity where we can play around without messing up our current codebase. We will later export what we have created and import that into our RockOn app. This way, we have proven to ourselves that we do have a reusable component.

Creating the Unity app

So, open Unity3D and create a new app. It does not matter what you call it, we are only interested in the code parts which we are going to write anyway. However, I do suggest you follow the steps I outlined at the beginning of this book to prepare the project for HoloLens. We want to test our code before exporting it, so we need to be able to run it. In case you forgot, these are the steps you need to take:

1. Set the camera position to **(0,0,0)**.
2. Set the camera **Clear Flags** to **Solid Color**.
3. Set the **Solid Color** to **Black (RGB: 000)**.
4. Set the **quality settings** to **Fastest**.
5. Set **Player Settings, Other** to **Virtual Reality Supported** | **Windows Holographic**.
6. Set the **Platform** to **Universal 10**.
7. Turn on **Create C# Projects**.

Those are the minimal basic steps you need to take in order to have something that runs on HoloLens. Since we will be using spatial audio, you should also set the audio settings for this example as follows:

1. In **Audio Settings**, set the **sample rate** to **48,000**.
2. In **Audio Settings**, set the spatializer plugin in to **MS HRTF Spatializer**.

Add a new GameObject to the scene. This empty game object will be a placeholder: later, you can add other child objects to it. The responsibility of this object is to provide a location from where the voice comes. I prefer to set the location to **(0,0,0)**, but you can choose your own settings here. I have also changed its name to `SpatialVoiceGenerator` because basically, that is what it will do.

Now, add to this GameObject an **AudioSource**. Set the settings for this audio source to look as follows:

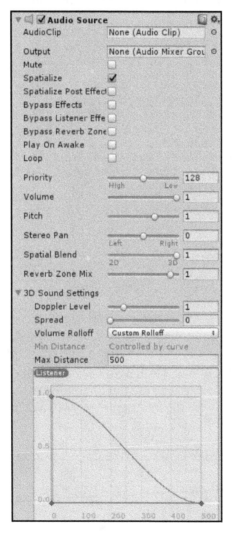

AudioSource settings for spatial voice

Adding the helper script

Now it is time for some scripting. We will first add a script that intercepts the air-tap so we can use that to test our code. You should know how to do that by now, but here it is anyway.

Add a new folder to the project, named Scripts. Add to that a script; let us call it GestureHelper. Remember, Unity3D adds the .cs extension to our file so we do not have to do this ourselves. The script should be attached to the camera, and it looks as follows:

```
using UnityEngine;
using UnityEngine.VR.WSA.Input;
public class GestureHelper : MonoBehaviour
{
    [SerializeField] [Tooltip("The object with an audiosource.")]
    private GameObject _objectContainingVoice;
    private void Start()
    {
        var rec = new GestureRecognizer();
        rec.SetRecognizableGestures(GestureSettings.Tap);
        rec.TappedEvent += RecOnTappedEvent;
        rec.StartCapturingGestures();
    }
    private void RecOnTappedEvent(
    InteractionSourceKind source,
    int tapCount,
    Ray headRay)
    {
        _objectContainingVoice.SendMessage(
        "PlayVoice",
        SendMessageOptions.DontRequireReceiver);
    }
}
```

Again, we should know this by now. We have a field that will contain the object with the AudioSource component. We initialize the GestureRecognizer. If the recognizer sees an airtap, we call SendMessage with the message PlayVoice on the GameObject we placed in _objectContainingVoice.

In Unity, we should drag the GameObject to the **Object Containing Voice** property of this script.

Creating the scripts for the asset

That is all the preparation we need to do. It is time to write our reusable object.

We can do this in our `Scripts` folder or we can do it in a new folder. Since we want things to be grouped together, I suggest you create a new folder as a subfolder under `Scripts`. I think `VoicePlayer` would be a nice name for this: this is what the component will do.

In that newly created folder, or in the Scripts folder if you decided to use that one, create two new scripts. One is called `SpatialVoicePlayer`, and the other is called `WaveFileParser`. The first one will be the one generates the voice, and the other one is used to convert the data.

The `WaveFileParser` is quite complicated. It reads the data from the stream and dissects it into the different parts of a Wave file. The Wave file (`.WAV` extension in Windows) is one of the standard formats Windows and Unity understand and the one that the synthesizer generates for us. However, Unity is not able to read the data from the in-memory stream the synthesizer generates. We need to read that data from the `SpeechStream` we saw in the previous part and turn that into a fake file we can supply to `AudioSource`.

I give you the code for this class as-is, without talking more about it. Of course, this code is also part of our RockOn example app, so you can find it there as well:

```
using System;
using UnityEngine;
#if WINDOWS_UWP
    using System.IO;
    using System.Threading.Tasks;
    using Windows.Media.SpeechSynthesis;
#endif
public class SpatialVoicePlayer : MonoBehaviour
{
    private AudioSource _source;
    [Tooltip("The string to say")]
    public string TextToSay = "Hello HoloLens";
    private WaveFileParser _wav;
    #if WINDOWS_UWP
        public void PlayVoice()
        {
            _source = GetComponent<AudioSource>();
            if (_source == null)
            return;
            var myTask = ReadSpeechStream();
            myTask.Wait();
            var clip = AudioClip.Create(
            "voiceClip",
```

```
                _wav.SampleCount,
                _wav.ChannelCount,
                _wav.Frequency,
                false);
                clip.SetData(_wav.LeftChannel, 0);
                _source.clip = clip;
                _source.Play();
        }
        private async Task ReadSpeechStream()
        {
                using (var speechSynt = new SpeechSynthesizer())
                {
                    var speechStream =
                    await speechSynt.SynthesizeTextToStreamAsync(TextToSay);
                    var stream = speechStream.AsStreamForRead();
                    _wav = new WaveFileParser(stream);
                }
        }
    #endif
}
```

Unity3D can use files as a source for audio, or you can use the WWW helper class to download streams from a website, provided you have set the correct capabilities (you need `InternetClient` or `PrivateNetworkClientServer` in the publishing settings to be set to true).

Our SpatialVoicePlayer script

Let us fill in the details of `SpatialVoicePlayer`. We will add this script as a component of our sphere. Just drag the script onto the `SpatialVoiceGenerator` object in the hierarchy window or in the scene editor. When you have done this and rebuilt the project, you can open Visual Studio and create the actual code.

I will first show you the complete file, and then I will tell you what is going on:

```
using System;
using UnityEngine;
#if WINDOWS_UWP
    using System.IO;
    using System.Threading.Tasks;
    using Windows.Media.SpeechSynthesis;
#endif
public class SpatialVoicePlayer : MonoBehaviour
{
    private AudioSource _source;
    [Tooltip("The string to say")]
```

```
    public string TextToSay = "Hello HoloLens";
    private WaveFileParser _wav;
    #if WINDOWS_UWP
        public void PlayVoice()
        {
            _source = GetComponent<AudioSource>();
            if (_source == null)
            return;
            var myTask = ReadSpeechStream();
            myTask.Wait();
            var clip = AudioClip.Create(
            "voiceClip",
            _wav.SampleCount,
            _wav.ChannelCount,
            _wav.Frequency,
            false);
            clip.SetData(_wav.LeftChannel, 0);
            _source.clip = clip;
            _source.Play();
        }
        private async Task ReadSpeechStream()
        {
            using (var speechSynth = new SpeechSynthesizer())
            {
                var speechStream =
                await speechSynth.SynthesizeTextToStreamAsync(TextToSay);
                var stream = speechStream.AsStreamForRead();
                _wav = new WaveFileParser(stream);
            }
        }
    }
    #endif
}
```

There is quite a lot going on here that we have not really talked about before. First, you will probably notice the `#if WINDOWS_UWP` / `#endif` structures in this file. There is, of course, a reason for this. Unity3D uses the **Mono** runtime. Now, although Mono looks a lot like the .NET things you already know and love, there is a big difference. For starters, it is built by other people. Mono is a cross-platform variant of the normal .NET framework. Anything that is put in .NET will one day or another be put into Mono as well. Of course, this means that it lags behind: not every feature can be in Mono the moment it is available in .NET.

What is it about these #if statements?

You might be wondering why Unity3D uses Mono. After all, why are we not using C# 6.0, the version which is available right now? The answer to is that Unity3D apps should run on a multitude of platforms. We are dealing with a system that can deploy to Windows, iOS, MacOS, Android, Samsung TV, Tizen, Play Station 3, and much more. Those platforms do not support .NET as Microsoft has made it available; it needs the open-source, open-platform variant, Mono.

HoloLens, however, runs on the latest version of .NET. On that device, we can use all the latest and greatest constructs and frameworks coming out of Redmond, as long as it is supported by the UWP platform. So, we have a problem here. If we restrict ourselves to what Mono is offering, we cannot use many of the features we need. If we use C# 6.0 features, the editor in Unity3D will start complaining about things in our code it does not understand.

The solution to this is what we did in this piece of code. Anything that might upset Unity3D, such as certain namespaces, will be surrounded with the #if WINDOWS_UWP / #endif construct. When the internal compiler in Unity3D sees this, it will ignore all the code inside that block. After all, Unity3D does not do WINDOWS_UWP. When we compile our code in Visual Studio in preparation for deployment to the device, emulator, or store, the define WINDOWS_UWP is set and thus the code will be part of our codebase. By doing it this way, you can mix the two platforms. However, a word of warning: do not clutter your files with #if statements. They can cause problems if they block out code other parts rely on. Those error messages from Unity can be very hard to solve, so be careful here.

There is a better way of dealing with this, one that removes those ugly if statements but that requires some work. I will explain how to do this in Chapter 8, *Speed Up Your Development - Advanced Unity3D*. For now, statements work just fine.

Asynchronous stream generating

We have two methods. One is the public `PlayVoice()`, the other is called `ReadSpeechStream()`. The first one is called by `SendMessage("PlayVoice")` in the `GestureHelper` class. The second one is the part that loads the voice data into the streams. Why did we do this?

The answer lies in the inner workings of Unity. The short answer is: we need to call several awaitable methods that work asynchronously, while also doing work that can only be done on the main thread.

Let us investigate. If we look at the work being done in the ReadSpeechStream method we can see the following steps:

1. Create an instance of the speech synthesizer.
2. Wrap that in a using statement so we are sure it will be disposed of.
3. Asynchronously create the SpeechStream from the given string.
4. Wait for this to finish.
5. Convert the SpeechStream to a ReadStream.
6. Create an instance of our WaveFileReader to parse the data from the stream.

This whole construct will be called from PlayVoice().

In PlayVoice we do the following:

1. Get the AudioSource component. If we do not have one, there is no use continuing.
2. Call ReadSpeechStream to make sure the string is converted into a wav object containing the spoken words.
3. Wait for this to be finished.
4. Create a new AudioClip component, giving it the properties from the stream (now stored in _wav).
5. Set the actual bytes in the _wav.LeftChannel (we do not care about left or right: the spatializer will take care of this for us) to the AudioClip.
6. Link the AudioClip to the AudioSource of our GameObject.
7. Play it. The AudioSource will play, using the spatializer constructs we have set up before so the voice will come from the same position as our sphere.

The things done in step 4 (create a new AudioClip) and 5 (copying the data) can only be done on the main thread of Unity. That is just the way it works. However, the streaming is done asynchronously and can be done on a different thread. If this happens you will get an exception during runtime.

If you put all the code in one method, place a breakpoint on line 1 of that method, and run it, you will see that it just works. This is because the debugger messes up with the internal threading algorithms of Unity and thus avoids the issues I just described. But if you happen to run this on the device without stepping through it, you will notice that there is no sound. An exception, of type `ArgumentException`, is thrown. This does not help you, but if you delve into the issue you will find something telling you it is not permitted to create an AudioClip or to set its data from outside the main Unity thread. This is exactly what we are doing: the reading of the stream is offloaded to another thread and that is where we do the creation.

So, we have this construct with the async/await patterns to help us deal with this.

You can run the app, do an airtap, and you will hear the voice come out of the sphere.

Creating the reusable asset

That was a lot of work with a lot of details. Luckily, we can turn that hard work into something we can reuse over and over again.

We first need to turn our GameObject into a prefab. You can think of a prefab as being a class in C#, something that you instantiate if you want to use it. The instantiation is the GameObject. Here we work the other way around: first we create the GameObject with all its properties and components, and then we create the prefab out of it.

To do this, all you need to do is create a folder in your **Assets** pane; I suggest you use the name `Prefabs` and drag the `SpacialVoiceGenerator` GameObject from the hierarchy to that folder. You will see it appear as a cube in the `Prefab` folder, and you will also see that the color of the GameObject in the hierarchy changes. The color tells you that you are working with a prefab instance.

Now we need to build our reusable prefab.

If you right-click on the `SpacialVoiceGenerator` prefab in the `Prefab` folder, you see a dialog such as the following:

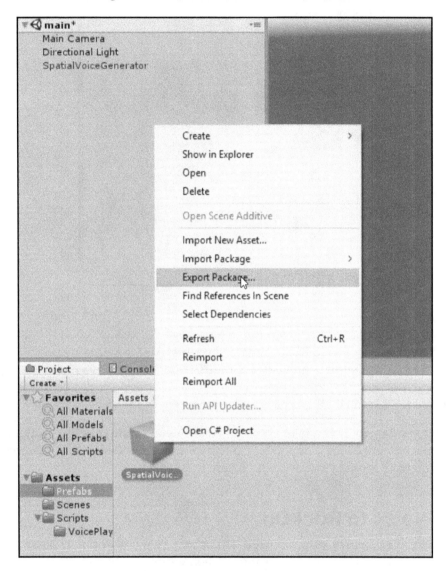

Exporting the package

When you select **Export Package...** you get the following dialog:

Here you can select what items you want in the package. Make sure you select the `Prefabs` subfolder the `Scripts` folder, and all contained scripts. Also, be sure Include dependencies is checked. Now, click **Export...**, and enter a location and a descriptive name. I suggest you use a name such as `SpatialVoiceGenerator`. I have a separate folder on my system where I store my custom HoloLens packages; you might do the same.

That is all we need to do! If you need a spatial voice in your HoloLens application, you can import this package, drag the component from the `Prefabs` folder to your hierarchy, set the properties you need for the location, and you are good to go.

Adding voice to RockOn

We will add this prefab to our RockOn app. Let us make a game out of it. We can add guitars to our world by tapping on a location. When we do that, we see the new guitar and we hear a sound coming from that location. Would it not be fun to have someone tell us to place an instrument somewhere? I suggest we make the following changes:

1. Have the `SpatialVoiceGenerator` prefab in our app.
2. Wait a little while, somewhere between five and ten seconds.

3. Let the system tell us: *Place the guitar here.*

4. The voice should come from the direction in which we want the instrument to be placed.

Later, we can change this to include multiple instruments. If we also have drums, bass, microphones, and so on, we can easily change the spoken text: it is all computer-generated anyway.

Open the RockOn app in Unity. Right-click on the `Assets` folder in the `Project Pane` and choose `Import Package` followed by `Custom Package...`:

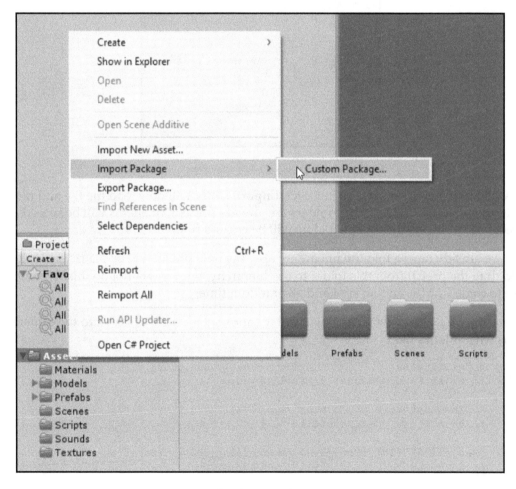

Importing the new package

Browse to the location where you saved the generated package and select the file. Click **Import**. You will get the following dialog:

Importing our package and selecting the content

We want all of this in our app, so just click **Import**. Unity will now load the file and place all the items in the right folder. If the folders are already present, the items will be placed in the correct folder. If they are not, the folders will be created first.

Since we already have a folder named `Prefabs`, the new prefab will be placed there. We could drag the prefab from this folder to our hierarchy, but we will not do this. We want the voice to come from a random spot and at a random time.

This means we need a new script. I will call it `RandomShouter` and link it to the camera. This is what it looks like:

```
using UnityEngine;
public class RandomShouter : MonoBehaviour
{
    // The next time the system should shout
    private float _nextShoutTime;

    [SerializeField] [Tooltip("The prefab that generates the voice.")]
    private GameObject _spatialVoiceGenerator;

    [SerializeField]
    [Tooltip("The text you want to be said.")]
```

```
private string _textToSay = "Place the guitar here.";

// Use this for initialization
private void Start()
{
    CalculateNewTime();
}

private void CalculateNewTime()
{
    var waitTime = Random.value*5.0f + 5.0f;
    _nextShoutTime = Time.time + waitTime;
}

// Update is called once per frame
private void Update()
{
    if (Time.time >= _nextShoutTime)
    {
        CalculateNewTime();
        CreateAndPlayVoice();
    }
}
private void CreateAndPlayVoice()
{
    // Calculate the position somewhere
    // around the user at 5 meters distance
    var position = Random.insideUnitSphere*3.0f;
    // Instantiate the object at that position
    // Rotation is of no importance
    var instance = (GameObject) Instantiate(
        _spatialVoiceGenerator,
        position, Quaternion.identity);
    // Set the text property
    var voiceScript = instance.GetComponent<SpatialVoicePlayer>();
    voiceScript.TextToSay = _textToSay;
    voiceScript.PlayVoice();

    // Kill the instance, two seconds after creation.
    Destroy(instance, 2.0f);
}
```

This code should be obvious. For the sake of brevity, I have omitted certain checks, things you obviously should be doing in production code, but again, none of this code should come as a surprise to you.

Save it, build it, and run it. You should hear the voice calling out to you to place the guitar *here*.

Making things more lifelike

This was all great fun. But there is still one thing bothering me: we still hear a clearly computer-generated voice. That would not be a problem if we were designing an 80s retro-game, but if we want things to be as lifelike as possible, we need to change things.

Fortunately, we can. We can tweak the way the computer says the words in a rather fine-grained way. It takes some work, but with some patience and careful planning you can achieve a much better experience. And that is what HoloLens apps should be all about: things should be as realistic as possible to provide a real immersive experience.

Introducing the SSML stream

If you go back to our source code, you might remember the following line:

```
var speechStream =
await speechSynth.SynthesizeTextToStreamAsync(TextToSay);
```

We have used this in both the DirectX sample and the Unity3D sample. The preceding line comes from the Unity-based app but we had a similar line in DirectX. This line tells the synthesizer to take the string we give it and turn that into voice. It does so by using the default settings, resulting in the robot-like voice we have heard so far.

You might have noticed, as you typed in the code, that there is an alternative:

```
var speechStream =
await speechSynt.SynthesizeSsmlToStreamAsync(TextToSay);
```

We could have used this line as well. However, that would have resulted in an error: this call expects the string to be in a certain format. This format is a variant of the XML standard, called **Speech Synthesis Markup Language** (**SSML**).

With SSML, you can break the text up into parts, defining for each part the characteristics you want for the voice. Let me show you an example of a very simple sentence:

```
<speak version='1.0'
xmlns='http://www.w3.org/2001/10/synthesis'
xml:lang='en-US'>
>
Hi there, my <emphasis>dearest</emphasis> reader.
</speak>
```

This is just a plain XML file as we know it, but slightly different.

The `xml:lang='en-US'` part is usually ignored by most developers. Here it is very important: this determines what voice the system should use. If I were to put `'nl-NL'` there, indicating I want a Dutch voice, the system will try to use Dutch pronunciation of the English text. This can be a funny effect, but it is usually not what you want. So, choose the correct language. For HoloLens, this means it has to be en-US because that is the only language it supports.

The markup starts with `<speak>` instead of `<xml>`. The plain text inside the body of the document is what the system will say. We can augment this with keywords such as `<emphasis>`, which will emphasize the word, words, or even syllables in between those elements. There is a lot of documentation available for SSML. I suggest you go out on the web and look for the official standards specification, but I will give you a brief overview of how to get results quickly.

Overview of the most important SSML tags

There are a lot of tags you can use to make your voice more lifelike. A lot of them are described in the standards, but some of the details are left to the supplier of the engine. In the following table, I give you an overview of the most important tags and how to use them in a way that the Microsoft synthesizer understands:

Element	Description	Attributes
break	A pause in the spoken text.	strength, time
emphasis	Makes the part in this element more prominent.	level
p	Paragraph.	-
s	Sentence inside a paragraph.	-
phoneme	Turns the pronunciation into a phonetic one. Used to spell out numbers and characters.	ph, alphabet
prosody	Controls the rate, pitch, and volume of the text inside the element.	pitch, contour, range, rate, duration, volume
say-as	The type of text inside the element. For instance, speak out a date or time.	interpret-as, format, detail
voice	The kind of voice you want for this part.	xml:lang, gender, age, variant, name

As you can see, most elements have attributes that you can use. In the following table, you can see what those attributes look like and what values they can have. Almost all attributes are optional; if you do not define them the defaults will be used:

Attribute	Owing element	Description
strength	break	The relative duration of the pause. Possible values: none, x-weak, weak, medium, strong, x-strong. Default: medium.
time	break	The absolute duration of the pause, in milliseconds.
level	emphasis	The level of emphasis to be used. Possible values: reduced, none, moderate, strong. Default: moderate.
alphabet	phoneme	The phonetic alphabet to use. Possible values: ipa, x-microsoft-sapi, x-microsoft-ups.
ph	phoneme	**Required**. The ph attribute contains the phonemes or phonetic codes telling the system how to pronounce certain words. If there is a mistake in this string, the whole file will be rejected and nothing will be heard, so be careful with this one.
pitch	prosody	The baseline pitch for the spoken words. You can give this either an absolute value followed by Hz (example: 400 Hz), a relative value that starts with a + or -, then a number, and then Hz or St (example: +80 Hz, or -2 St, meaning down two semitones), or one of the following options: default, x-low, low, medium, high, x-high.
contour	prosody	A set of pitch changes, defined as a percentage of the duration. Example: (0%, +20 Hz) (40%, +80 Hz), (75%, -20 Hz).
rate	prosody	The speed of the spoken words. Can be a relative number (0.5 means half the speed) or one of the following: x-slow, slow, medium, fast, x-fast.
duration	prosody	The total duration of this segment, in milliseconds.
volume	prosody	The volume level of the voice. Can be absolute, ranging from 0.0 to 100.0, relative (indicated by + or -, so -10 means -10%), or one of the following: silent, x-soft, soft, medium, loud, x-loud, default. Default is 100%.
interpret-as	say-as	**Required**. This is the content type of the string within the element. Possible values are as follows: • Date (with format) • Cardinal • Ordinal • Characters • Time (with format) • Telephone
name	voice	The name of the voice. We have seen the voices that are available on the HoloLens; you can specify that name here.
gender	voice	The preferred voice to be used. Options are: male, female, and neutral.
age	voice	The preferred age for the voice. Options are 10 (child), 15 (teen), 30 (adult), 65 (senior).
xml:lang	voice	The language you want. Example: en-US. This is the only available option for HoloLens.

As you can see, there are quite a few options you can choose from to make the voice more realistic. Of course, the hard part is to figure out which part goes where. What does it take to make a voice sound more human? I suggest you listen carefully to people when they speak and try to learn their pattern of speech. Where do they put the emphasis? When do they raise or lower their voice? When do they increase or decrease the volume?

The nice thing about SSML is that you can implement all of this in code. We could, for instance, say, *Please look to your* **left**, with the emphasis on the word left. It would be very easy to change that to: *Please look to your* **right**. After all, all that it takes is an XML document containing the right words and tags. It is very easy to do this in software by using a `XMLWriter` object. For instance, I use the following class quite frequently:

```
internal class SsmlSpeechCreator
{
    public enum PauseTime
    {
        Short,
        Medium,
        Long
    }

    public enum Side
    {
        Right,
        Left
    }

    private XmlWriter _writer;

    public string CreateSpeechSsml(Side side)
    {
        var stringBuilder = new StringBuilder();

        _writer = XmlWriter.Create(stringBuilder);
        using (_writer)
        {
            AddStartDocument();
            AddNormalText("Please,");
            AddPause(PauseTime.Medium);
            AddNormalText("Look at the ");

            switch (side)
            {
                case Side.Right:
                    AddEmphasizedText("right.");
                    break;

                case Side.Left:
                    AddEmphasizedText("left.");
                    break;
            }

            _writer.WriteEndElement();
```

```
            _writer.Flush();
        }
        var result = stringBuilder.ToString();

        return result;
    }

    private void AddStartDocument()
    {
        _writer.WriteStartDocument();
        _writer.WriteStartElement("speak",
"http://www.w3.org/2001/10/synthesis");
        _writer.WriteAttributeString("version", "1.0");
        _writer.WriteAttributeString("xml", "lang", null, "en-US");
    }

    private void AddNormalText(string text)
    {
        _writer.WriteString(text);
    }

    private void AddPause(PauseTime pauseTime)
    {
        _writer.WriteStartElement("break");
        string pauseIdentifier;
        switch (pauseTime)
        {
            case PauseTime.Short:
                pauseIdentifier = "x-weak";
                break;

            case PauseTime.Medium:
                pauseIdentifier = "medium";
                break;

            case PauseTime.Long:
            default:
                pauseIdentifier = "x-strong";
                break;
        }
        _writer.WriteAttributeString("strength", pauseIdentifier);
        _writer.WriteEndElement();
    }

    private void AddEmphasizedText(string text)
    {
        _writer.WriteStartElement("emphasis");
        _writer.WriteAttributeString("level", "strong");
```

```
        _writer.WriteString(text);
        _writer.WriteEndElement();
    }
}
```

This class helps me create convincing-sounding voices. With SSML, you can create all sorts of effects, but be cautious: not all of the standards are implemented in UWP and thus not in HoloLens. For instance, the **Prodisy Contour** setting does not do much yet. I advise you to test everything you want to use to be sure it works on HoloLens at the time you create the software. Then again, things such as Prodisy might not work yet but they are not doing any harm either. They will not break the synthesizer. Other mistakes might, but this is just ignored.

Listen up - voice commands

We have been listening to the HoloLens giving us hints, tips, and commands for quite some time. Now it is time to do the reverse: we are going to give the HoloLens some commands.

Before we begin exploring the world of speech recognition, I want to show you something very important. I start out with this for one simple reason. In every single class I teach, people come to me complaining that they cannot get their code to work: the system just does not listen to their voice commands. Yet they have done everything I taught them, so the HoloLens must be broken!

I can assure you: you will do this as well. The reason I know this is because it also happens to me every now and then, even though I am a trainer on this subject. I am talking about capabilities.

As we have discussed before, a **Universal Windows Platform** (**UWP**), app is sandboxed. This means the app cannot do much besides render itself on the screen and listen to keyboard, mouse, and touch input. If you want to do something a bit more interesting, you will have to tell the operating system exactly what it is you want to do. By doing so, you make sure that when the user installs your app he will get a dialog telling him your intentions. The user can then opt in to this, or opt out, and thus not use your app.

In our case, we need to request access to the microphone. Next to that, we also need to have access to the network connection: a lot of the speech recognition can be done in the cloud so we have to make sure we can access that as well. I have shown you how to set those capabilities in Unity; I have not shown you how to do that in the DirectX samples.

If you create a project in Visual Studio, you will see a file called `Package.appxmanifest` in the `solution` folder. Open that file and you will be presented with the settings for your app. The third tab on that settings page is the **Capabilities** page. By default, none of the options are selected. I encourage you to make it look more like the following:

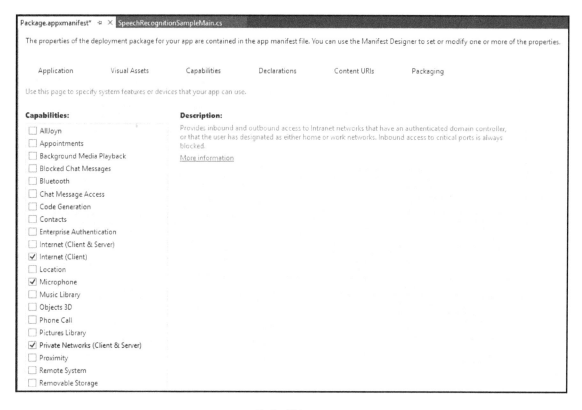

The Capabilities page

As you can see, I have chosen the following options:

- **Internet (Client)**: This means I can access web services out there in the cloud.
- **Private Networks (Client & Server)**: I can access devices on my local network. You might think this is not needed, but you will need it later on when we talk about sharing holograms between devices, so it is best to have it in your app from the beginning.
- **Microphone**: Well, this goes without saying. We cannot give the HoloLens voice commands if we do not support a microphone.

As far as the other options are concerned, enable them if you need them. Do not think, *Hey, I might as well check everything in case I need them later on.* This will have the effect that your app will permitted in the store. Someone at Microsoft will think something like, *Why would this app need all this? That sounds fishy...,* and reject your app. Only apply what you need. However, these three options are always needed, including a fourth one I am not showing you here but which will become obvious when we start talking about spatial understanding.

So, with that out of the way, let us get started with voice recognition.

Default commands

Out of the box, HoloLens listens to whatever you are saying. Since the interaction with the world is limited to one gesture, the air tap, the designers had to make sure people could work the device without having to go through all sorts of menus. To solve this, they implemented a list of voice commands you can use. If you are building your own app and want to use voice commands, you need to be aware of those that already exist.

Select

You are probably already familiar with this one. This is the equivalent of an airtap or a click with the clicker. The HPU actually processes this one and hands it to the CPU as a mouse click. You can use this in the same way you use the other two events.

Hey, Cortana

Since HoloLens is a Windows 10 device, it comes preinstalled with Cortana. Cortana is the digital assistant in Windows. You usually interact with her through the use of voice commands. You start a conversation with Cortana by saying *Hey, Cortana,* after which the familiar Cortana interface will show up.

You can use all sorts of commands. You can ask Cortana to tell a joke, ask her where she comes from, and other funny things. Of course, she can also help you handle your agenda and inform you of the weather.

Next to these standard Cortana commands there are a bunch of special commands for HoloLens, as follows:

- What can I say?
- Go home / Go to start (same as the Bloom gesture)
- Launch <app name>
- Move <app> here
- Take a picture
- Start recording
- Stop recording
- Increase/decrease brightness
- Increase/decrease volume
- Mute/unmute
- Shut down the device
- Restart the device
- Go to sleep
- How much battery do I have left?

As you can see from the preceding list, a lot of things can be done by just talking to the device. It is just another example of how natural user interface systems work.

App commands

You have probably noticed this before: if you hover over a button in an app, a label will appear underneath that button, displaying an icon of a microphone and text next to it. This indicates that you can just say that text to perform the same action:

Done as a voice command

As you can see, when I am working on adjusting the puppy from the Holograms app (which I started by saying, *Hey Cortana, start Holograms*), I have a visual aid telling me I can select the **Done** button just by saying the word *Done*.

I suggest you use the same technique in your applications: help the user to discover the voice commands you have supplied in your app.

Hologram manipulations

When working with holograms, there are several commands you can use. This is true for both three-dimensional and two-dimensional apps. These commands are as follows:

- Face me
- Bigger
- Enhance
- Smaller

Try them out on any app and see what happens. I think they are pretty self-explanatory.

Dictation

Input in HoloLens is tricky. We can use a Bluetooth keyboard to facilitate text entry, but we have already decided this is not what we want: a user will not carry a keyboard around all the time. There is an alternative: the on-screen keyboard. However, using this is not as easy as it seems. It can be quite hard to enter text; people get quite tired after using it.

Luckily, we can use speech here as well. In front of the text entry field there is a button with a microphone on it. Select that (using an airtap, the clicker, or just by looking at it and saying *Select*), and you can dictate your text. The words you say will appear in that box.

Try it out by opening the Edge browser (*Hey Cortana, start Edge.*), and select the address bar (*Select*). The on-screen keyboard will appear. Next to the input box at the top there is a microphone. Select that and say something, such as, *HoloLens.* You will see that it picks up your speech and puts it in the address bar of the Edge browser, showing you results immediately:

Voice input with the keyboard

Troubleshooting speech recognition

I have to say: the speech recognition works extremely well. In the past, I have worked on other systems that utilized speech and they always had problems. You needed to train the devices to recognize your voice and even then, it was a hit-or-miss game. Sometimes it worked, sometimes it did not.

With the new Cortana-based system we have a pretty reliable system in place. This is helped a lot by the placement of the microphones in the device. Remember, we have four of those, placed in such a way as to focus on the area just in front of your mouth. This means other sounds can be filtered out and the device will only pick up your voice commands, not those of your co-workers who find it funny to shout, *Hey Cortana, restart!* from across the room.

However, it does fail. When that happens, just repeat the words again. If that does not help, try to be a bit clearer and speak a bit slower.

Also, a noisy environment might be the problem. Try to move to another area that is a bit quieter. That being said, it is amazing how well this device performs: I have tested it out on the floor of one of the large casinos in Las Vegas infamous for its noise. Even there it worked just fine.

One last remark: the device is built for the US-English market. This means that it is optimized for that language as well. So maybe trying an American accent will help you get the message across, if all else fails.

Building a VoiceRecognizer in DirectX

It is not that hard to build this kind of code in our app. Most of the hard work has been done by the teams at Microsoft that build the UWP framework and the HoloLens framework.

It is important to realize that the code that is provided by the teams uses a special set of audio categories. All audio streams, both input and output, need to be marked by the developer, indicating what kind of audio this is. Voice recognition in HoloLens is marked as follows:

- `AudioCategory_Communications`: This means it is optimized for calls and narrative scenarios. It uses a 16 kHz, 24 bit mono stream.
- `AudioCategory_Speech`: Customized for the speech engine, also 16-kHz, 24-bit mono.

- `AudioCategory_Other`: Used for ambient sound recording a, 48-kHz, 48-bit stereo stream.

The audio we use will fall into these categories. The HoloLens hardware has hardware acceleration for these three types, meaning the processing of this data is done by the hardware and not on the CPU. We will get the data we need from these hardware algorithms, so it is not advisable to just open the microphone and do all the heavy work yourself. If you do, you will use the CPU and thus take away some performance, and possibly even drain the battery. Just follow what I am showing you here and you will be fine.

The VoiceRecognizer class

As usual, begin a new Holographic project in Visual Studio. I called mine `SpeechRecognitionSample`. We will begin our `VoiceRecognizer` class with some standard code and place it next to the `SpinningCubeRenderer` in the `Content` folder and namespace. This is what it looks like:

```
using System;
using System.Collections.Generic;
using System.Threading.Tasks;
using Windows.Media.SpeechRecognition;

namespace SpeechRecognitionSample.Content
{
    internal class VoiceRecognizer : IDisposable
    {
        private readonly Dictionary<string, Action> _actions = new
Dictionary<string, Action>();
        private SpeechRecognizer _speechRecognizer;

        public void Dispose()
        {
            GC.SuppressFinalize(this);
            Dispose(true);
        }

        protected void Dispose(bool isDisposing)
        {
            if (isDisposing)
            {
                _speechRecognizer.Dispose();
                _speechRecognizer = null;
            }
        }
```

```
        ~VoiceRecognizer()
        {
            Dispose(false);
        }
    }
}
```

Nothing special here. We have made the class `IDisposable` so we can clean up after ourselves when we are done. The only new thing here is the `_actions` field and of course the `_speechRecognizer` field. We will use these later on, but for now I can tell you that the actions will contain all the phrases and words we want to recognize. We make a link between these terms and the callbacks in the shape of actions we want to call if we recognize a spoken word.

The instantiation of this class is done next to the instantiation of the `SpinningCubeRenderer`. Since we have been doing this all along, I am sure you know where we do this. But just to help you out a bit, I have placed this code in the `SpeechRecognitionSampleMain` class in the `SetHolographicSpace` method:

```
// Initialize the sample hologram.
spinningCubeRenderer = new SpinningCubeRenderer(deviceResources);
_voiceRecognizer = new VoiceRecognizer();

spatialInputHandler = new SpatialInputHandler();
```

Again, nothing special. Do not forget to add the field to the class:

```
private VoiceRecognizer _voiceRecognizer;
```

Let us also take care of the cleaning up. After all, we did not implement the `IDisposable` method for nothing. Change the `Dispose` method in `SpeechRecognitionSampleMain` to look as follows:

```
public void Dispose()
{
#if DRAW_SAMPLE_CONTENT
    if (spinningCubeRenderer != null)
    {
        spinningCubeRenderer.Dispose();
        spinningCubeRenderer = null;
    }
    if (_voiceRecognizer != null)
    {
        _voiceRecognizer.Dispose();
        _voiceRecognizer = null;
```

```
    }
#endif
}
```

Again, nothing new is happening here.

Now, let us make it a bit more interesting. We return to our class and add the following method. I will walk you through it step-by-step:

```
public async Task Instantiate(params Tuple<string, Action>[]
keywordsAndActions)
{
    foreach (var keywordAndAction in keywordsAndActions)
    {
        _actions.Add(keywordAndAction.Item1, keywordAndAction.Item2);
    }

    _speechRecognizer = new SpeechRecognizer();

    var constraintList = new
SpeechRecognitionListConstraint(_actions.Keys);
    _speechRecognizer.Constraints.Clear();
    _speechRecognizer.Constraints.Add(constraintList);

    await _speechRecognizer.CompileConstraintsAsync();

    _speechRecognizer.ContinuousRecognitionSession.ResultGenerated +=
        OnPhraseRecognized;
    await
_speechRecognizer.ContinuousRecognitionSession.StartAsync(SpeechContinuousR
ecognitionMode.Default);
}
```

First of all, we have some asynchronous calls here, so we need to mark this method as `async`. We pass in the parameters in `Tuple<string,Action>`. This way we can call this method and give it as many commands and callbacks as we want. These tuples will be torn apart and stored in the dictionary we created earlier.

Then we create an instance of the `_speechRecognizer` field we saw before. As you can see, there is nothing special going on here: we do not need to give it any parameters.

We create an instance of a `SpeechRecognitionListConstraint`. This is the list of words and short phrases the recognizer will understand. In the constructor, we need to pass an `IEnumerable<string>` so the keys of our dictionary look like a good candidate for this. Next, we need to feed those constraints to the `_speechRecognizer`. First, we clean up any possible remaining words and then add our list to the `Constraints`.

These words need to be compiled. This means the phonetics of all these words and phrases need to be distilled and stored in such a way that the recognizer can work with them efficiently. Remember, this is all done in hardware-optimized code so it needs some attention. For us, this means all we have to do is call `CompileConstraintsAsync`. Since this might take a while we need to call this asynchronously.

When this is all done, we set up a callback. This will be called whenever the `speechrecognizer` hears something it knows about. We call this method `OnPhraseRecognized` and we will deal with it shortly.

All that is left to do is switch on the recognizer. We call `StartAsync` on it. I have passed in the option `SpeechContinuousRecognitionMode.Default`. This means the recognizer will keep on running even though it is currently processing another input. You can set it to `PauseOnRecognition` to prevent multiple calls from entering.

Now, let us have a look at the callback:

```
private void OnPhraseRecognized(SpeechContinuousRecognitionSession sender,
    SpeechContinuousRecognitionResultGeneratedEventArgs args)
{
    var calledWord = args.Result.Text;
    if (!_actions.ContainsKey(calledWord)) return;

    var action = _actions[calledWord];
    action?.Invoke();
}
```

The recognizer calls this whenever it hears something it has learned about. We take the `args` argument and from that we take the text. This will hold the text we have put in the `Constraints` list before, if it recognizes this.

The `Result` member of `args` is of type `SpeechRecognitionResult`. This has some interesting properties, next to the `Text` we just saw. It gives you information about the time the text was spoken, the duration, the confidence (how sure is the system that this is correct?), and so on. Have a look at this class and see what you can do with it.

The confidence is something you actually should be using, although we do not do that here. You could say that you only act upon words that the system is more than 50 percent certain it got right. That way you can filter out a lot of errors. Of course, this depends on your scenario. If you have very little phrases, all very much different from each other, you might not need this.

We have the word in the variable `calledWord`, so we look up the corresponding action in `_actions`. If we find it, we call it.

That is all we need to do. It is time to get this working.

Go back to the `SetHolographicSpace` method in the `SpeechRecognitionSampleMain` class. Below the creation of the `_voiceRecognizer` field, call our new initialize method thus:

```
var voiceTask = _voiceRecognizer.Instantiate(
    new Tuple<string, Action>("Place", OnPlaceCalled));
voiceTask.Wait(1000);
```

We add one word here, `Place`, and give it the `OnPlaceCalled` callback. We wait for this to be ready and I have given it a timeout of one second. Again, it might take some time and I did not want to make `SetHolographicSpace` async as well. This works pretty well, so I stick to this solution.

The `OnPlaceCalled` method is very boring, but it looks as follows:

```
private void OnPlaceCalled()
{
    _isPlacing = true;
}
```

I have added a field `_isPlacing` to the class. We will use that shortly. All I do in `OnPlaceCalled` is set that Boolean field to `true`.

The last thing we need to do is go to the `Update` method in this class. Find the piece where the tap gesture is intercepted, where the cube is placed at the position the user is looking at. It will be in the part marked with the `#if DRAW_SAMPLE_CONTENT` directive. Change it to look like the following:

```
#if DRAW_SAMPLE_CONTENT
// Check for new input state since the last frame.
var pointerState = spatialInputHandler.CheckForInput();
if (null != pointerState)
{
    // When a Pressed gesture is detected, the sample hologram will be
repositioned
    // two meters in front of the user.
    spinningCubeRenderer.PositionHologram(
        pointerState.TryGetPointerPose(currentCoordinateSystem)
        );
}

if (_isPlacing)
{
    var pointerPose =
```

```
SpatialPointerPose.TryGetAtTimestamp(currentCoordinateSystem,
prediction.Timestamp);

    spinningCubeRenderer.PositionHologram(pointerPose);
    _isPlacing = false;
}
#endif
```

The first part is the normal code. Then we start with a check of the _isPlacing variable. If it is set to true, we can assume the VoiceRecognizer has been doing its work. We get the gaze from the user by calling SpatialPointerPoise.TryGetAtTimestamp. Then we place the cube there. Of course, we finish by setting _isPlacing to false.

Run the app and look away from the cube. Call *Place* and notice the cube moves to the new location.

That is all there is to it. That was not too hard, was it?

Building the VoiceRecognizer in Unity3D

As you might have expected, our work in Unity3D is even simpler. Let me walk you through it.

Open the RockOn app. Add a new C# script to the Scripts folder, call it VoiceRecognizer, and attach that to the main camera.

The implementation looks as follows:

```
using UnityEngine;
using UnityEngine.Windows.Speech;
using Random = System.Random;

public class VoiceRecognizer : MonoBehaviour
{
    [Tooltip("The object you want to place")]
    public GameObject objectToPlace;

    private void Start()
    {
        var keywordRecognizer = new KeywordRecognizer(new[] {"Place"});
        keywordRecognizer.OnPhraseRecognized += OnPhraseRecognized;
        keywordRecognizer.Start();
    }

    private void OnPhraseRecognized(PhraseRecognizedEventArgs args)
```

```
    {
        var confidence = args.confidence;
        if (args.text == "Place" &&
            (confidence == ConfidenceLevel.Medium || confidence ==
ConfidenceLevel.High))
        {
            Place();
        }
    }

    private void Place()
    {
        if (objectToPlace == null)
            return;

        var distance = new Random().Next(2, 10);
        var location =
            transform.position +
            transform.forward*distance;

        Instantiate(
            objectToPlace,
            location,
            Quaternion.LookRotation(transform.up, transform.forward));
    }
}
```

This should look very familiar by now. Let us have a look. We have a GameObject called `ObjectToPlace`. This will hold our `GuitarPrefab`, so please add that to the script in Unity. In the `Start` method we create an instance of the `KeywordRecognizer` class. This is the equivalent of the `VoiceRecognizer` class we created in the DirectX sample. In the constructor, you pass it an array of strings that holds all the keywords this should understand.

Next, we add a callback that is called whenever the recognizer recognizes something. Then we call `Start()`. And that is basically all you need to do.

In `OnPhraseRecognized` we get the args containing the text the system recognized and the level of confidence. The biggest difference with the DirectX sample is that, instead of a double representing a percentage, we now get an `enum` telling us how sure the system is. This could be `Rejected`, `Low`, `Medium`, or `High`.

If it is medium or high, we accept it and call the `Place` method.

The `Place` method is identical to the one we saw in the `GestureHandler` class in our app: this takes a random position and places the prefab at that place.

If you have not forgotten to add the `GuitarPrefab` to this script and you have attached this script to the camera, you should be able to run the app, look at a point and say, *Place*. The guitar will appear there.

Things could not be simpler.

What is next?

We have covered a lot in this chapter. We have added sounds to our app, which makes the whole thing even more realistic. But we are not there yet. To make the system truly integrate with our world, we need to add some awareness of that world to our app. We need to use the spatial mapping, and an understanding of the real world, and then blend that with our virtual world. It is time to really go mixed reality.

Summary

In this chapter, we have spent a lot of time looking at spoken words and listening to them as well. We learned how to create voices and generate speech in different ways. We took a look at the SSML markup language that defines the characteristics of a voice and of a spoken sentence. Then we implemented this in DirectX, made it spatial, and then moved on to create classes in Unity3D that do the same thing. We created realistic-sounding voices we can use in our apps and put them in reusable assets and packages, so next time we need voices we can just import them. In short, we have made our app more human-like.

6
Take a Look around You - Spatial Mapping

This is it. This is the one. The party piece, the thing that makes the HoloLens a unique device--Spatial Mapping.

Why is this so important, you might ask? Well, the answer lies in the definition of Mixed Reality, or MR in short. If you remember what we have discussed previously, there are three different kinds of reality, other than the one we live in:

- Virtual reality
- Augmented reality
- Mixed reality

VR, AR, and MR

Let me outline the differences here:

Scenarios	Virtual Reality	Augmented Reality	Mixed Reality
Augments the real world by adding objects to it.		X	X
Invisibly blends virtual objects with real-world objects.			X
Makes the user believe the experience.	X		X
Replaces the real physical world with sound and vision.	X		

Virtual reality

As you can see, virtual reality replaces the real world with a digital one but does so in such a way the user actually believes, on a more subconscious level, that what she experiences is the real thing. By this, I mean that, although the user is aware it is all fake, on a lower level she will accept the virtual world as the real world. You can see this by observing someone who rides a virtual rollercoaster in a VR environment: if she does not sit down she will probably fall down because she will compensate for the fake movements of the car. On another level, we see a similar behavior: people who see scary things in a VR world will actually be frightened, more so than they would if watching the scene on a television or in a movie theater.

Augmented reality

Augmented reality is on the other side of the spectrum: it does not replace the world but just adds information to it. Although this does have its uses, no user will feel it is completely real. We can see this in the many different popular AR games that are available: people will enjoy them but not believe there really is a dinosaur walking by. This is partly because they are holding a device through which they are observing this fake world, usually a mobile phone or a tablet. If they look past the device they see nothing but the real world, which our bodies translate into *it is fake*. Another reason we do not buy this is that the objects have no understanding of the real world. There is no interaction. Things might appear to sit on a table, for instance, but only when we place a piece of paper with a marker in the right spot.

Mixed reality

Mixed reality does this differently. Because a good MR device is worn and not carried, we cannot see past it. But the more important reason users believe what they are seeing (again, on a subconscious level) is that the objects are integrated into the world. Virtual objects are placed on top of physical objects. Virtual objects can be hidden and thus be invisible when placed behind real-world objects. Even better: these objects can be placed in front of some real object but the user can walk away. When the real-world object is in front of the virtual object, the user will not see, or will only partially see, the digital object. Our bodies accept this as perfectly natural behavior and thus accept it as being the real thing. This is what I mean when I say MR systems can invisibly blend objects with the real world.

In order to do this, devices have to have a deep knowledge of the world. We examined its sensors in `Chapter 1`, *Let's Begin!*, so you know how HoloLens does this. The depth sensor is the main component responsible for making this happen. In this chapter, I will show you how you can use this in your own application.

Spatial mapping, or surface mapping (choose the term you feel most comfortable with), is the API we can use to get data out of the depth sensor and into our application. It is unique: there are no other systems besides Windows Holographic that can do this.

Usages of spatial mapping

I told you that spatial mapping is what makes MR possible. However, there are several things we can do with spatial mapping that enhances this feeling of realism. The following sections look at what we have so far.

Occlusion

We have discussed this one. In the real world, things hidden behind other things are not visible. So, our virtual objects should behave the same way. Objects behind other objects such as tables, walls, boxes, and so on should be occluded. If the user walks around the room the objects will appear from behind the real-world things. This will make the whole scene much more realistic and believable. The reverse is true as well: if this does not happen the user will feel ill at ease. The world does not work like that!

Partially occluded dog

You can see an example of this in the preceding image. This is the holodog, part of the standard app, Holograms. It is more or less occluded by the chair.

However, sometimes we do want to achieve the opposite. Sometimes we want the user to be able to see objects through other objects. It would be like giving the user superpowers. Imagine building an app that shows a plumber where the water pipes are in a wall. Would it not be cool if he could just put on a HoloLens and see the pipes inside the wall? This is not hard to build, but if we do this we need to make it obvious to the user he is getting these superpowers--we can adjust the brightness of the pipes.

Sometimes we want the user to see objects even though they are hidden, just because they are vital to the application. Imagine having a switch that does something important. If this switch is hidden away around a corner the user may not even know it is there and may not be able to achieve the goal he set out to achieve. In this case, you can decide to make the switch visible but in a less bright way, or just by showing the outline. You can even draw it in such a way it looks like it was an X-ray photograph. Of course, the moment the user walks around the corner of that wall and is able to see the switch for real, we have to make sure the object is drawn in a normal way. You would be amazed at how quickly users accept this behavior:

Meshes of the spatial mapping

The meshes you see in the preceding image are those of the cupboard around the corner. You can see that they are rendered as if they are visible through the wall. If you look even closer, you might even see my wife sitting at the kitchen table, which is on the other side of this wall, something not really possible in real life.

Navigation

Our apps live in the real world. This means we can take advantage of the physical structures around us in our app. Imagine we are writing a game where we have to follow a character around the living room. At the time of writing this game, we have no idea what the user's living room looks like. We can safely assume there are walls, a floor, and a ceiling, but that is about it. So, we must use the spatial mapping feature to detect these structures and place our game objects in the right position. But we also have to make sure the user finds the character, the pot of gold, the wizards, the dinosaurs, or whatever it is we want the user to interact with. We could do this in several ways. We can place markers on the floor pointing in the right direction. Or we can place an arrow in front of the user, guiding him as to which way to go. As soon as he needs to turn left the arrow shows this by changing into a left-pointing arrow.

As you can see, we have plenty of ways to show the user where to go and where to discover the elements in our app. But we can only do so when we have a good understanding of the physical layout of the user's world. Again, we do not know this beforehand: each user has his own room and layout. This is where spatial mapping comes into play. We can use spatial mapping to make a map of the physical world so we can guide the user toward interesting things happening in our virtual world.

The great thing about this is that it feels very natural to the user. We are accustomed to systems like this that help us find our way. Most people who drive cars have satellite navigation and thus are familiar with such a system. Again, all this helps in making the virtual world more believable. After all, what could be more realistic than having a virtual kitten that hides behind our couch and a system that tells us where to find it?

Placement

Since we do not know what the area the user is in looks like, we have to scan for this. By scanning and using spatial mapping we can make educated guesses about where things are. We can deduce where the floor is, where to find walls, and so on, by processing the data the spatial mapping engine gives us. I will tell you more about this later on, but for now, just accept that we can do this. However, this is not always enough. Sometimes you will want to give the user control of the layout of the virtual world.

If we are writing a holographic version of chess we want the user to be able to place the board on the table. We can find out where the table is, but we do not know where the user wants to sit, especially if it is a large table. So, we need to give the user this option. The one thing we do not want is to burden the user with the task of positioning the board at exactly the right height so that it does not float above the table or, worse, falls through it. The user merely points at a place on that table and we will put the board there. We know where the table is, so we can do this:

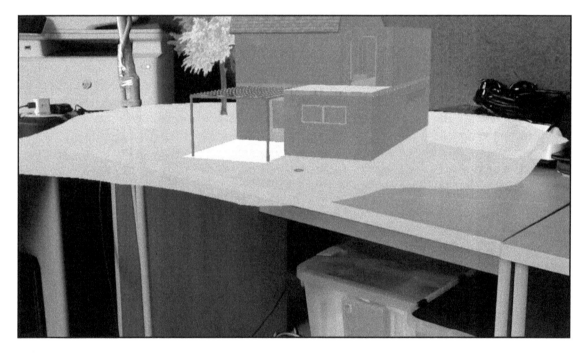

A dollhouse, placed on a workbench

There are many scenarios where this could be handy. We want to create a portal into another dimension, by punching a hole in the wall. The system knows where the walls are; all the user needs to do is the point at the place on that wall where they want that multi-dimensional hole to appear.

Again, this is very natural. In real life, we place things on top of things all the time. You are reading this book and if you are reading the hard copy you will probably put it down on your desk sometime. The book will not fall through it or float above it. It would be weird if this happened, so why would we accept that in a mixed-reality world? We do not. So make sure the system acts naturally.

Visualization

The spatial mapping part of the HoloLens does its work quietly, in the background. All it does is calculate where the surfaces are and return a set of points that form triangles, which form the areas of the world. Our app can take these triangles and do things with them. Usually, we just use them to occlude objects or provide navigation. Sometimes, however, it would be nice to actually show these triangles and draw the surfaces the HoloLens sees. First, it is a pretty cool effect. But secondly, we can use this to show the user what the HoloLens sees so that they can do something with it. For instance, the app we will be building later on in this chapter will give the user X-ray vision: showing rooms in his house through walls and ceilings. It can also help during the placement of objects: by showing the surfaces, the user will be more aware of the places he can put his virtual object. If we want to build an app that creates a virtual skylight in a ceiling, there comes a time in the app where we want to ask the user to place that skylight somewhere. By visualizing the meshes on the ceiling, we can help the user find a suitable place for this skylight and thus prevent them from making a hole in the floor from which they can see the sky: that would be weird.

This is something that doesn't happen in the real world: we never see a table light up when we want to put something on it. But in this kind of scenario, it feels very natural to the user and they will become used to it pretty quickly.

Physics

When we want to achieve as realistic an environment as possible, we need to make sure our virtual objects interact with the physical objects as much as possible. Imagine you have a football and you drop it on the floor. What happens is that it will bounce and eventually roll away, especially when you drop it on a sloped surface.

The virtual football you might have created does no such thing. It will drop when we have gravity and keep on dropping, right to the center of the earth. But if we have spatial mapping, we can have the ball stop falling when it reaches the floor—have the ball bounce or roll off that sloped surface. We can have balls bouncing off the table, onto the chair, and then onto the floor, if the user decides to start dropping the ball in such a place. To do this, we need to know where the table, chair, and floor actually are. Spatial mapping to the rescue! Again, everything is done to make things as believable as possible.

Masquerading imperfection

As you can see, there are a lot of things we can do with spatial mapping, all helping to achieve a level of realism other systems in the VR and AR world cannot match. This helps to convince the user the virtual objects and the physical objects around him blend seamlessly as if it is all really there. However, there is another nice side-effect: since all our virtual objects are a bit more believable and rooted in the real world, the user's brain tends to filter out things that are not perfect, since this does not happen in the real world.

Let me clarify that. The tracking mechanism in HoloLens is pretty good. In fact, the system is one of the best out there. But there are problems. If the user moves around a lot or moves his head rather quickly, sometimes the system loses track of where we are. Objects will drift around a bit. They will not always stay perfectly in place as they are supposed to. But since we expect things to remain sitting still on a table, for example, our brain will correct this for us and convince us the object does not move at all. Do not forget: we see with our brains, not our eyes. The eyes are just sensors, providing data to the graphical processing unit between our ears. Since that GPU expects things to remain static in place, it dismisses the slight movement as a sensor error and ignores it, resulting in a steady, static image. This is an oversimplification of course, but that is what happens. We simply do not see very small jittering.

Things to be aware of in spatial mapping

Spatial mapping is a great way to achieve all of the above. The hardware in the HoloLens is rather impressive and does a great job at getting three-dimensional data from the real world and relaying it to the apps. If you consider the amount of mathematics and physics involved in achieving this you would be even more surprised that it works at all. But it does. That being said, this does not mean the system is perfect. There are still a lot of things we as developers need to take care of, or a least be aware of.

Errors in the spatial mapping

The system is fast and accurate. Yet things go wrong every now and then. As a developer, you have to be aware of this so you can take precautions. The most common errors are holes in the meshes, fake surfaces, and misaligned surfaces.

Holes

The system does not look at a floor and return one big quad. Instead, it returns a whole set of triangles that together form the area of the floor. These triangles, or meshes, are pretty messy, something you will see later on when we start writing the code. So, it can happen that the system misses a triangle or two. It can miss parts of the mesh.

Sometimes the environment is not very spatial-mapping-friendly, making these holes even more apparent.

Fake surfaces

It can happen that the system sees surfaces that are not there in the real world. It will report meshes where there are none. This happens less frequently than the holes, but it does happen.

Misaligned surfaces

The surfaces the spatial mapping mechanism returns should lie flat on top of the surface of the real world. However, this does not always happen. You will notice the triangles are reported to be a couple of centimeters below or above the real surface. This means that if we place that chess board we talked about before on a table, it would appear to hover a bit above the table instead of lying on top of it. While this is a cool effect, after all, you do not encounter many floating chess boards in real life, it takes away from the realism.

Causes for errors

Sometimes the system just makes mistakes. The good news is that it usually corrects itself. As you might recall, the depth sensor is continuously working on getting data and feeding this to the HPU. The HPU is thus continuously working on perfecting the surface scan and updating the mapping. The bad news is that external factors the system cannot do anything about may be the reason things go wrong.

The user's movements

A scan takes about 0.2 seconds. This means that a user running through a room while wearing the HoloLens does not give the device enough time to scan the environment. It simply does not get the chance to do a proper scan.

The reverse is also a possibility: the system scans everything from 0.8 meters to 3.1 meters away from the users. Everything closer is ignored, so the system will not scan the user's hands. Everything further away is also not scanned: the hardware just cannot do this with the limited power it has. So, when we start up the HoloLens in a new environment, only items and surfaces in that limited area, within an arc of 70 degrees, will be scanned. If we want the system to scan more, the user has to walk around a bit. Not too fast of course, but just a relaxed walk around the room.

Another thing might be a problem: users tend not to look toward ceilings. Floors are something we do look at when walking since we want to avoid tripping over things, but ceilings are usually ignored. If we do not look at something, it will not be scanned. The same goes for areas around corners, under tables, behind couches, and so on. The user needs to walk around and look at everything before the system can build up a coherent picture. We as humans understand that if a couch is standing on a floor the floor will continue behind that couch, but the HoloLens does not make these kinds of assumption. So, if we want the HoloLens to be aware of that floor behind the couch, we have to make sure the user walks toward that area and looks at it for at least 0.2 seconds.

I said the system scans a cone of about 70 degrees. However, things that are looked at from a direct perpendicular angle are scanned in higher definition than things that are more on the side. The fidelity of the scan will benefit if the user looks directly at surfaces, so the user has to move her head all the time while scanning.

The good news is that the surface mapping is updated all the time, so when the app is running, you will get new and updated data all the time.

The physical qualities of the surfaces

The system relies on the reflection of infrared light to work reliably. Some surfaces, however, are very bad at reflecting this light that is emitted from the depth sensor. I once had to give a demo at the board room of a large bank. This demo took place in a beautiful room that contained a huge black marble conference table. No matter what I did, I could not get the device to recognize this area. In my surface mapping, it appeared as a black hole in my virtual universe. Black marble is very bad at reflecting infrared light so the system will think there is nothing there.

Mirrors and windows can be troublesome also. I have had mixed results with these but I found that reflective surfaces work when scanned directly head-on. Mirrors are a problem. The system gets confused. It will probably think the room continues in the mirror, but with lots of holes in the meshes.

Dark objects, in general, can be troublesome, but they get picked up in the end if the user walks around enough. Again, scanning head-on helps here.

Lighting

The spatial mapping works with infrared light. So, when you have a source of lots of infrared light around, such as the sun, things might work less than optimally. Normal light should not be a problem but I have found it sometimes does this temporarily. The system will adjust for this but it might take a couple of scans.

Other HoloLens devices in the room will usually not be a problem due to the timing of the infrared beams being sent out. If you happen to have more than five devices within relatively close range of each other, you will notice errors being more prevalent.

Moving objects

A lot can happen in 0.2 seconds. A person entering your view might take less than 0.2 seconds to walk out of that view again. Cars passing by will also be gone in less than that time. A co-worker might enter the room and stand in front of you. Or, he might get bored and walk away again. All these things cause a change in the spatial mapping. Fast-moving things tend to get ignored: it usually takes a couple of scans for the system to decide things have changed. This is a good thing if you want to ignore the car passing by, but it might be a bad thing if you want to occlude your virtual object because your colleague stands in the way. You will see that at the first second the object will be visible before the newly arrived obstacle. Only after that time will the system decide there is something new and, based on the new scans, perform the occlusion.

It also works the other way around. If your colleague walks away again it might take a second before the formerly occluded virtual object becomes visible again.

App-specific requirements

How we deal with these errors and their possible causes is highly dependent on your specific use case. Sometimes your app needs spatial mapping, sometimes it does not. It all depends.

If your app does not require spatial mapping at all, then life is easy. Just do not use this and do not read on. This could be the case if all you do is materialize objects in front of the user that she can interact with. However, even in this bare-bones scenario, it might be worthwhile to make sure the objects that are being instantiated are reachable. Let us assume we have created a simple sphere one meter away from the user. What happens if the user is about 50 centimeters away from a wall? Do we place the sphere inside the wall? Or do we provide some sort of feedback? If we want to do the latter, we need to know about this wall, and thus we need spatial mapping in its most rudimentary form.

Let us examine another case. I mentioned the imaginary portal to another dimension above. Our portal is an ellipsis with a width of 80 centimeters, about 120 centimeters high. Since we require the user to look through the portal, we want it to be at such a height that the eyes of the user are about two-thirds of the height of the portal itself. We can do this of course, but we need a flat wall-like area at least 100 centimeters wide and 220 centimeters high (I assume the user's eye to be at 1.7 meters, so one-third of our portal will be above eye level; I also add about 10 centimeters for some padding between the top of the portal and the ceiling). Again, we need spatial mapping to decide if we do have enough space to place the portal.

How about a game where we hide stuff in the room so the user has to look for it? We must have a coherent image of the room beforehand, so we need to make sure the room is scanned before we start the actual game play.

A final example is an app where the user communicates with an alien that materializes out of thin air. We know the alien moves about a bit in an area one meter by one meter by one meter. We know this since we programmed it this way. We can only start this when the user has an empty area of at least one cubic meter in front of her.

To achieve all this, we need to guide the user. The first scenario is simple. If the player is standing too close to a wall, we can have a voice tell her, *Please step back a little*, until we have reached a good distance.

In the second example, the one with the portal, we can project a preliminary version of our portal and have the app say, *Place this on a wall to start the experience* and let the user select a wall. We will not accept the input until the user has walked around and we have found a suitable area.

In the third option, we can tell the user to walk around, using the visualization to show what we have scanned, or use a fog-like environment to show what we have not yet sampled. I suggest, however, you do the former--just show the mesh or planes that have been processed instead of using fog. Fog should take up the entire view of the HoloLens when the app first starts up and this will clearly show the limited field of view of the device.

In the final example, we can do two things. We can wait until we have discovered a cubic meter's worth of nothingness before we start the alien sequence, or we can have the user position a wireframe cube of one by one by one meter in the air, where the alien will begin to appear. Again, this all depends on your use case.

Depending on your needs you can require the user to first scan the room or parts of the room, or you can have the app update the environment all the time to perfect the mapping. Whatever you do, make sure you make the user aware of what is happening. You will find most apps use some sort of starting scene in which the user is required to scan the area. Most apps will not accept a starting point or will just not begin until the special requirements are met. Do not let the user guess what is needed; make sure she knows what we want her to do. Tell her to find an empty wall, to find an empty space in the room, or to walk around a bit. Then, when you have enough information, let her begin the experience.

Optimizing meshes

Errors in meshes can create an experience that is less than optimal. Remember, the system updates itself all the time so problems will go away eventually, given sufficient time and enough scans. Some errors, such as the ones caused by IR-unfriendly materials, will persist no matter how many scans are done. You could take care of this in your app.

Removing holes sounds like a good plan. If you have found a set of meshes that are somewhere between 1.5 and 2 meters below the user's eye level, you may safely assume that that is the floor. If you find a hole there that is not big enough to hold a staircase, you can decide to fill that hole with a new mesh.

Windows and ceiling lights are a bit harder. You just do not know how big or how small the windows are, or what shape they are. So how do you determine what is a hole and what is real? You have to decide if that is important enough to spend time on. If you decide to make a game where things come out of walls, you might decide to disregard these errors: they will probably be small enough and the wall is probably big enough to find a suitable place to, say, place your multi-dimensional portal for your aliens to come through.

I have used the word *probably* since you never know for sure. I have worked in environments where the walls did have irregular-shaped small holes in them. The system picked them up nicely since the materials were surface-scanning friendly, but you cannot know this in advance. It is up to your best judgment to decide if this works for you.

The problem with misalignment with the actual surfaces is a tough one. You have no way to learn about this. If the floor detected hovers two centimeters about the real physical floor, then you have to accept this. If this is not an option, you can give the user some way of correcting this. You could ask the user to maneuver the floor up or down a bit so that it sits nicely on the physical floor. This might take away from the sense of realism, but if accuracy is what you need then this is a solution.

Another thing I have seen people doing is to use QR markers. They place these markers in well-known locations on a wall or in the corner of the room, scanned them, and then used this as a reference point to help the surface-scanning mechanism place the fake floor at exactly the right position. This is not something the average user will use, but if your use case calls for this kind of precision, this might be a trick you can use.

However, most of the time it is not a problem. Most errors in scanning are fixed during subsequent scans. If your user moves about in the area he is using the app in, the scanning mechanism will constantly update the meshes and fix whatever errors it can. Usually, the old rule of *good enough is good enough* applies here as well. I would not worry about it until you run into a problem and then think of a solution.

Spatial understanding in DirectX

We have had enough talk about the ideas and principles behind spatial mapping. It is time to put this to practice.

Initial app

Let us start the way we always start. Start Visual Studio and create a new Universal / Holographic C# app with SharpDX as our library. You know the drill by now. Set the target as **x86** if it is not already, and deploy this first version of the emulator or the device. This will be our starting point.

I have called my app `SpatialDemo`.

Spatial capabilities

Spatial surface detection is done by the depth sensor in cooperation with the HPU. This means we have to access these. Now, accessing a processing unit is not a problem in UWP apps, but accessing sensors is. You cannot simply get data from the microphone, the webcam, and other sensors in UWP apps. The apps are running as a sandbox, meaning you cannot do much more than render on a screen and get input from a keyboard, mouse, and in our case, gestures. That is all. As we have seen in the chapters about voice, we need to ask the system for permission to use the microphone. The same goes for spatial mapping. We need to have consent from the user to use these devices. But, as you can imagine, a spatial mapping capability is not something you will find in an ordinary Windows 10 app.

Most devices have no idea what this is, so the designers of the SDK for Windows 10 did not include this capability into the development environment. Therefore, you cannot double-click on the `Package.appxmanifest` file and set the capability in the UI editor. You need to go into the code.

So, right-click on the `Package.appxmanifest` and choose **View Code**. Visual Studio might warn you that the file is already open and ask you if you want to close it. Just say **yes**: you want to leave the UI and go into the actual XML file underneath.

In the `Package` part, we need to add a new namespace. It should look as follows:

```
<Package
   xmlns="http://schemas.microsoft.com/appx/manifest/foundation/windows10"
   xmlns:mp="http://schemas.microsoft.com/appx/2014/phone/manifest"
   xmlns:uap="http://schemas.microsoft.com/appx/manifest/uap/windows10"
   xmlns:uap2="http://schemas.microsoft.com/appx/manifest/uap/windows10/2"
   IgnorableNamespaces="uap uap2 mp">
```

We have added the `uap2` namespace and the `IgnorableNamespaces` section as well. Now find the `Capabilities` section. If you have not declared any yet, you have to type it in yourself. In our case, I have not asked for any capabilities such as the microphone or webcam, so I also have to enter the whole thing myself. If you already have one, just change it to include the new capability:

```
<Capabilities>
   <uap2:Capability Name="spatialPerception"/>
</Capabilities>
```

This should be added somewhere below, as a subsection of the `Package` section.

If you do not do this, you will find your app just does not work. Trust me: adding this by default to your projects will save you a lot of debugging later on.

Initial classes

We need to add three extra classes to our app. In previous samples, we have worked with the `SpinningCubeRenderer` and adapted that to fit our needs, but this will not work anymore. Spatial mapping is quite complex, so we cannot add that in one class if we want to keep a bit of structure in our app. We will keep `SpinningCubeRenderer` just to see it running and to have a reference point in our virtual world, though, so do not remove it.

We will add three extra classes to the `Content` folder and namespace, right next to `SpinningCubeRenderer`:

Class	Responsibilities
SpatialSurfaceRenderer	This class is the equivalent of `SpinningCubeRenderer`. It is set up in the main code and called whenever we need to update and render our spatial meshes.
SurfaceMeshList	Our spatial environment consists of many, many meshes. This list is responsible for maintaining them.
SurfaceMesh	This is the actual mesh. It will have many triangles and this class will render them all.

Add the following classes to the `Content` namespace. First, `SpatialSurfaceRenderer`:

```
using SpatialDemo.Common;
using System;
using System.Linq;

namespace SpatialDemo.Content
{
    class SpatialSurfaceRenderer : Disposer
    {
        public async void CreateDeviceDependentResourcesAsync()
        {
            // To be filled in later
        }

        public void ReleaseDeviceDependentResources()
        {
            // To be filled in later
        }
    }
}
```

Then we will add `SurfaceMeshList`:

```
using System;
using System.Linq;

namespace SpatialDemo.Content
{
    class SurfaceMeshList
    {
        public void ReleaseDeviceDependentResources()
        {
```

```
            // To be filled in later
        }
    }
```

Finally, the `SurfaceMesh` class:

```
using SpatialDemo.Common;
using System;
using System.Linq;

namespace SpatialDemo.Content
{
    class SurfaceMesh : Disposer
    {
        public void ReleaseDeviceDependentResources()
        {
            // To be filled in later
        }
    }
}
```

We have subclassed `SpatialSurfaceRenderer` and `SurfaceMesh` from `Disposer`: these classes will contain valuable and expensive resources; we need to make sure we clean them up when we are done. If you do not do this, you will notice the system uses lots of memory. After all, after each update of the surface scanner, new meshes will be created. If we do not get rid of the old stuff, we will run out of memory pretty soon.

I have also added the signatures for the `CreateDeviceDependentResourcesAsync()` and `ReleaseDeviceDependentResources()` methods to the `SpatialSurfaceRender`, and the `ReleaseDeviceDependentResources ()` method to `SurfaceMeshList` and `SurfaceMesh`. We have encountered them before but they are slightly different here.

First, we have made the method that creates resources asynchronously. The spatial mapper works in its own thread, so we need to take care of that. Next, we have omitted the creation method in the `SurfaceMesh`. The reason for this is that the resources we need to update and render will be created elsewhere and just given to the `SurfaceMesh`. It just needs to clean them up when necessary.

Checking capabilities

We have set the capabilities in the XML file. However, that is not enough. We need to specifically request access to the spatial data. We do this in a method called `CheckAccess()`. In this case, we will just throw an exception if we are not allowed to access the spatial data, but in your case you might do something else. Sometimes, you might want to continue anyway but have your app run in limited mode. For our `SpatialDemo`, it does not make sense to go on without spatial data, so we just throw in the towel and quit.

We call this method from the constructor in `SpatialSurfaceRenderer`. And while we are at it, we also set some initial data:

```
DeviceResources _deviceResources;
SpatialCoordinateSystem _spatialCoordinateSystem;
RasterizerState _state;
SurfaceMeshList _surfaceMeshList = new SurfaceMeshList();

public SpatialSurfaceRenderer(DeviceResources deviceResources,
SpatialCoordinateSystem spatialCoordinateSystem)
{
    _deviceResources = deviceResources;
    _spatialCoordinateSystem = spatialCoordinateSystem;
    CheckAccess();

    var desc = RasterizerStateDescription.Default();
    desc.FillMode = FillMode.Wireframe;

    _state = new RasterizerState(deviceResources.D3DDevice, desc);

    SurfaceMeshList.CoordinateSystem = _spatialCoordinateSystem;
    _surfaceMeshList.DirectXDevice = deviceResources.D3DDevice;

    CreateDeviceDependentResourcesAsync();
}

async void CheckAccess()
{
    var res = await SpatialSurfaceObserver.RequestAccessAsync();

    if (res != SpatialPerceptionAccessStatus.Allowed)
        throw new Exception("No access to spatial data.");
}
```

We pass in the `DeviceResources` as before. We also pass the `SpatialCoordinateSystem` we use: spatial data needs to map itself to this coordinate system so we need it as soon as possible.

Another thing we do here is set the `RasterizerStateDescription`. This class tells the GPU how to render things: either in solid mode or in wireframe mode. For our meshes, we want wireframe. If we were to render all the surface meshes in solid mode, we would get a homogenous mass of one color everywhere we look. We will tell the GPU to use this `RasterizerState` later on.

The `CheckAccess` method I talked about is next. What we do is call the static method `RequestAccessAsync` on the `SpatialSurfaceObserver` class. This class is defined in the namespace `Windows.Perception.Spatial.Surfaces`, so do not forget to include that namespace in your using statements.

We can get several results from this call. It can be `Allowed`, in which case we can continue, or it can be `Unspecified`, `DeniedByUser`, or `DeniedBySystem`. In those cases, we give up and stop.

I also pass the `spatialCoordinateSystem` and the `D3Device` from the `deviceResources` to the `SurfaceMeshList` instance we have in our class.

Do not forget to add the auto properties, `CoordinateSystem` and `DirectXDevice`, to the `SurfaceMeshList` class; otherwise, things will not compile.

Setting up device-dependent resources

The `CreateDeviceDependentResourceAsync()` method should look very familiar, but with one tiny difference:

```
public async void CreateDeviceDependentResourcesAsync()
{
    ReleaseDeviceDependentResources();

    _usingVprtShaders = _deviceResources.D3DDeviceSupportsVprt;

    var folder = Package.Current.InstalledLocation;

    var vertexShaderFileName = _usingVprtShaders
        ? "Content\\Shaders\\VPRTVertexShader.cso"
        : "Content\\Shaders\\VertexShader.cso";

    var vertexShaderByteCode =
        await DirectXHelper.ReadDataAsync(await
```

```
folder.GetFileAsync(vertexShaderFileName));

    _vertexShader = ToDispose(new VertexShader(
        _deviceResources.D3DDevice,
        vertexShaderByteCode));

    var vertexDesc = new InputElement[]              {
        new InputElement("POSITION", 0, Format.R32G32B32_Float, 0, 0,
InputClassification.PerVertexData, 0),
        new InputElement("COLOR", 0, Format.R32G32B32_Float, 12, 0,
InputClassification.PerVertexData, 0)
    };

    _inputLayout = ToDispose(new InputLayout(
        _deviceResources.D3DDevice,
        vertexShaderByteCode,
        vertexDesc));

    if (!_usingVprtShaders)
    {
        var geometryShaderByteCode =
            await DirectXHelper.ReadDataAsync(await
folder.GetFileAsync("Content\\Shaders\\GeometryShader.cso"));

        _geometryShader = ToDispose(new
GeometryShader(_deviceResources.D3DDevice, geometryShaderByteCode));
    }

    var pixelShaderByteCode =
        await DirectXHelper.ReadDataAsync(await
folder.GetFileAsync("Content\\Shaders\\PixelShader.cso"));

    _pixelShader = ToDispose(new PixelShader(
        _deviceResources.D3DDevice,
        pixelShaderByteCode));

    BuildSpatialSurfaceObserver();
}
```

We create the shaders as we have done before. I leave it to you to declare the fields
containing these shaders and other structures we create here. However, we do not specify
the vertices and indices as you see done in SpinningCubeRenderer. We cannot do this: the
vertices and indices are dependent on the spatial environment we are in.

Creating the SpatialSurfaceObserver

The creation of the vertices and indices is done for us by the `SpatialSurfaceObserver`
class, which is what we build in the call to `BuildSpatialSurfaceObserver()`:

```
void BuildSpatialSurfaceObserver()
{
    _spatialSurfaceObserver = new SpatialSurfaceObserver();

    var positionFormat = DirectXPixelFormat.R32G32B32A32Float;
    var normalFormat = DirectXPixelFormat.R32G32B32A32Float;

    _spatialSurfaceMeshOptions = new SpatialSurfaceMeshOptions
    {
        IncludeVertexNormals = false,
        VertexPositionFormat = positionFormat,
        VertexNormalFormat = normalFormat,
        TriangleIndexFormat = DirectXPixelFormat.R16UInt
    };

    var boundingBox = new SpatialBoundingBox
    {
        Center = new Vector3(0f, 0f, 0f),
        Extents = new Vector3(10f, 10f, 10f)
    };
    var bounds = SpatialBoundingVolume.FromBox(_spatialCoordinateSystem,
boundingBox);

    _spatialSurfaceObserver.SetBoundingVolume(bounds);

    _spatialSurfaceObserver.ObservedSurfacesChanged +=
SpatialSurfaceObserverOnObservedSurfacesChanged;
}
```

The `BuildSpatialSurfaceObserver` class creates an instance of the
`SpatialSurfaceObserver` class. This is the workhorse of our application: it creates all
meshes for us.

We need to tell it how to do its job, though. The `SpatialSurfaceMeshOptions` is a class
that we can use to tell the system what we want and how we want it.

In my case, I decided not to use `VertexNormals`. We can use normals if we want to texture
the meshes, but I am only using the wireframe, so the normals are not used anyway. Next,
we tell it we want all data to be formatted as `R32G32B32A32Float` data, meaning for each
of the colors red, green, blue, and alpha, we want the data to be expressed as floats, or
`System.Singles`. We also want the triangle indices to be a 16-bit unsigned integer.

Now we have to tell the observer what area we want to track. We can do several things here. We can tell it to track everything in a cube-like shape, in a cube with a certain orientation, in a sphere, or in a frustum. The last option is the volume defined by what the user can currently see: a pyramid defined by six planes.

I am satisfied with using a box centered around the initial position of the user, with an extent of 10 meters in all directions. So I create that box, then I create bounds with that box, and that is what I give to SpatialSurfaceObserver in the call to SetBoundingVolume().

Getting the surface data

The last line in the method sets the event handler for the ObservedSurfacesChanged event. We could have done this otherwise: instead of being called every time the surfaces change, and that happens quite a lot, we could just call a GetObservedSurfaces method as a regular interval. If you do not need high-fidelity tracking but need high performance, you could call that method every 10 frames or so. That will save you a lot of performance. Again, this is all dependent on your use case. I want it to be called every time the system changes the surfaces it sees.

Let us have a look at that method:

```
async void
SpatialSurfaceObserverOnObservedSurfacesChanged(SpatialSurfaceObserver
sender, object args)
{
    var observedSurfaces = _spatialSurfaceObserver.GetObservedSurfaces();

    foreach (var surfacePair in observedSurfaces)
    {
        var spatialSurfaceInfo = surfacePair.Value;
        await _surfaceMeshList.AddOrUpdateAsync(spatialSurfaceInfo,
_spatialSurfaceMeshOptions);
    }

    var allIds = (from item in observedSurfaces
                    select item.Key).ToList();
    _surfaceMeshList.Prune(allIds);
    _loadingComplete = true;
}
```

This is the method that is called whenever the surfaces change. First we call `GetObeserverdSurfaces()`. This will give us a list of surfaces the system has detected. Now, these surfaces can be completely new surfaces, or they can be surfaces we have seen before but that are better defined now. Remember when I told you the system is constantly updating so we could fix errors just by waiting? This is where that is done.

We get a dictionary containing keys and `SpatialSurfaceInfo` instances. The key identifies this surface so we can check if we have already seen this one or not. `SpatialSurfaceInfo` is what contains all our data. Next to the ID, it also has a timestamp that indicates when this was last updated. You could check this to see how old this data is. It would be a nice effect to change the colors of the meshes depending on their age, but we are not going to do that now.

The surface it contains consists of many triangles. If you do not care about this, since you only want to know where the floor is or where the walls are, you can call the `TryGetBounds()` method on this `Info` class. This will give you a `SpatialBoundingOrientedBox` telling you the dimension of the surface. This is an easy way to construct rough structures such as walls, which tend to be rectangular anyway.

We do not do this. Instead, we hand this info down to the list, which will do the rest of the work for us.

We will return to the renderer class shortly.

Getting the actual mesh data

Use the following code to get the actual mesh data:

```
public async Task AddOrUpdateAsync(SpatialSurfaceInfo spatialSurfaceInfo,
SpatialSurfaceMeshOptions options)
{
    var mesh = await spatialSurfaceInfo.TryComputeLatestMeshAsync(1000.0d,
options);

    if (mesh == null)
        return;

    var tempList = new Dictionary<Guid, SurfaceMesh>(_internalList);
    // See if we already have this one....
    var hasOne = tempList.ContainsKey(mesh.SurfaceInfo.Id);

    if (hasOne)
    {
        // Update
```

```
            var surfaceMesh = tempList[mesh.SurfaceInfo.Id];
            if (surfaceMesh.UpdateTime < mesh.SurfaceInfo.UpdateTime)
            {
                surfaceMesh.CalculateAllVertices(mesh);
                surfaceMesh.UpdateTime = mesh.SurfaceInfo.UpdateTime;
            }
        }
        else
        {
            // Add new
            var newMesh = new SurfaceMesh
            {
                Id = mesh.SurfaceInfo.Id,
                UpdateTime = mesh.SurfaceInfo.UpdateTime,
                CoordinateSystem = CoordinateSystem,
                DirectXDevice = DirectXDevice
            };

            newMesh.CalculateAllVertices(mesh);
            tempList[newMesh.Id] = newMesh;
        }

        lock (_lockObject)
            _internalList = tempList;
    }
```

The `AppOrUpdateAsync` method in the `SpatialMeshList` class gets all the mesh details for us. This is called from the event handler in the renderer.

First, we call `TryComputeLatestMeshAsync()` on `spatialSurfaceInfo`. This will try to calculate all the triangles, normals (if needed), and indices for us. We tell it the density we want, in our case 1,000 triangles per cubic meter, and give it the options that define how we want our data to look. We define this as `R32G32B32A32Float` for both vertices and normals, and R16UInt for the triangles.

It can happen that it fails—we call it Try for a reason. In that case, the mesh will be null, so be careful to check for that.

The next thing we do is create a dictionary. This dictionary is a copy of a field in our `SurfaceMeshList` class, so we can work in this copy without interfering with the original. Since we are using async methods, it could happen that the renderer reads our list and tries to render it while we are in another thread updating the list. This is why we make a copy.

We check if we already have this surface on our list. If we do, and if the creation or update time of that mesh is newer than the old update time, we need to update the data. If we do not, it is a new one and we need to add it to the list. We do both by creating or updating an instance of the `SurfaceMesh` class.

When we are done processing them, we assign the `internalList` dictionary to point toward our `tempList`. We apply a lock so other threads will not interfere here. The lock is a field defined in the class as follows:

```
public object _lockObject = new object();
```

Pruning the list

In the event handler in the renderer, we also called a method called `Prune` on the list. This is the method that looks at all the meshes we have in our list and removes all the ones the surface observer does not see anymore. There is no point in keeping those meshes around if we are no longer going to draw them. So, we go through the list of surfaces, and if we have surfaces identified by IDs that are no longer available, we remove them. Of course, we first call `ReleaseDeviceDependentResources` so all non-garbage-collected items will be cleaned up:

```csharp
public void Prune(List<Guid> allIds)
{
    var removableIds = new List<Guid>();

    var tempList = new Dictionary<Guid, SurfaceMesh>(_internalList);

    foreach (var id in tempList.Keys)
        if (!allIds.Contains(id))
            removableIds.Add(id);

    for (var i = 0; i < removableIds.Count; i++)
    {
        tempList[removableIds[i]].ReleaseDeviceDependentResources();
        tempList.Remove(removableIds[i]);
    }

    lock (_lockObject)
        _internalList = tempList;
}
```

The SurfaceMesh class

Let us have a look at the `SurfaceMesh` class. In essence, it is just a class that contains the vertices and triangles and therefore knows how to render and update itself onto the screens.

Let me start by giving you all the private fields:

```
object _lockObject = new object();
static Vector3 color = new Vector3(1.0f, 0.0f, 0.0f);
Buffer _indexBuffer;
int _indexCount;
Buffer _modelConstantBuffer;
ModelConstantBuffer _modelConstantBufferData;
Matrix4x4 _transformMatrix;
Buffer _vertexBuffer;
```

Some of these you have seen before: the `indexBuffer`, the `modelConstantBuffer`, the `_modelConstantBufferData` and the `_vertexBuffer` are fields that are also used in `SpinningCubeRenderer` to define the vertices and indices. Since each surface has its own set of data, we have to define them here.

We also have to add two using statements that help us later on:

```
using Buffer = SharpDX.Direct3D11.Buffer;
using Device3 = SharpDX.Direct3D11.Device3;
```

The `CalculateAllVertices` method gets the data from the observer and translates it into meaningful data for this class. Here it is:

```
public void CalculateAllVertices(SpatialSurfaceMesh mesh)
{
    VertexPositionColor[] vertices;
    ushort[] indices;
    Matrix4x4 transformMatrix;

    CalculateVertices(mesh, out vertices, out indices, out
transformMatrix);
    _transformMatrix = transformMatrix;

    SetVertices(vertices, indices);

    NeedsUpdate = true;
}
```

We get a `SpatialSurfaceMesh` instance containing all raw data from the observer. We call `CalculateVertices`, which will give us the vertices, indices, and transformation we need to apply. Then we call `SetVertices`, which actually calls the code that sets up the buffer for the rendering pipeline for the GPU.

When that is done, we set the auto property, `NeedsUpdate`, to `true`, so the `Update` method we will write later on knows that this mesh needs to be updated.

First, we examine `CalculateVertices`. Again, this takes the raw data and creates everything we need to set up the GPU:

```
void CalculateVertices(SpatialSurfaceMesh mesh,
    out VertexPositionColor[] vertices,
    out ushort[] indices,
    out Matrix4x4 finalMatrix)
{
    var transformMatrix = Matrix4x4.Identity;
    var tryTransform =
mesh.CoordinateSystem.TryGetTransformTo(CoordinateSystem);
    if (tryTransform != null)
        transformMatrix = tryTransform.Value;

    var vertexByteArray = mesh.VertexPositions.Data.ToArray();
    var vertexStride = (int)mesh.VertexPositions.Stride;
    var vertexCount = mesh.VertexPositions.ElementCount;

    var triangleIndexByteArray = mesh.TriangleIndices.Data.ToArray();
    var triangleCount = mesh.TriangleIndices.ElementCount;

    var vertexScale = mesh.VertexPositionScale;
    var scaleMatrix = Matrix4x4.CreateScale(vertexScale);
    finalMatrix = Matrix4x4.Transpose(scaleMatrix * transformMatrix);

    vertices = new VertexPositionColor[vertexCount];
    for (var i = 0; i < vertexCount; i++)
        TranslateVertices(vertices, vertexByteArray, vertexStride, color,
i);

    indices = new ushort[triangleCount];

    var indexOffset = 0;
    for (var i = 0; i < triangleCount; i++)
    {
        var index = BitConverter.ToUInt16(triangleIndexByteArray,
indexOffset);
        indexOffset += 2;
        indices[i] = index;
```

```
        }
    }
```

There is a lot going on here, but it is not that hard if you read it line by line.

First, we create the transformation. As mentioned previously, we have a `SpatialCoordinateSystem` in our app that we need to use to convert the coordinates of our meshes. The meshes we are given are more or less normalized. They have their own coordinate system, depending on the bounds we give the system. Next, to that, they are not up to scale: they are scaled down. So, we create a `transformMatrix` that will help us translate the coordinates.

Next, we get the raw data from `VertexPositions`. We create an array out of this by including the namespace using `System.Runtime.InteropServices.WindowsRuntime;` This contains the extension method `ToArray()`, so do not forget that one!

We get the stride, which is the spacing between each element, and we get the number of vertices.

We do a similar thing for the triangle indices. If we were to use normals, we could do the same thing here with the `mesh.NormalPositions` collection.

We get the scale we need to translate all vertices and create a matrix out of it. We then combine the `transformMatrix` we created earlier with this scale so we can get the final translation.

We create an array that will hold all `VertexPositionColor` structures. This is the same kind of structure we have seen before. It just holds a position and a color, exactly as it does in `SpinningCubeRenderer`.

We iterate through all our data and create instances of the `VertexPositionColor` items that we store in the array.

When we have done that, and I will tell you shortly precisely how we do that, we do the same for the triangle indices. We convert the raw data, which is in R16UInt format, to an actual R16UInt: the data is passed to us as arrays of bytes. We store this in the indices array:

```
static void TranslateVertices(
    VertexPositionColor[] vertices,
    byte[] vertexByteArray,
    int vertexStride,
    Vector3 colorAsVector,
    int vertexNumber)
{
    var vertexPositionX = BitConverter.ToSingle(vertexByteArray,
```

```
vertexNumber * vertexStride + 0);
    var vertexPositionY = BitConverter.ToSingle(vertexByteArray,
vertexNumber * vertexStride + 4);
    var vertexPositionZ = BitConverter.ToSingle(vertexByteArray,
vertexNumber * vertexStride + 8);

    var vertexPositionColor =
        new VertexPositionColor(new Vector3(vertexPositionX,
vertexPositionY, vertexPositionZ), color);

    vertices[vertexNumber] = vertexPositionColor;
}
```

This is `TranslateVertices`. Similar to the indices, we see that the data for the vertices is passed to us as an array of bytes. We need to translate that to the floats we require. We calculate the X, Y, and Z values, and then create a `VertexPositionColor` out of that. We add that to our array.

Now it is time to create the structures for the GPU: the `SetVertices` method takes care of that one:

```
void SetVertices(VertexPositionColor[] cubeVertices, ushort[] cubeIndices)
{
    lock (_lockObject)
    {
        ReleaseDeviceDependentResources();

        _vertexBuffer = ToDispose(Buffer.Create(
            DirectXDevice,
            BindFlags.VertexBuffer,
            cubeVertices));

        _indexCount = cubeIndices.Length;

        _indexBuffer = ToDispose(Buffer.Create(
            DirectXDevice,
            BindFlags.IndexBuffer,
            cubeIndices));

        _modelConstantBuffer = ToDispose(Buffer.Create(
            DirectXDevice,
            BindFlags.ConstantBuffer,
            ref _modelConstantBufferData));
    }
}
```

This code should be very familiar. We create the `vertexBuffer`, the `indexBuffer`, the `_modelConstantBuffer`, and the `_modelConstantBufferData`. This is the same code as we have seen in `SpinningCubeRenderer`, only in another position and in a different class. Of course, we first clean up any old resources we do not need anymore:

```
public void ReleaseDeviceDependentResources()
{
    RemoveAndDispose(ref _modelConstantBuffer);
    RemoveAndDispose(ref _vertexBuffer);
    RemoveAndDispose(ref _indexBuffer);
}
```

Again, nothing new here. We clean up the resources we just saw being created.

Updating and rendering

If you look at the code in `SpinningCubeRenderer`, you will see the main app code calls update and render on that class. We will do the same for our `SpatialSurfaceRenderer`, so let us add these two methods to our class:

```
public void Update()
{
    var allMeshes = _surfaceMeshList.GetAllUpdatedMeshes();
    foreach (var mesh in allMeshes)
        mesh.Update(_deviceResources.D3DDeviceContext);
}
public void Render()
{
    if (!_loadingComplete)
        return;

    var context = _deviceResources.D3DDeviceContext;

    // Attach the vertex shader.
    context.VertexShader.SetShader(_vertexShader, null, 0);

    if (!_usingVprtShaders)
        context.GeometryShader.SetShader(_geometryShader, null, 0);

    // Attach the pixel shader.
    context.PixelShader.SetShader(_pixelShader, null, 0);

    context.InputAssembler.InputLayout = _inputLayout;
    context.InputAssembler.PrimitiveTopology =
PrimitiveTopology.TriangleList;
    context.Rasterizer.State = _state;
```

```
    var allMeshes = _surfaceMeshList.Meshes();
    foreach (var mesh in allMeshes)
        mesh.Render(context);
}
```

In `Update`, we simply call `surfaceMeshList` to give us all the meshes that require updates. This is a simple query over the internal dictionary, which returns all items that have the `NeedsUpdate` flag set. Then we call `Update()` on each of those items.

Just to be thorough, this is what `SurfaceMeshList.GetAllUpdatedMeshes()` looks like:

```
public IList<SurfaceMesh> GetAllUpdatedMeshes()
{
    return (from item in _internalList.Values
                where item.NeedsUpdate
                select item).ToList();
}
```

Nothing fancy here.

Render is also not very complicated. First, after checking if we are ready to render, we set the shaders. We only need to do that once for all of our meshes, so this is a good place to do so. All meshes use the same shader, after all. The thing that is new is the call to set `context.Rasterizer.State`. Remember we set the state to use WireFrame in the constructor of this class? This is where we use it.

We could have set this in the constructor. However, this setting is used for all renderers for this context. Thus, all objects in our scene, including our spinning cube, will be rendered with WireFrame.

You should rewrite `SpinningCubeRenderer` in such a way that it does a similar thing there, only using a solid state to render.

After all this, we simply call `Render()` on all the meshes we have.

The meshes are retrieved from the list by accessing the property:

```
public IEnumerable<SurfaceMesh> Meshes() => _internalList.Values.ToList();
```

Mesh updating and rendering

So, let us now have a look at the actual updating and rendering code. This work is done in the `SurfaceMesh` class. Here is the implementation:

```
public void Render(DeviceContext3 context)
{
    context.VertexShader.SetConstantBuffers(0, _modelConstantBuffer);

    var stride = Utilities.SizeOf<VertexPositionColor>();
    var offset = 0;
    var bufferBinding = new VertexBufferBinding(_vertexBuffer, stride,
offset);
    context.InputAssembler.SetVertexBuffers(0, bufferBinding);
    context.InputAssembler.SetIndexBuffer(
        _indexBuffer,
        Format.R16_UInt,
        0);

    context.DrawIndexedInstanced(_indexCount, 2, 0, 0, 0);
}

public void Update(DeviceContext3 context)
{
    _modelConstantBufferData.model = _transformMatrix;

    if (!NeedsUpdate)
        return;

    context.UpdateSubresource(ref _modelConstantBufferData,
_modelConstantBuffer);
    NeedsUpdate = false;
}
```

In `Render`, we set the buffers and then we call `DrawIndexedInstanced()`, just like we did in the `SpinningCubeRenderer` class.

The `Update()` method is also very similar. First we apply the `transformMatrix` we calculated earlier, the one that contains the scale and the transformation from the `SpatialCoordinateSystem` of the mesh combined with the current `SpatialCoordinateSystem`. Then, if we need updating, we call `UpdateSubResource()`, passing the buffers. Of course, we finish by setting `NeedsUpdate` to `false`.

Cleaning up

All that is left is some cleaning up. Here is the code for `SpatialSurfaceRenderer`:

```
public void ReleaseDeviceDependentResources()
{
    _loadingComplete = false;
    _usingVprtShaders = false;
    RemoveAndDispose(ref _pixelShader);
    RemoveAndDispose(ref _vertexShader);
    RemoveAndDispose(ref _geometryShader);
    RemoveAndDispose(ref _inputLayout);

    _surfaceMeshList.ReleaseDeviceDependentResources();
}
And here it is for SurfaceMeshList:
public void ReleaseDeviceDependentResources()
{
    foreach (var surfaceMesh in _internalList.Values)
        surfaceMesh.ReleaseDeviceDependentResources();

    _internalList.Clear();
}
```

The implementation for `SurfaceMesh` has already been discussed.

Putting it all to work

We have finished the work on our classes. Now we need to call them and make sure it all works as we intended.

To do this, we make some minor changes to the main class, which in my case is called `SpatialDemoMain`.

Similar to what we did before, we need to instantiate the renderers. These are the steps we need to take:

1. Add a new member field:

```
private SpatialSurfaceRenderer _spatialSurfaceRenderer;
```

2. Create an instance of this in the `SetHolographicSpace` method. However, make sure you do this after the part where `referenceframe` is set. We need this to get `SpatialCoordinateSystem`:

```
// This line is the original, the second is new
referenceFrame =
locator.CreateStationaryFrameOfReferenceAtCurrentLocation();
_spatialSurfaceRenderer = new
SpatialSurfaceRenderer(deviceResources,
referenceFrame.CoordinateSystem);
```

3. In `Dispose()`, get rid of the following instance:

```
if(_spatialSurfaceRenderer != null)
{
_spatialSurfaceRenderer.Dispose();
_spatialSurfaceRenderer = null;
}
```

4. In the `Update` method, call the update:

```
_spatialSurfaceRenderer.Update();
```

5. In the `Render` method, call the render:

```
_spatialSurfaceRenderer.Render();
```

6. In the `OnDeviceLost()` method, call `ReleaseDeviceDependentResources();`.

7. In the `OnDeviceRestored()` method, call `CreateDeviceDependentResourcesAsync();`.

And that is it! Save your project, run it, check to make sure you did not forget to initialize some fields, such as the `_internalList` dictionary in `SurfaceMeshList`, and then run it.

This is what my attic looks like: you can see the stairs going down through the floor, if you look closely. Try it out yourself. Walk around while this app is running and see the walls behind the walls. You have got X-ray power!

Spatial Mapping in action

Spatial understanding in Unity3D

In Unity3D there are two ways to handle spatial mapping. Well, to be honest, there are three, but I will leave the third option for `Chapter 8`, *Speed up Your Development – Advanced Unity3D*. For now, we will focus on the things Unity3D gives us out-of-the-box.

There is an easy way and a harder way. The easiest way is a matter of just dropping one or two components into your scene. The harder way is to write the code to do yourself what those components do for you. Needless to say, the harder way is the more flexible way. You can achieve things you cannot achieve doing it the easy way.

However, rest assured, the harder way is nowhere near as complicated as the things we looked at in the part about DirectX. There are a lot of similarities, of course, but you will find the code is a lot easier to understand. So, we will start with the harder way and conclude with the easier way.

Writing scripts for spatial mapping in Unity3D

We will work on our RockOn app a bit more in the next chapter. There, we will combine what we learned in this chapter with what we discussed there so that it makes more sense. For now, we will work on an empty app. Follow along, please:

1. Create a new project. Let us call it `SurfaceTest`.
2. Apply all the settings we need to apply: the camera, the virtual reality, the platform, and so on. You know the drill by now.
3. Create a new folder for our scripts. Let us call it `Scripts`.
4. Add a new script to this folder, called `DropHandler`.
5. Attach `DropHandler` to the camera.
6. Add a sphere, floating two meters in front of the user's eyes. Make it 20 centimeters in diameter.
7. Add a `RigidBody` component to the sphere, but turn `Use Gravity` off. We will do this later on.

Things should look more or less as follows:

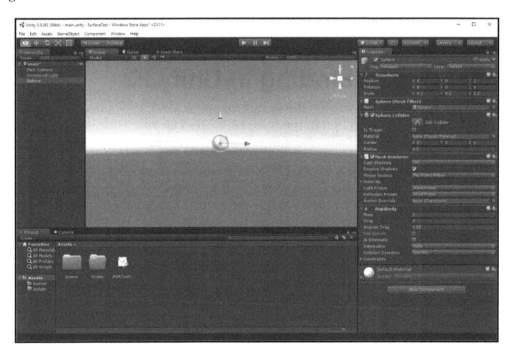

The setup of our Unity app

Now, add the following code to the `DropHandler` script:

```
using System.Collections;
using System.Collections.Generic;
using UnityEngine;
using UnityEngine.VR.WSA.Input;

public class DropHandler : MonoBehaviour {

    // Use this for initialization
    void Start () {
        var gestureRecognizer = new GestureRecognizer();
        gestureRecognizer.SetRecognizableGestures(GestureSettings.Tap);
        gestureRecognizer.TappedEvent += OnTapped;
        gestureRecognizer.StartCapturingGestures();
    }


    private void OnTapped(InteractionSourceKind sourceKind, int tapCount,
Ray headRay){
        RaycastHit hitInfo;
        if(Physics.Raycast(headRay, out hitInfo)){
            var hitObject = hitInfo.transform.gameObject;
            var hitRigidBody= hitObject.GetComponent<Rigidbody>();
            if(hitRigidBody != null)
                hitRigidBody.useGravity = true;
        }
    }
}
```

Just to make sure we have not made any mistakes, build this and deploy it to the HoloLens. You should see the sphere. If it is in the center of your view, tap on it and it should fall. But, as you can see, it falls and keeps on falling. There is no floor or table stopping it. That is not very realistic, if you ask me, and violates one of the principles of mixed reality: it should enhance the sense of realism, not take away from it. Even in our fictional universe, things should behave in ways the user expects them to, no matter how weird it may seem in the real world.

Adding surface mapping

If we want the ball to stop falling once it reaches the ground, we should change our app in such a way that it knows where the ground is. Guess what: we can use spatial mapping to do this.

There are a lot of similarities between the DirectX code and the code we will write now, but the code for Unity3D is much simpler.

Capabilities

Before we begin writing code, however, there is one thing we need to do first. Since the outcome of a Unity3D project is another UWP app, the same restrictions with regards to using sensors apply. We cannot access any sensor data unless we express our intentions first. Just like we did before, we need to set the capabilities.

In Unity3D, this is done under the **Capabilities** tab, which can be reached by going through the menus **Edit** | **Project Settings** | **Player**, and then navigating to the bottom of the **Inspector** window. There you will find the **Publisher** settings. This is the same screen where we enabled microphone access in earlier chapters. This time, however, I want you to scroll down the list of capabilities and check **SpatialPerception**:

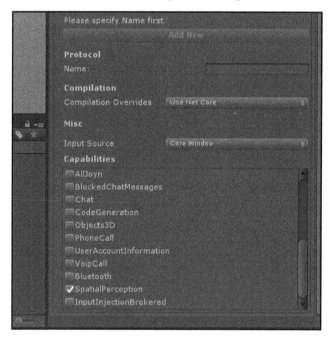

SpatialPerception capability

If you do not do this, there will be no errors, no exceptions, and no warnings, but also no spatial mapping. I always turn this on in a new project: I will need it for sure and I do this at the beginning of every single project. That way I cannot forget it.

Spatial mapping in code

Add another script to the project and then to the camera. I have called it `SurfaceHelper`. The initial version looks as follows:

```
using System.Collections;
using System.Collections.Generic;
using UnityEngine;
using UnityEngine.VR.WSA;

public class SurfaceHelper : MonoBehaviour {

    SurfaceObserver _observer;
    void Start()
    {
        _observer = new SurfaceObserver();
        _observer.SetVolumeAsAxisAlignedBox(Vector3.zero, new Vector3(10f,
10f, 10f));
    }
    private void HandleSurfaceChanged(
        SurfaceId surfaceId,
        SurfaceChange changeType,
        Bounds bounds,
        System.DateTime lastModification)
    {
        // This is where we handle all changes

    }
}
```

In the `Start()` method, we initialize the whole thing. First, we create an instance of the `SurfaceObserver` class. This class needs to know what the area it needs to map is, so we give it a cube, centered around 0,0,0, extending 10 meters in width, height, and depth. We could also have used other shapes such as a sphere, an oriented box, and a frustum. Sound familiar?

I have also added a method called `HandleSurfaceChanged`. This gets called whenever the surface is changed and new data is available. You will be given an id that identifies this surface, the reason for the change (either Added, Updated, or Removed), the bounds of the surface, and the time it was done.

Now, there is one caveat. The scanning and processing takes a lot of time, so we should, preferably, do this in a different thread. And that is exactly what we will do. Add the following to the `Start()` method:

```
StartCoroutine(UpdateSurfaceData());
```

This starts a new thread (more or less). The code running inside it looks as follows:

```
IEnumerator UpdateSurfaceData()
{
    var wait = new WaitForSeconds(1.0f);
    while (true)
    {
        _observer.Update(HandleSurfaceChanged);
        yield return wait;
    }
}
```

This method, called a co-routine in Unity3D, runs outside the normal update loop. It starts by creating a wait object, one that blocks execution for, in our case, one second. The infinite loop calls `Update()` on our observer instance, and gives it the callback. We already wrote that one, so it knows what to do. Then it waits that one second and continues.

Okay, now on to the good stuff - the implementation of the `HandleSurfaceChanged` method.

Handling changes in the surfaces

First, we need to add a dictionary to our class. This will contain all the objects we create. Again, we have seen this before. We did a similar thing when we created the `_internalList` dictionary in our `SurfaceMeshList` class:

```
System.Collections.Generic.Dictionary<SurfaceId, GameObject> _meshList =
    new System.Collections.Generic.Dictionary<SurfaceId, GameObject>();
```

Change `HandleSurfaceChanged` to look as follows:

```
void HandleSurfaceChanged(
    SurfaceId surfaceId,
    SurfaceChange changeType,
    Bounds bounds,
    DateTime lastModification)
{
    // This is where we handle all changes
    switch (changeType)
    {
        case SurfaceChange.Added:
        case SurfaceChange.Updated:
            HandleNewOrUpdated(surfaceId, bounds, lastModification);
            break;
        }
}
```

I handle the add and update in the same method—they are almost identical.

New and updated surfaces

First, `HandleNewOrUpdated()`:

```
void HandleNewOrUpdated(SurfaceId surfaceId, Bounds bounds, DateTime
lastModification)
{
    if (!_meshList.ContainsKey(surfaceId))
    {
        // It's a new one
        GameObject newSurfaceObject = new GameObject("hl_sm_" + surfaceId);
        newSurfaceObject.transform.parent = this.transform;
        newSurfaceObject.AddComponent<MeshRenderer>();
        _meshList[surfaceId] = newSurfaceObject;
    }

    // It's an update or a new one, but we can now treat
    // them the same
    var surfaceObject = _meshList[surfaceId];
    var sd = new SurfaceData(
        surfaceId, // surfaceId,
        surfaceObject.GetComponent<MeshFilter>() ??
surfaceObject.AddComponent<MeshFilter>(), // mesh filter
        surfaceObject.GetComponent<WorldAnchor>() ??
surfaceObject.AddComponent<WorldAnchor>(), // world anchor
        surfaceObject.GetComponent<MeshCollider>() ??
surfaceObject.AddComponent<MeshCollider>(), // mesh collider
        1000, // triangles per cubic meter
        true // bake meshes
        );
    _observer.RequestMeshAsync(sd, MeshesReady);
}
```

We start by checking to see if we already have a mesh with this particular ID in our collection. If we do not, we are dealing with a new one.

We create a new `GameObject`, give it a name, set the transform to be the transform of the camera, and add a default `MeshRenderer`. We could add custom material if we want to, and add it to the `MeshRenderer`, but I chose not to do that here.

Then, we add it to the dictionary.

So, our dictionary now contains a `GameObject`, which is linked to this `SurfaceId`. We can now combine the code for the new and updated cases.

First, we retrieve `GameObject` from our dictionary. If it is an update, it will be there. If it is a new one, it will also be there, since we just added it ourselves.

Now, we create an instance of a `SurfaceData` class. This is comparable to our `SurfaceMesh` class: this is the mesh that will be rendered to show what the surface looks like. This `SurfaceData` class needs properties. If the previous version of this class had those properties, we copy them. If it did not, we create new ones.

The properties we create are as follows:

- An ID in the form of `SurfaceId`: This is basically comparable to the GUID we used before.
- A `MeshFilter`: This is what gives us access to the actual mesh data; this is used when you created objects in code--so-called procedural meshes.
- A `WorldAnchor`: This is used to stabilize meshes, and it enables sharing objects. We will talk about this in depth in the next chapter.
- A `MeshCollider`: This is what enables us to detect collisions between other objects and our mesh.
- The density, indicated as the number of triangles per cubic meter. We set this to 1,000.
- A Boolean, indicating we want to bake the meshes. This means we get the data back when all work is done. We want this: we want to be able to give the user an indication the surface mapping is done.

Finally, we call `RequestMeshAsync`, giving it the newly created `SurfaceData` and a callback that is called when it is done.

The callback in this case is empty; I just want to show you how to declare one:

```
void MeshesReady(
    SurfaceData surfaceData,
    bool outputWritten,
    float ellapsedBakeTimeSeconds)
{
}
```

This method gets called whenever the baking is done, so we know when the meshes are ready. This might take up to five seconds, so do not worry if it takes a long time.

Wireframe

If you run it now and wait for a couple of seconds, you will see a screen filled with one color and a sphere. This is probably not what you expected, but this makes sense. The code we just wrote generates meshes and, since we gave it a `MeshRenderer`, it will draw these on screen. We did not specify a material, so it will use the default material and fill our whole world with it.

Add the following couple of lines to your class:

```
private void OnPreRender()
{
    GL.wireframe = true;
}

private void OnPostRender()
{
    GL.wireframe = false;
}
```

This turns the wireframing on during the PreRender of our class, and turns it back off again when rendering is done.

Now run the app and have a look. You will see the meshes being rendered as the spatial mapper does its work.

But, we are not quite done. Look at the sphere. Tap on it. See that it falls, reaches the surfaces, and stops falling. If you disable `MeshRenderer` in the created `GameObject`, the meshes will not be visible. The result will be that it seems like the physical floor stops our virtual ball from falling. This will feel very natural, but now that you know what it takes to do this, I am sure you are amazed at the power of all this.

The easy way

I promised you there is an easier way of doing this. You will be surprised how easy it is. You may even wonder why we bother with all the hard code we used above. The reason is that I want you to know how things work underneath. You will need that knowledge if you want to have more control over what is happening under the covers. However, that being said--most of the time you just want to be able to use the surface mapping and spatial discovery. Here we go.

These are the steps you need to take.

1. Create a new project in Unity3D.
2. Set all the settings required for a HoloLens project (camera, player, and so on)
3. In your scene, add a new empty game object. Call it "Managers"
4. Add two components to this new game object
    1. **Spatial Mapping Renderer**
    2. **Spatial Mapping Collider**
5. Run…

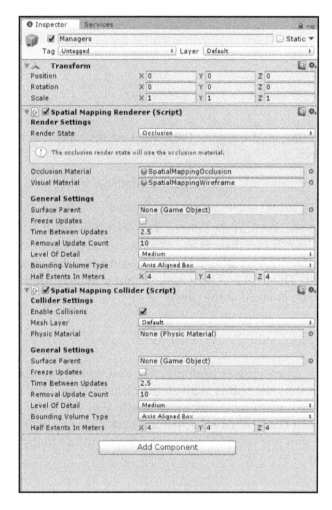

Settings for spatial mapping and collider

And that's it. These two components take care of the things we discussed earlier. There are just C# scripts that do what I have just shown you, but now you do not have to write it yourself.

There are a lot of properties you can set in these components, but they are similar to what I have shown you so far. So you should be able to play with them and have a go.

Now, that was easy, wasn't it?

Occlusion

We have covered a lot so far. However, we have not discussed one very important thing: how to hide virtual things behind physical things.

I have shown you the virtual puppy hiding behind my living room chair. How do we do this? The answer is: using the right kind of shader.

We have mentioned shaders before, but now it is time to delve a little bit more deeply into them.

In DirectX, we have a whole set of shaders: we have seen `pixelshaders`, `geometryshaders`, and `vertexshaders`. There are a lot more, but we will not go into those at all.

In Unity3D we only have one, simply called the shader. The shader we use is a property of the material we apply.

Let us create a new one. In our Unity3D project, create a new shader. Call it Occlusion. You do this by right-clicking in the **Assets** pane and selecting the relevant menu options, as shown in the following screenshot:

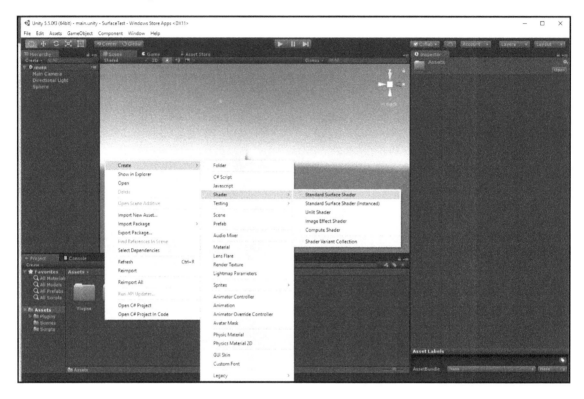

Creating a shader

Double-click on the newly created file and you will get the following code:

```
Shader "Custom/Occlusion" {
    Properties {
        _Color ("Color", Color) = (1,1,1,1)
        _MainTex ("Albedo (RGB)", 2D) = "white" {}
        _Glossiness ("Smoothness", Range(0,1)) = 0.5
        _Metallic ("Metallic", Range(0,1)) = 0.0
    }
    SubShader {
        Tags { "RenderType"="Opaque" }
        LOD 200
        CGPROGRAM
        // Physically based Standard lighting model, and enable shadows on
all light types
```

```
#pragma surface surf Standard fullforwardshadows

// Use shader model 3.0 target, to get nicer looking lighting
#pragma target 3.0

sampler2D _MainTex;

struct Input {
      float2 uv_MainTex;
};

half _Glossiness;
half _Metallic;
fixed4 _Color;

void surf (Input IN, inout SurfaceOutputStandard o) {
      // Albedo comes from a texture tinted by color
      fixed4 c = tex2D (_MainTex, IN.uv_MainTex) * _Color;
      o.Albedo = c.rgb;
      // Metallic and smoothness come from slider variables
      o.Metallic = _Metallic;
      o.Smoothness = _Glossiness;
      o.Alpha = c.a;
}
ENDCG
}
FallBack "Diffuse"
}
```

This is the standard shader code. We will not talk about this too much—there are lots of good resources out there that explain everything that is going on—but we will change some things.

First, the `Properties` at the beginning of the file. These are the properties you also see in the material editor. Shaders, and thus materials, have colors, textures, glossiness, and a value for the amount of metallic they have. Since we do not want to have anything rendered at all, we can simply empty this out:

```
Properties
{
}
```

The rest of the code I will not discuss here, but just copy and paste this into your editor. This is the whole shader file, so just replace everything with the following:

```
Shader "Custom/Occlusion" {
    Properties {
    }
    SubShader {
            Tags { "RenderType"="Opaque" }
    Pass
      {
        ColorMask 0
        Offset 50, 100
        CGPROGRAM
        #pragma vertex vert
        #pragma fragment frag
        #pragma target 5.0
        #pragma only_renderers d3d11
        #include "UnityCG.cginc"
        struct v2f
        {
            float4 pos : SV_POSITION;
            UNITY_VERTEX_OUTPUT_STEREO
        };
        v2f vert(appdata_base v)
        {
            UNITY_SETUP_INSTANCE_ID(v);
            v2f o;
            o.pos = mul(UNITY_MATRIX_MVP, v.vertex);
            UNITY_INITIALIZE_VERTEX_OUTPUT_STEREO(o);
            return o;
        }
        half4 frag(v2f i) : COLOR
        {
            return float4(1,1,1,1);
        }
        ENDCG
      }
    }
}
```

What happens here is that we set `ColorMask` to 0, meaning we will not render any color at all.

Save the file and, in Unity3D, create a new material. Call it Occluded.

In the **Inspector**, choose the new shader as the shader for this material:

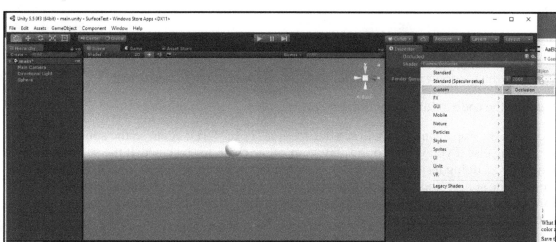

We need to make some small changes to our code. In our `SurfaceHelper`, we add a publicly accessible field:

```
public Material MeshMaterial;
```

This is the material we will use to paint our meshes with. Save this file and, in Unity3D, assign our new material with the new shader to this `MeshMaterial` field (if you select the camera you will see it in the **Inspector**).

Back in Visual Studio, change the line where we add the `MeshRenderer` component to the following:

```
var renderer = newSurfaceObject.AddComponent<MeshRenderer>();
renderer.material = MeshMaterial;
```

We store the renderer in the variable renderer and assign the material to it.

Remove the code to turn the wireframe on and off.

Now run the app again. You will see the sphere. Try to start it again so the sphere is behind something else if you walk around. Try your office chair, for instance. If the surface mapper has finished doing its job you will not see anything happening. But, if you place the chair in front of the sphere and wait a couple of seconds, you will see the occlusion kicking in. You cannot see the sphere until you walk around the chair, or whatever object you have placed between you and the sphere.

Again, this will feel very natural to the user, but as you can see, there is a lot going on behind the scenes.

Now, let us put this all to good use and dive more deeply into this topic when we try to communicate with other devices. Yes, these two topics are very much related!

Summary

This chapter was the hardest of them all. We have looked at surface mapping, the technique that allows the HoloLens to understand what the actual, real world looks like. We have seen how the device does this investigation with its sensors. We spent most of our time creating the code in DirectX that allows us to read the data from the depth sensors and map it into a grid. This resulted in a sort of superpower that gave us the ability to look through walls. Along with that, we looked into the Unity3D code to do more or less the same.

We also learned how to draw wireframes, and we learned a bit more about optimizing apps when drawing more than one figure; our wireframes consist of many polygons, so we had to make our code a bit smarter. We did not spend any time working on RockOn, but we will deal with that later on.

7
Lets Talk! Communications between Devices

In the previous chapter, we took a look at how HoloLens spatial mapping works. This is the way the machine learns about its environment. It is important for a couple of reasons. Firstly, if we want to have a great mixed-reality experience, the holograms need to know where things are. Secondly, we need information about the real-world surface to help the user. We talked about different scenarios where, for instance, the user needs to place something in the world, or where we need to guide the user to a certain place in her room.

There is one more thing knowing about the physical layout of the world, and that is what this chapter will be about.

The position of holograms

I have to make a confession: I have not been completely honest with you. In previous chapters, I boasted about the perfect inner workings of the HoloLens. It knows where you are all the time, so it can place the holograms at the right position all the time. The truth is: this is not what is happening. Yes, the device knows where you are, but it does not know this to the millimeter. It needs to make educated guesses and sometimes, it gets this wrong. In fact, this does not only happen sometimes; it happens frequently. If you pay close attention, you will notice that the holograms move about a bit the whole time. We usually do not notice this. There is a good reason for this. Again, our brains come to the rescue. If we look at something in the real world, such as a coffee mug, we expect it to be standing still on the table. It would be weird if it started to move all of a sudden. So, when our eyes detect slight movement in an object that is not supposed to move, our brains filter this out and decide we did not see that. Of course, if the movement persists and is quite obvious, then we will see this. And we will probably be scared or amazed to see this happening.

In the HoloLens, the same thing happens. The objects move slightly but we do not see this happening. But they do. And although we do not really register this consciously, it does take away from the realism.

If you walk around your room, you will see it happen even more. The movement of the holograms will be quite obvious. Let me explain what is going on.

Let us assume we have a hologram of a coffee mug. We place this object one meter away from the user. Now the user moves one meter to the left. This means the HoloLens has to notice this and move the coffee mug one meter to the right so that it seems to stay in the same place. But, the user might not move one meter to the left, and instead she moves 0.98 meters to the left. Is the HoloLens accurate enough to measure this tiny difference? The answer is no. So, it will make a mistake in positioning the mug in the right place. Apparently, using the position of the user as the origin of all holograms is not a good way to do this kind of thing. We need something else.

Local coordinate systems

In all the code samples we have used previously, we always started out with a coordinate system in which the user is in the center of the world. At least, she is initially. Every item we place something somewhere, it is positioned relative to the user's position. As we have seen, this might lead to undesirable behavior. If we express the position of each object relative to the user, we are talking about one global coordinate system.

Another approach might be to have a local coordinate system for each object. Let us assume each object has its own coordinate system and that the center of that coordinate system - thus, position (0,0,0) - is at the heart of the hologram. If we do this, we can easily move objects about. If we want to move that object one meter to the left, we just tell it to position itself at (1,0,0). This is independent of the position of the user, so it simplifies things. Well, not really, of course. It is not enough to say that each object has its own system. The system needs to know where our coffee mug's position (0,0,0) is, relative to the rest.

We could do that. We could, of course, calculate the origin of our objects relative to all the other objects. If we have two mugs, *Mug A* and *Mug B*, we could say that they both have their own coordinate system, but A sits 1 meter to the left of B. This way, we can calculate the position of everything else.

We need a reference point. We need a starting point. It would be obvious to use the only thing we know everything about: the user's position. This is not enough. As we have discussed, this is not accurate enough, so we need to find another solution.

Spatial mapping and coordinate systems

As a matter a fact, we have a solution. In fact, we have more than one. They are all based on one general idea. We do have access to things we know the location of and that stay in their place all the time--our walls, floors, and ceilings. So why do we not use these? Well, we will!

The nice bonus is that the system constantly updates its knowledge about the world it sits in. If we express the position of the local coordinate systems in relation to the actual physical objects around it, they tend to be fairly stable. Mistakes made by the sensors will be corrected as soon as there is an update. This sounds like a great solution. Actually, this is such a great solution, the team behind the HoloLens decided to use this and have it available to you more or less automatically.

From this point on we can choose between three strategies to fix our holograms at their position:

- Spatial anchors
- Stationary frame of reference
- Spatial locator-attached frame of reference

We will go through these one at a time.

Spatial anchors

Spatial anchors are anchor points. We can create a new coordinate system that we place somewhere in the world. Initially, it will be placed relative to the initial coordinate system, defined by the position of the user and the HoloLens. However, as we move on and the device learns more about its environment, the coordinate system based on the device will differ from fixed coordinate systems. Fixed or anchored systems will be repositioned every time the depth sensors decide the world looks a bit different than it initially thought; tiny mistakes will be corrected all the time.

So, assume we create a new coordinate system. Its origin will be placed two meters in front of the user when the system starts up. We can rotate this as well, so that the positive Z axis points at a 45-degree angle away from us.

If we now want to position a hologram at the center of this coordinate system, we need to do some calculations. But once we have done this, we can be assured that the object stays where it is, no matter where the user goes and no matter how many corrections the system makes to its knowledge about the environment.

This sounds like a great solution, so you might be tempted to place these coordinate systems everywhere. You might even think about creating a grid of systems that each define a cubic meter of area in your scene and have your holograms placed there. If this is what you are thinking, then I want you to stop doing that.

Coordinate systems are not expensive in terms of resources or calculations, but they do come with a cost. It is best not to use too many of these; the system has to keep track of them all of the time. Next to that, we have found that objects placed at coordinate systems far away from the user tend to appear to move a bit. The reason for this is that the corrections the system makes seem to be larger at greater distances. So, objects placed there are more subject to changes. Holograms placed nearby, say, within three meters of the device, will be more stable.

You might consider instead having one new coordinate system, fixed in the center of the room, and placing all objects relative to that one. Again, you would be wrong. Objects placed far away from the origin of the coordinate system are also susceptible to changes in the awareness of the real world. Again, try to place holograms within three meters of the origin to minimize slight movement and jittering.

Using the spatial anchors in DirectX

It is time to look at what this is and how it all works. We will, as we have always done, start with a new application, based on the template *Universal DirectX Holographic* app in C#.

Before we begin our coding, let me remind you that spatial anchors depend on the information the depth sensors give us. Therefore, we need to set the right capabilities in our app. If you do not do this, the whole thing simply will not work. So, open the `Package.appxmanifest` file and add the correct capabilities. Just as a reminder, we do so by adding the correct namespace to the `Package` element:

```
<Package
  xmlns="http://schemas.microsoft.com/appx/manifest/foundation/windows10"
  xmlns:mp="http://schemas.microsoft.com/appx/2014/phone/manifest"
  xmlns:uap="http://schemas.microsoft.com/appx/manifest/uap/windows10"
  xmlns:uap2="http://schemas.microsoft.com/appx/manifest/uap/windows10/2"
  IgnorableNamespaces="uap uap2 mp">
```

And then we add the `Capabilities` section below the `Application` section:

```
<Capabilities>
  <uap2:Capability Name="spatialPerception"/>
</Capabilities>
```

So, what is a spatial anchor? Well, simply put, a spatial anchor is a fixed point in place that remains in that position by referencing the physical objects around it.

In practice, you can think of it as a point in space expressed by coordinates relative to the things that are in the real world. In practice, what the system does is look at the meshes given by the spatial mapping mechanism and try to match that with a cached version of those meshes. By doing this, you can be fairly sure the anchor will be placed at that precise point every time.

Once you got access to that anchor, you can use the corresponding coordinate system to place items or to define transformations against those coordinates.

So, let's create one.

Creating the anchor

In the app, find the method `SetHolographicSpace` in your main class (in my case, `SpatialAnchorsDemoMain`).

At the end of this method, add the following line:

```
_cubeAnchor =
SpatialAnchor.TryCreateRelativeTo(referenceFrame.CoordinateSystem);
```

Of course, you need to set the private member in that class somewhere, so we can reach it when we need it.

We call the static method `TryCreateRelativeTo` and give it the default `CoordinateSystem`, the one based on the current position of the current user. This method could return null when there is no more room for more anchors, but this will not happen frequently. Still, it would be a good idea to test for it before you attempt to use the anchor.

Now, we have created an anchor with a new coordinate system. The coordinate system will be exactly the same as the one we used before. Its offset (0,0,0) is at the same position as the default coordinate system. Of course, once HoloLens decides it made a mistake and that the world is not quite what it expected it to be, it will shift our new coordinate system so that it remains in place with respect to the walls, furniture, and other things it has found.

We could have used an overload:

```
_cubeAnchor = SpatialAnchor.TryCreateRelativeTo(
    referenceFrame.CoordinateSystem,
    new System.Numerics.Vector3(0f,0f, -2f));
```

This would have placed the origin (0,0,0) of our new system at the coordinates (0,0,-2), which is where the spinning cube is. This all depends on your needs. All that matters now is that we have a new coordinate system we can use, which will stay in place, no matter what happens. There is also an overload that accepts a quaternion to determine the rotation of the system.

Now it is time to use it.

In the `Update` method of this same class, you will find the sample code that takes care of the repositioning of the cube. We will do the same here; this time, however, we will not use the normal coordinate system but our new, more stable one.

So, this is what the new code looks like. Compare it to the default version you have got right now and see the differences:

```
#if DRAW_SAMPLE_CONTENT
// Check for new input state since the last frame.
SpatialInteractionSourceState pointerState =
spatialInputHandler.CheckForInput();
if (null != pointerState)
{
    // When a Pressed gesture is detected, the sample hologram will be
repositioned
    // two meters in front of the user.

    var spatialPointerPose =
pointerState.TryGetPointerPose(_cubeAnchor.CoordinateSystem);
    spinningCubeRenderer.PositionHologram(spatialPointerPose);
}
#endif
```

As you can see, all I did was replace the `CoordinateSystem` in `TryGetPointerPose`.

`TryGetPointerPose` is one of the many methods that rely on coordinate systems to do their work. In this case, it will return the position of the user and the orientation of the user's head. We do not want those positions in relation to the original coordinate system (where the center (0,0,0) was the place we started up), but we want it expressed in relation to the anchor we created.

If you run this, you will probably not notice a lot of different behavior. However, if you keep on running the app for a long time, or if you run it in an environment HoloLens knows little about yet, you might notice that it does not move about as much as it used to. We have successfully created an anchor and used it to place our cube.

But that is not all. The anchor has some interesting properties and one interesting event that we can use as well.

We have used the `CoordinateSystem` property in the preceding example. This is what we call a system with easing applied. What this means is that, when the system suddenly decides to move our hologram because of errors, it will do so over the course of a couple of frames. This results in a smooth glide into place, if you will. The holograms do not jump around.

We could have used `RawCoordinateSystem`, which is another coordinate system but without the easing.

You will also find the `RawCoordinateSystemAdjusted` event. This is called when the system decides it needs to update the location of the holograms. We could assign a handler to this method and implement it as follows:

```
private void RawCoordinateSystemAdjusted(
    SpatialAnchor sender,
    SpatialAnchorRawCoordinateSystemAdjustedEventArgs args)
{
    Matrix4x4 transform =
args.OldRawCoordinateSystemToNewRawCoordinateSystemTransform;
    // Apply that to the cube...
}
```

The matrix can then be used to move the cube's position to the right spot. This is just another transform you can apply in the `Update` method of `SpinningCubeRenderer`, something we have already seen before. I am leaving that to you for now.

One thing that you need to be aware of is that the position of the cube might change every single frame. Even if you do not tap to reposition the cube two meters in front of you, the system might decide to change the position, simply because it thinks the environment needs adjusting. So, in the `Update` method, you need to check for this constantly.

This is not that hard to do--you can use the `TryGetTransformTo()` method from the coordinate system in the anchor to get the transform. If you apply that to the cube's position you will see it will be updated as soon as the depth sensors think it is necessary.

Persisting and loading the anchor

Anchors have one nice capability: they can be persisted. What this means is that, whenever you create an anchor and store it on the device, you can load it again the next time the app starts up and use it immediately. This means that the location of the cube is persisted during shutdown and restart. You start your app, place the cube two meters away from you, walk around, reposition the cube, shut down the app and then restart it, only to notice it is in the same spot. This leads to a pretty nice experience. After all, we expect things to stay where we put them last time, right? The same goes for holograms.

How do we do this?

First, we need to get access to the place where the anchors are stored. This is a class named `SpatialAnchorStore`. You cannot create one of those; you need to ask a helper class for it:

```
_anchorStore = await SpatialAnchorManager.RequestStoreAsync();
```

`SpatialAnchorManager` is the class that loads and saves the anchor store. What happens is that all anchors will be persisted to the SSD drive in the HoloLens, in a sandboxed place that only your app can access. So, all anchors belong to an app and cannot be shared with other apps. Well, that does make sense-- the anchors define where your holograms should go so, they are no use in other apps.

Once you get a reference to the anchor store, you can use it to store your anchors in. Obviously, it would be a great idea to check if your anchor is not there already, something that will happen if you load your app a second time.

All anchors are identified by a unique string. Unique, of course, only in the context of your app.

Let us find our anchor. I have named it `"myCube"`:

```
IReadOnlyDictionary<string, SpatialAnchor> allAnchors =
_anchorStore.GetAllSavedAnchors();
if (allAnchors.ContainsKey("myCube"))
    _cubeAnchor = allAnchors["myCube"];
```

So, I call `GetAllSavedAnchors`, which gives me a dictionary containing the keys and the anchors. If this dictionary already contains the `"myCube"` key it should have my anchor there as well, so I can use it.

If it does not, I can create an anchor in the usual way and store it in the store. That way it cannot get lost anymore:

```
_anchorStore.TrySave("myCube", _cubeAnchor);
```

The method is called `TrySave`. It might fail, so you need to check for that. But if all goes well you do not need to do anything else about it: it will be persisted to the SSD automatically.

If you tap during the runtime of the app, the cube will be relocated. Since we have a guideline advising us to place objects within three meters of the origin of the spatial anchor's coordinate system, it might be a great idea to create a new coordinate system instead of moving the cube.

If we do this, we need to update the stored anchor as well. Unfortunately, we cannot do this. There is no `Update()` method on the store. What you need to do is remove the anchor from the store, create a new one, and store that one instead.

Here it is (I am omitting the code to calculate the new position of the origin of our spatial anchor):

```
// Remove it from the store
_anchorStore.Remove("myCube");

// Recreate the anchor
_cubeAnchor = SpatialAnchor.TryCreateRelativeTo(currentCoordinateSystem,
newOrigin);

// Try to save it
if (!_anchorStore.TrySave("myCube", _cubeAnchor))
    Debug.WriteLine("Save failed");
```

We remove it from the store by calling `Remove` and giving it the identifier. Then we create a new anchor and try to save that one. Again, this could fail, so make sure you check for that.

The template gives us two methods `SaveAppState` and `LoadAppState`, which will be called whenever the app is suspended and then resumed again. This would be a great place to save and load all the anchors. This can be time-consuming, so it is best not to do it during the `Update` method as I just have shown you. However, do not forget to initially call the loading code from `SetupHolographicSpace()`. After all, `LoadAppState` is only invoked after a resume, so it will not get called during start up.

Using SpatialAnchors in Unity3D

Again, things in the Unity3D world are simpler. Not much, though: the mechanics are very similar. The biggest difference is that anchors are not placeholders for coordinate systems as they are in the DirectX world, but instead are properties of our holograms or a group of holograms. We can create an empty `GameObject` that has child objects and give it an anchor.

Let us do that in our *RockOn* app. But before we can do that, remember to set the **SpatialPerception** capability in the **Player Settings**. If you do not do that, it will not work:

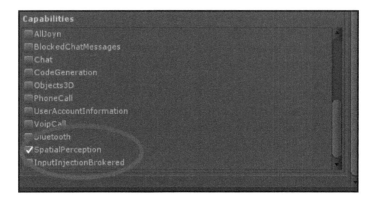

SpatialPerception capability needs to be checked!

Changing GestureHandler.cs

We need a script where we can write the code to handle the anchors. We could create a new script, but in this case it would be much wiser to reuse an existing script. We have the GestureHandler script that is responsible for creating new instances of our guitar. It makes sense to use this. GestureHandler creates new instances of our guitar. One additional task along with creating that instance is to store its position in relation to a spatial anchor and store that anchor in the store. That way, it will be persisted, and we can load them up again when we restart our app. This implies that we have two ways of creating our guitars: one by tapping somewhere, as we have done until now, and the other when the app starts up. In that case, the app will load all previously created guitars and place them at the right spot.

Let us do that! Open up `GestureHandler.cs` and add a new private field:

```
private WorldAnchorStore _store;
```

In DirectX, we had `SpatialAnchorStore`; in Unity3D we have `WorldAnchorStore`. Not surprisingly, the anchors themselves are not called Spatial Anchors in Unity3D, but World Anchors instead. They serve more or less the same purpose so it is just a different name.

Loading the store

In the `Start()` method, add the following line to the bottom:

```
WorldAnchorStore.GetAsync(WorldAnchorStoreLoaded);
```

This static method loads the store asynchronously. It is similar to the
`RequestStoreAsync()` method we have seen in DirectX. Of course, we need to create the
callback `WorldAnchorStoreLoaded()` as well:

```
private void WorldAnchorStoreLoaded(WorldAnchorStore store)
{
    _store = store;
    LoadAllAnchors();
}
```

We store the store instance in our field so we can reuse it later on, and then we call
`LoadAllAnchors()`. This is what that looks like:

```
void LoadAllAnchors()
{

    var allIds = _store.GetAllIds();
    _guitarCount = allIds.Length;

    foreach(var id in allIds)
    {
        var newGuitar = Instantiate(objectToPlace);

        _store.Load(id, newGuitar);
    }
}
```

First, we load all the IDs from the store in `_store.GetAllIds()`. As you will remember,
anchors have a string that uniquely identifies them in the scope of the app. These are all the
strings we might have stored and persisted before.

`_guitarCount` is an integer I have added as a field to keep track of the number of guitars.
That way I can give each anchor belonging to a guitar a unique name.

Next I iterate through all the IDs and create a new instance of our guitar prefab. The
`objectToPlace` field is the same we used before, when we handled the tap event.

The last line is the most interesting one: we call `Load(id, newGuitar)` on the store and
that will do several things:

- Load the data associated with the anchor from the SSD
- Create the coordinate system, with the center at the pivot point of the guitar
- Create a new component in our `GameObject` of type `WorldAnchor`

- Attach the coordinate system to that `WorldAnchor` internally
- Move the combination of the coordinate system and the `GameObject` to the right position

Yes, you read it right. The `WorldAnchor` takes care of the positioning. So, you do not have to deal with the transformations in Unity3D, as the `WorldAnchor` does this for us. All we need to do is attach a `WorldAnchor` and the object will remain fixed in place.

Moving objects with anchors

This is very different from DirectX. There, we had a coordinate system we could move the object in. Here we cannot do that. It is even stronger than that: once you have attached a `WorldAnchor` to a `GameObject` you cannot move it anymore. If you want to move it, you will have to do following:

1. Remove the `WorldAnchor` component.
2. Destroy the `WorldAnchor` component.
3. Remove it from the store by calling `_store.Delete(id);`.
4. Reposition the `GameObject`.
5. Call `CreateComponent<WorldAnchor>()`.
6. Store that newly created `WorldAnchor` in the store.

You cannot update anchors. You have to delete them and make new ones.

Creating another anchor

Let us finish our code: we need to create an anchor when we tap somewhere, resulting in a new guitar.

At the bottom of the `GestureRecognizerOnTappedEvent()` method add the following:

```
var worldAnchor = newGuitar.AddComponent<WorldAnchor>();
_guitarCount++;
var anchorName = string.Format("Guitar{0:000}", _guitarCount);

_store.Save(anchorName, worldAnchor);
```

In that event, you create a new instance by calling Instantiate, and give it a position and a rotation. The result is stored in the `newGuitar` variable. We continue by adding a `WorldAnchor` component to the guitar, giving it a unique name, and storing it in the store.

Try it out. Run it, place some guitars, and stop the app. Start the app again while you are standing at a different spot and you will see all the guitars reappear in the same physical location as they were when you created them.

Problems with anchors

This is all nice and handy, but sometimes there are issues. It does not work all the time.

Most of the issues are self-explanatory. Once you realize how anchors work, you can think of this yourself and be aware of the potential problems.

So, how does this work? Well, it is not that hard to understand. A spatial anchor or world anchor is just a place where the system stores information about a group of meshes. When the system needs to place something at a certain fixed place, it tries to match up the meshes it sees with the meshes it has stored. If it finds something that is close enough, it will store the objects or the coordinate system at that spot. When the meshes update because the depth sensors get more data, the internal mesh collection gets updated as well.

So, imagine the following scenario: you are in a room. You create a spatial anchor or world anchor. The system will store the meshes. Then you switch off the device and walk to another room with a different layout. Turn on the device again and load the app.

The app will load all anchors and place the objects in the right place. But it has no idea where to put them: there are no meshes it can see that are similar to the ones it has stored internally. So what happens? Well, that depends on the environment you are in. In DirectX code, the calls to `SpatialCoordinateSystem.TryGetTransformTo` will return null, `TryGetTransformTo` will return null. This means you cannot transform the positions, which makes sense.

In Unity3D it works slightly differently. It loads the anchors, it creates the objects, but it does not show them until you move it back to a room it recognizes. So it does no harm, but it does use resources!

Besides being in another room, there are some other reasons things might not work. They are related, however, and they all come down to the same problem: the system does not see enough meshes it recognizes to do its work. Some reasons for this could be as follows:

- The room has changed
- It is a very dynamic environment with lots of moving people and things
- The sensors are covered or dirty
- You are in a room very similar but not quite the same; the system will get confused

If you are experimenting with this, it might be worth cleaning out the persisted anchors. There is an easy way to do this during development.

In Visual Studio, right-click on your project in the Solution Explorer. This goes for both DirectX and the Unity3D version. Select Properties. In the Properties window, open the Debug Tab.

There you will find an option named **Uninstall and then re-install my package. All information about the application state is deleted.** Check that:

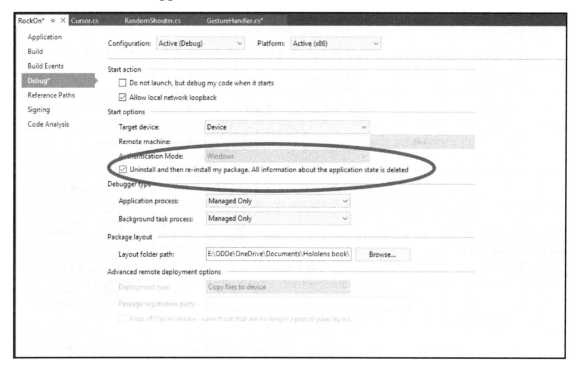

Option to clear anchor store

If you have checked this, it will remove everything related to your app from your device and do a clean install.

Stationary frame of reference

Spatial or world anchors are references to real-world objects. A coordinate is located in reference to the physical stuff around us. This means we can express the position of a hologram in relation to things that are actually there. So, you would say that a virtual dinosaur is to be placed three meters left of that wall, about 30 centimeters above the floor, and so on. The device will take care of the placement since it knows about these objects. This is what makes HoloLens unique in the world of virtual and augmented devices.

However, you do not always need this kind of behavior. Most of the time you can get away with less precision; especially when you have items that move about, such as following the user or leading the way to something interesting, you do not want things to be fixed in place.

In those cases, you are better off using a stationary frame of reference. This is quite a mouthful, but it is really quite simple. All it means is that you have one coordinate system that you use throughout your app. Of course, you can mix it with the other coordinate systems that the spatial or world anchors provide. That way, you can use the easy-to-use stationary frame of reference for most parts of your app, but have a fixed-in-place, anchor-based solution for holograms you want to keep in their place.

Using the stationary frame of reference in DirectX

One of the classes the framework provides is the `SpatialLocator`, in the `Windows.Perception.Spatial` namespace. You can get a reference to one by calling the static method `GetDefault()` on that class. You never instantiate one yourself: there is no public constructor available.

This class is a helper class that helps you find the frame of reference. To do this, all you need to do is call the extremely long-named `CreateStationaryFrameOfReferenceAtCurrentLocation()` method. This creates a new coordinate system for you, centered around the current position of your device, with the heading in the direction you are looking at. The template we have been using so far does exactly this: in your main class, you will find the `SetHolographicSpace` method, and there you will find this call. The result of this method call is stored in the field `referenceFrame`. Again, we have seen this before: this has a `CoordinateSystem` property that holds that coordinate system that has just been created.

You could call this method over and over again, if you decide you need a new position. However, be warned: if you do this, all your holograms will shift. They have a position which is relative to this frame of reference; thus, if the origin changes in either position or orientation, the holograms will move as well. An object placed two meters in front of the origin will remain two meters in front of the origin, no matter how often you move the origin about.

Of course, you are not obliged to position the origin at the current position of the HoloLens. You can use one of the given overloads and supply a position, a rotation, or a combination of those. That way, you can control where the origin is and use it like that.

As you probably know by now, the position and orientation of the origin of this coordinate system might, or rather; will, change over time. As the device learns more about its environment and as the user moves about, it will shift the origin a bit. Since all holograms are located with respect to this origin (except for those with spatial anchors) they will move as well.

Using the stationary frame of reference in Unity3D

Unity3D does not allow you to change this frame of reference. It does not even know such a thing exists. The moment you start Unity3D you are given a coordinate system. As you know, we start with the camera in position (0,0,0), although the camera might move about the scene. Actually, it will move about: the user is not able to keep her head still all the time and we do not want her to, either. So, the camera position will change but the origin of the coordinate system will remain fixed.

You can use world anchors in your scene so you can place items fixed to their surroundings, but you cannot decide to move every other hologram one meter to the left instantaneously by changing the main coordinate system. So, I cannot show you any code for how to do this. Luckily, you never need to do this in real life.

Spatial locator-attached frame of reference

Let us do something fun. First I will tell you what to do and then I will tell you why you want to do this. This is something you cannot do in Unity3D, at least not this easily, so I will omit that part. But you can do this in DirectX and that is what we will do. We will create something called `SpatialLocatorAttachedFrameOfReference`.

Using the locator attached frame in DirectX

Start a new HoloGraphic project. Do not do anything special; we only need to have our cube floating in front of us.

In the main method, we will make some changes. First, find the `referenceFrame` field and change its type to `SpatialLocatorAttachedFrameOfReference`.

In the `SetHolographicSpace` method, this field is set. Change it to look as follows:

```
referenceFrame = locator.CreateAttachedFrameOfReferenceAtCurrentHeading();
```

This was a call to `CreateStationaryFrameOfReferenceAtCurrentLocation`, but we do not want a stationary frame; we want an attached frame.

In the `Update()` method, we use this to assign a coordinate system to the `currentCoordinateSystem` field. Change it to look as follows:

```
SpatialCoordinateSystem currentCoordinateSystem =
referenceFrame.GetStationaryCoordinateSystemAtTimestamp(prediction.Timestamp);
```

We call `GetStationyCoordinateSystemAtTimestamp` and give it the time for the next prediction. This will give us the desired coordinate system.

We do the same thing in the `Render()` method: find the line that sets the local variable `coordinateSystem` and change it in the same way:

```
var coordinateSystem =
referenceFrame.GetStationaryCoordinateSystemAtTimestamp(prediction.Timestamp);
```

Now, run the app.

You will see the cube, spinning slowly about two meters in front of you. However, when you move about you will notice it moves with you. It will not rotate (besides the spinning) but it will move. Is that not cool?

What this does?

Imagine you want to build a game. You might want to have something like a bulletin board floating in front of the user indicating that he should start the game by saying "Go." Something like that. You want it to be visible no matter where the user walks, but you do not want it to be "in his face" all the time. This is why we need this frame of reference. It is a coordinate system that, once defined, stays in the same rotation but moves with the user.

There are a couple of overloads available. These are similar to the ones we saw with the stationary frame of reference.

I did not mention this before, but there is a fourth overload that might be a bit misleading. This overload is available for both frames. You can supply an angle to rotate the frame before positioning. That way, it is much easier to position the frame at the correct place.

Let us assume you want to create an attached frame, which is two meters in front of the user; but also two meters to the left of the user. You know by now how to do that. But what if you want something else, such as having a frame that is about two meters away from the user but not right in front of him. Instead, you want it to be away from the line of sight and about 45 degrees to the left. You could do the calculations yourself and come to the conclusion that you need to move the object two meters to the front and two meters to the right, then rotate it counterclockwise for 45 degrees. So, you have to calculate the right quaternion for that.

It is much easier to use the overload specified for this:

```
var position = new Vector3(0f, 0f, -2f);
var rotation = Quaternion.Identity;
var heading = (45f / 180f) * Math.PI;

referenceFrame = locator.CreateAttachedFrameOfReferenceAtCurrentHeading(
    position,
    rotation,
    heading) ;
```

You can then use the coordinate system from this referenceFrame to position your holograms. If you want to rotate an object around the user or around any arbitrary point, you can simply modify the last parameter. This specifies the rotation of the coordinate system before the translation is applied. Remember, the order in which these things take place is important! Moving an object two meters ahead and then rotating it 90 degrees means you will still see it right in front of you but you are now looking at its side. First rotating it and then moving it two meters means you move it to the side.

Using the locator-attached frame in Unity3D

As I said, I cannot show you how to do this in Unity3D. There is no such thing as different coordinate systems in that tool. But how would we go about achieving the same effect? Well, we need to write a script for that!

```
The following snippet is just for illustration purposes; it is not part of
our RockOn app. But I want to show you how it is done anyway, so here it
is:
public class AttachedFrameBehaviour : MonoBehaviour {

    [Tooltip("The distance from the camera, in meters", order=1)]
    public float DistanceFromCamera;

    // Update is called once per frame
    void Update () {

        var cameraPos = Camera.main.transform.position;
        var myPos = cameraPos + new Vector3(0f, 0f, DistanceFromCamera);
        this.transform.position = myPos;
    }
}
```

You should attach this script to the objects you want to be in that attached frame, specify the distance, and off you go.

Quite simple, is it not?

Sharing

As my favorite artist once sang: *"Two hearts are better than one."* That is true for holographic experiences as well. To me, the two biggest differentiators between mixed reality as experienced in the HoloLens and other devices that are currently available, is untethered way of working and the possibility to see what other people are doing.

So, if you have more than one device, it is possible to share data between these two devices. We can even share holograms, thus enforcing the effect of believing objects are actually there. After all, if you see something and someone else sees the same thing and can point out things, it must be real. Right?

We will dive into this now. But first we need to do some system administration.

Setting up networking

We have everything set up: we understand the world and we can map our objects to real-world coordinates. It is time to share these objects with other HoloLenses. However, chances are you do not have access to more than one device. If you or your company have more than one device, it is very likely your colleagues, spouse, or kids will claim the other device. If you want to test out sharing, you have to think of another solution. The answer is pretty obvious--you DO have access to another machine. You have access to the emulator. We can use this to test our scenarios. But we do have one small problem. If you install the emulator, you might have noticed in the top-left corner of the start menu a tiny icon saying you are disconnected from the internet.

Let us have a go at fixing this first.

The reason the emulator does not have an internet connection is that by default, the device in that emulator is connected to a virtual switch. This virtual switch acts like a real hardware-based switch that routes all network traffic, but it is only connected to itself. We need to change that.

First, we need to start the HoloLens emulator. We can do this more easily from Visual Studio. Just open one of our previous DirectX apps or create a new one, it does not really matter what we use. We just need to make sure the HoloLens emulator is running. Start the app and check the emulator is actually running.

On your host machine, which is the machine you are working on, open Hyper-V Manager:

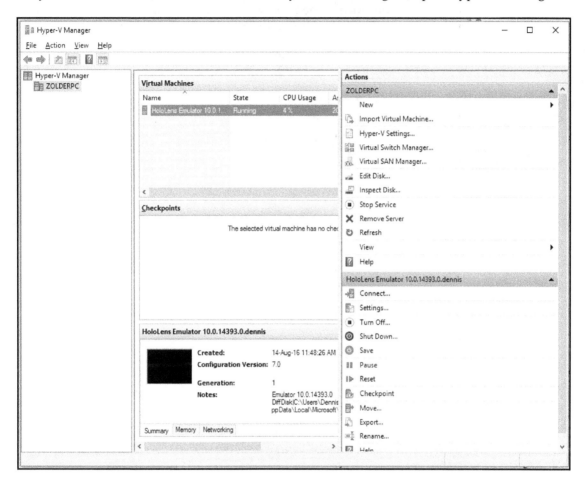

Hyper-V Manager, showing the emulator

As you can see, my PC is called **ZOLDERPC** (which is Dutch for Attic-PC, where I write this book), and I have got one instance of the HoloLens emulator running. On the right-hand side, you can see the **Actions** panel. Choose the **Virtual Switch Manager...** here:

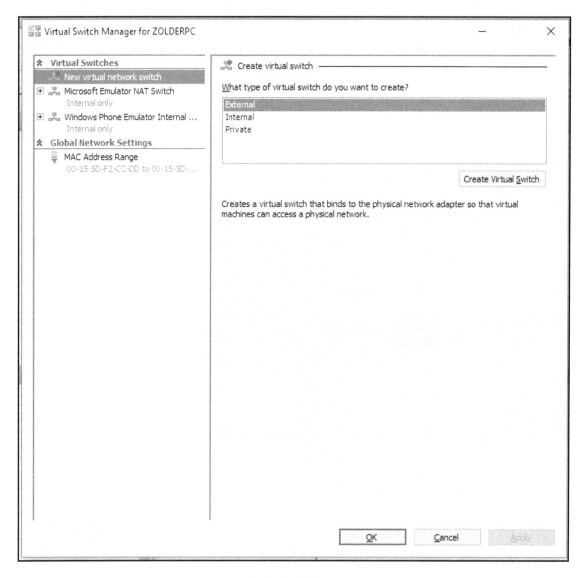

The Virtual Switch Manager

Click on **Create Virtual Switch** and select **External** as the type you want to create.

Give it a name. I called mine `Emulator with Internet`. Connect this switch to your main network connection. In my case it is a wired Ethernet connection, but it could just as easily have been a Wi-Fi connection. It does not matter, as long as you make sure the check next to **Allow management operating system to share this network adapter** is set.

Click **OK**:

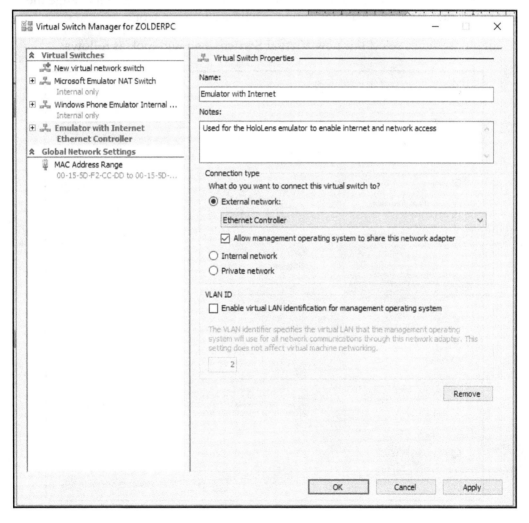

Our new switch

We have now successfully created a new switch. We could have changed the existing ones, but since we do not know (yet) who uses the other switches, we just leave them as they are and create a new one.

Go back to the Hyper-V Manager main screen and right-click on the running instance of the Emulator.

Click **Settings.** In the settings screen you see now, find the entry for the network card that says **Emulator NAT Network Adapter**. There are two adapters; we do not change the **Emulator Internal Network Adapter**, otherwise things will not work.

In the adapter settings, select our new **Virtual Switch**. It should look as follows:

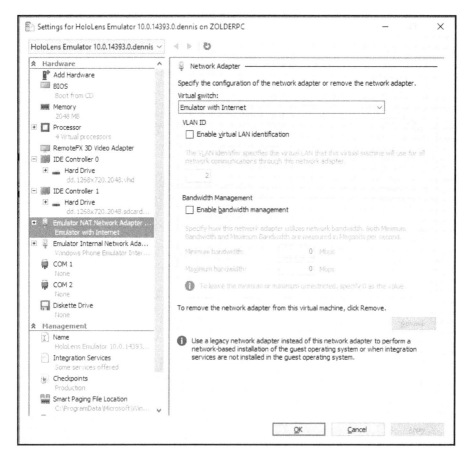

New switch assigned to the network adapter

Click **OK** and go back to the emulator. Notice the start screen of the HoloLens. It still says **Disconnected**. However, if you open Edge browser and navigate to a page, you will see that it does work. My guess is that the Start menu message telling us it is still disconnected has a bug somewhere. The important part is that we now have an emulator we can use to connect to the internet and other HoloLens devices. If your machine has enough memory, or if you have multiple machines, you could even have two emulators talking to one another. Or you can have your emulator talk to an actual device. No matter what your options are, we are going to exchange information between devices now.

Sharing scenarios

Everything we have in our app can be shared. Data, holograms, coordinate systems, you name it. But there are different ways we can set this up. Of course, it all depends on the scenario and what it is you want to achieve. Let us have a look at some of these along with the way to set up networking.

First, we can load data from an external server. This is something we have been doing for ages, but it is a good starting point. A lot of data resides in a cloud solution somewhere and it would be nice to have access to that.

Things get a bit more interesting if we want to talk to another HoloLens. We have two choices here:

* Use a hub or centralized server
* Connect directly to the device

Again, what you choose depends on your needs.

If you need to have multiple devices sharing data, I suggest you go the hub route. This scales much better and you have much better control over the life cycle of the data flow. Remember, *Holographic* apps are *UWP* apps and therefore they may suspend and resume at any given time. It would be a bad thing if the HoloLens that acts as the central server suddenly becomes unreachable because it is suspended.

However, if all you need to do is have two devices sharing information about the coordinate systems they are using, you might as well use a direct peer-to-peer connection.

In the case of the hub scenario, you once again have two choices. First you could use a local server that accepts connections, routes data to the devices, and makes sure nothing weird happens. This is by far the most common scenario. The other option is to use a cloud solution that hosts that same server but can be reached from all over the world by anyone who has the right credentials. That way you can share data and holograms with people all over the globe.

I will not go into the cloud solution. The technology from the HoloLens standpoint is nearly identical for both scenarios and there is tons of information out there on how to host servers on the cloud. I want to focus on the HoloLens-specific technology and how to achieve the results we want in our holographic world.

Using a hub

So, we have decided we have a couple of devices. We need to transfer data from one item to another. To do this we need a server. This can be a very lightweight device, as long as it accepts TCP/IP data coming in over a Wi-Fi connection. It can have any operating system you wish, but I am going for a Windows solution here.

For our demo server, I am writing a very simple console application. These are lightweight and very easy to understand: there is nothing else going on besides the code we write.

Start a new blank solution in Visual Studio. I called mine `SharingSolution.sln`.

Add a new console application to the solution. I called mine `Server`. I will be typing this name in the command line quite a lot to start it up, so I want it to be short and easy to remember. What you decide to name yours it is entirely up to you, of course.

We need to think of some data we want to send. In this very simple example, I will send some coordinates for where we want the cube to appear. Since I want to teach you all about HoloLens and mixed-reality development I will not dive too deep into the intrinsic details of network programming in *UWP* and *Windows* apps. After all, there are tons of great sources of knowledge about this to be found elsewhere; we will focus on what is relevant to us.

Setting up the data

In our server we will serialize data to a string representation. The reason for this is three-fold:

- It is very easy to do
- It allows for many other sources we can connect to
- It is very easy to debug

In our main `Program.cs` file I have added a new class:

```
public class SomeDataStructure
{
    public float X { get; set; }
    public float Y { get; set; }
    public float Z { get; set; }
}
```

As you can see, this is just a Vector3 in disguise. Now, if you want to serialize or deserialize data to a string, one solution jumps to mind: Json.NET from *Newtonsoft*. Add that package through the NuGet Package Manager.

Setting up the TCP/IP layer

If we want to connect our HoloLens to a server application, we need to know where that server is. Since we will be using TCP for our data transfer, we also need to have a port available. I have added the following code to the `Main()` method, so it will run as soon as the console application starts:

```
static void Main(string[] args)
{
    var portNumber = 8000;
    var host = Dns.GetHostEntry(Dns.GetHostName());

    Console.WriteLine("Please use one of these addresses:\n");
    foreach (var address in host.AddressList)
    {
        var addresType = address.AddressFamily.ToString();
        Console.WriteLine($"{address} ({addresType})");
    }
    // Next code will appear here
}
```

I have decided to use port number 8000. I know for a fact there is nothing on my system that uses this port, but you are free to use whatever you want.

Next I get the hostnames of the machine. Since my machine has multiple adapters and each adapter may have more than one IP address, such as a V4 and V6 version, I want to print them out and then I can select one of them. On my machine, the result looks as follows:

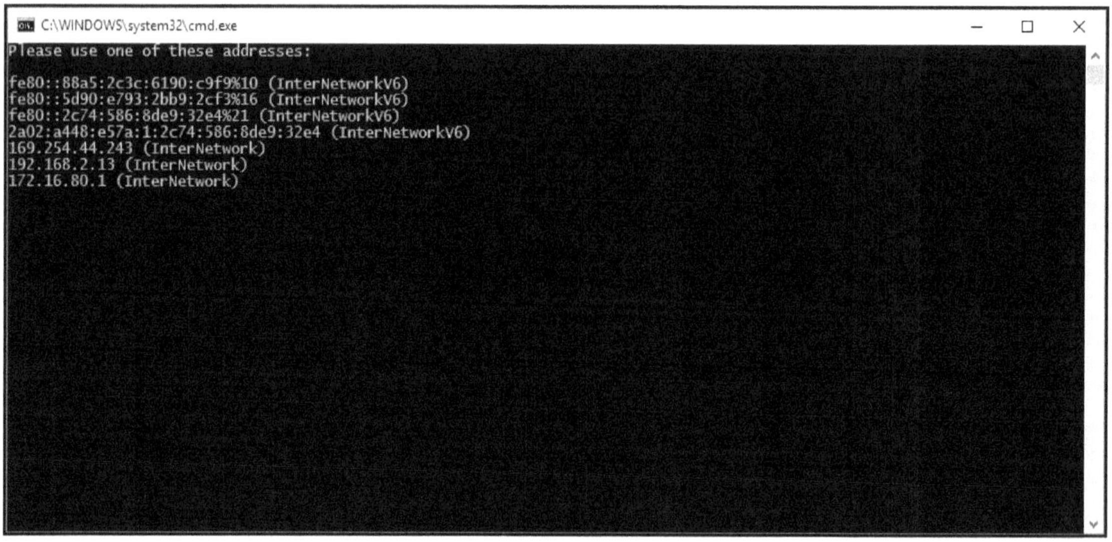

Our server running, showing addresses

Creating the thread for handling data traffic

We want to start a server listening for incoming connections on these IP addresses on port 8000. I want to do this in a separate thread so I can do other stuff in the main program while the server is waiting for something to connect in the background.

Replace the comment line //. The next code will appear here, with the following code:

```
var listener = new
    TcpListener(IPAddress.Any, portNumber);
var connectionHandler = new ConnectionHandler();

var workerThread =
    new Thread(connectionHandler.HandleConnections);
workerThread.Start(listener);

while (!Console.KeyAvailable) { }

Console.WriteLine("Shutting down");
listener.Stop();
workerThread.Abort();
```

This will not compile yet, as we are still missing an important piece. But allow me to walk you through it.

We create an instance of the `TcpListener` class and tell it to use any IP address on our machine, but use port 8000 for this. I have also created a `ConnectionHandler` class, something we will look at next. This connection handler is given to a new thread and we tell this thread to call `HandleConnections` on that class the moment it starts. Then we start the thread, giving it our listener as parameter.

Then we wait. We wait until the user presses any key, after which we kill the listener and the thread. And that is it.

Handling connections

We need to handle the incoming connections. To do this, we need to use the following code:

```
public class ConnectionHandler
{
    TcpListener _listener;

    public void HandleConnections(object dataToPass)
    {

        _listener = dataToPass as TcpListener;
        if (_listener == null)
            return;

        _listener.Start();

        Console.WriteLine("We are waiting for a connection");
        // More code follows here
    }
}
```

This is the start of our `ConnectionHandler` class. We have a private field `listener` of type `TcpListener`. We have the `HandleConnections` method with a parameter called `dataToPass`. Since we call this from `main` and give it the `TcpListener`, we can cast that parameter to the right type and store it. Then we tell the listener to start listening.

Sending data

Now, replace that last comment line with the following:

```
while (true)
    {
        var client = _listener.AcceptTcpClient();

        Console.WriteLine("We are connected");

        var dataStructure = new SomeDataStructure()
        {
            X = -2.0f,
            Y = 0.5f,
            Z = -1.5f
        };

        var dataToSend = JsonConvert.SerializeObject(dataStructure);
        using (var writer = new StreamWriter(client.GetStream()))
        {
            writer.Write(dataToSend);
            writer.Flush();
        }
        client.Close();
    }
```

This is an endless loop. Well, it is endless until somebody presses a key in the main thread that will kill this thread. We call `AcceptTcpClient`. This is a blocking call that waits until someone actually tries to connect to our server on port `8000`. The moment this happens, we create a new instance of our data structure, make a string representation of it using Json.NET, and send it over the network by using the `StreamWriter` class. The constructor of this class gets the stream from our client and we write the data.

Then we kill the connection, so we are ready for another one.

And that is all there is to it. We now have a TCP/IP-based server application that can send out cube coordinates to any HoloLens app willing to use it. This is what we will build now.

Creating the mixed-reality client app

In the same Visual Studio solution start a new *Holographic* app. You know, the one with the cube; the one we have been using all the time.

First, we will add a new class to our app. Use the same code as before to define the `SomeDataStructure` class. In an ideal world, you would set up some sort of library that handles all these data structures, but for now a simple copy will do.

Next, add a reference to Json.NET from NuGet. At the time of writing , the latest version was 10.0.1, but that version is incompatible with the other packages the HoloLens template uses, so I had to downgrade it to version 9.0.1. You might have to do to the same: if you get any error while installing the package, try an earlier version.

I called my `DataCapableApp`. In the main class, where most of the work happens, I have added a new method called `SetupTcpConnection()`. I call this method from the end of the `SetHolographicSpace` and `LoadAppState` methods. You have seen these before; this is the same way we dealt with the anchor store.

I also added a `private` field to the class:

```
private StreamSocket _socket;
```

This is what we will use to communicate with our server.

In the `SaveAppState` method I do some cleaning up:

```
public void SaveAppState()
{
    //
    // TODO: Insert code here to save your app state.
    //       This method is called when the app is about to suspend.
    //
    //       For example, store information in the SpatialAnchorStore.
    //
    if (_socket != null)
    {
        _socket.Dispose();
        _socket = null;
    }
}
```

I have also added that code to the `Dispose()` method. After all, we do not want connections to remain open all the time. These are the kind of thing we need to clean up after usage.

Setting up the connection

It is time to set up the connection. To do this, we need to check if we have a socket or not. If we do not, something is wrong and we just abort. If we do have one, we can use it to set up the connection, as follows:

```
private void SetupTcpConnection()
{
    if (_socket != null)
        return;

    _socket = new StreamSocket();

    var hostName = new HostName("192.168.2.13");
    var socketConnectionAwaiter = _socket.ConnectAsync(hostName, "8000");
    var handler = new
AsyncActionCompletedHandler(SocketConnectionCompleted);
    socketConnectionAwaiter.Completed = handler;
}
```

I set (hardcoded) the IP address of my server and the port number 8000. As you can see, the code here is slightly different than we saw on the server side, but that is the nature of UWP apps; they are different.

Now, we call `ConnectAsync`. In the documentation you will see that the correct usage of this is different from what I will show you here. It should look as follows:

```
await _socket.ConnectAsync(hostName, "8000");
// Handle the data coming out of the socket
```

Unfortunately, for some reason this does not work in a HoloLens app, although this is the correct way to do this. Instead, we have to do it the way I am showing you.

The result of the `ConnectAsync()` method is an `IAsyncAction`. In the next line, I create a new instance of an `AsyncActionCompletedHandler`, which is some sort of event that gets called the moment the method is done or, in our case, as soon as the connection has been made. We give it a callback method named `SocketConnectionCompleted`. Then we tell the awaiter to actually use this event handler when it is completed.

Consuming the connection

The event that is being called, SocketConnectionCompleted, should of course consume the connection and send data on it. That is what it is all about. This is what it looks like:

```
void SocketConnectionCompleted(IAsyncAction action, AsyncStatus status)
{
    if (status != AsyncStatus.Completed)
    {
        // Something went wrong.
        // We should probably deal with this
        _socket.Dispose();
        _socket = null;
        return;
    }

    // Read the data
    using (var reader = new
StreamReader(_socket.InputStream.AsStreamForRead()))
    {
        var data = reader.ReadToEnd();
        var newCubePosition =
JsonConvert.DeserializeObject<SomeDataStructure>(data);

        spinningCubeRenderer.PositionHologram(
            new Vector3(
                newCubePosition.X,
                newCubePosition.Y,
                newCubePosition.Z));
    }
}
```

The SocketConnectionCompleted method is not that hard. First, we check the status: did we actually get a connection or not? If we did not, we clean up. Something went wrong and there is no use continuing.

If we did get the connection, we can create a StreamReader. This class is an IDisposable so we use the using statement. We give it our _socket.InputStream to read from, which we convert to a readable stream first.

Now we read all available data, put that in a string, deserialize that string into an object, and make a new Vector3 out of that data.

I have also slightly altered our `SpinningCubeRenderer` class and given it an overload of the `PositionHologram` method, so that it places it at the given spot:

```
public void PositionHologram(Vector3 newPosition)
{
    this.position = newPosition;
}
```

Not exactly rocket science, is it?

And that is all there is to it. Make sure you run both the server and the HoloLens app at the same time and see the cube appear in its new position. We have managed to control our HoloLens app from the outside!

Connecting from Unity3D

We can use our server as a source for Unity3D apps as well. But I have to warn you: the code will look ugly. We will fix this more or less in the next chapter, but for now we just have to live with it.

Create a new Unity3D project and set it up to target the HoloLens. Add something interesting to the scene, such as a cube somewhere. Attach a new script to that cube. This should not pose a problem anymore as we have done it numerous times.

Open the script in Visual Studio.

We do not need Json.NET here. Unity3D has built-in support for JSON. However, the way this library handles JSON data is slightly different, so we have to modify our data structure a bit. This is what I added to my code file:

```
[Serializable]
public class SomeDataStructure
{
    public float X;
    public float Y;
    public float Z;
}
```

I have to mark the class with the `[Serializable]` attribute. Next I changed all auto-properties to be public fields. But otherwise it is just the same. After all, the data that is being transferred over the network is just a data representation, looking as follows:

```
{"X":-2.0,"Y":0.5,"Z":-1.5}
```

As you can see, the class name is not important and neither is the type of the fields or properties. All that matters is the order of the fields, their names, and their types, so our change does not interfere with the data. It will work.

In the `Start()` method of the new class I have added the following code:

```
async void Start()
{
    var socket = new StreamSocket();
    var hostName = new HostName("192.168.2.13");
    await socket.ConnectAsync(hostName, "8000");

    using (var reader =
        new StreamReader(socket.InputStream.AsStreamForRead()))
    {
        var data = reader.ReadToEnd();
        var cubePosition =
            JsonUtility.FromJson<SomeDataStructure>(data);

        _newPosition =
            new Vector3(
                cubePosition.X,
                cubePosition.Y,
                cubePosition.Z);
        _dataHasBeenLoaded = true;
    }
}
```

I also added two new fields to the class:

```
bool _dataHasBeenLoaded;
Vector3 _newPosition;

And I have changed the Update() method:
void Update()
{
    if (_dataHasBeenLoaded)
    {
        this.transform.position = _newPosition;
        _dataHasBeenLoaded = false;
    }
}
```

Let me walk you through it.

We created a socket and connected that to the server app we created previously. The connection can be made with the await keyword this time, so there is no need for the callback mechanism I showed you earlier.

The moment the connection is made, we start to read the data. We get that from the streams, put it in `StreamReader` and get the resulting string. The built-in `JsonUtility.FromJason<>()` method will transform this.

We take the result and store this in the `_newPosition` field. You may wonder why we do not put it in the `transform.position` field immediately. The answer is that, due to the way this code works, this is being done in another thread. Unity3D does not allow us to handle the transform in a thread other than the main thread, so we have to store it somewhere and wait for `Update()` to pick it up. This will be done the moment the `_dataHasBeenLoaded` flag has been set.

Run the server application we created previously and then start this app. You will see the splash screen, followed by nothing. If you look to the left and expect the cube to be there, just like it was in the DirectX sample, you might be surprised not to see anything. The reason is quite straightforward: you should be looking behind you. Remember, in Unity3D positive Z-values point to the front; in DirectX positive Z points to the back. So the Z-values are flipped and the cube appears somewhere else.

This is something to consider if you share coordinates like this: the server sends out some data but the actual meaning of this data is dependent on the receiving application. It is not a big problem but it might be something to keep in mind while developing.

If you switch back to Unity3D you will see that it does not like the code we just have written. There will be error after error.

Why does this happen and why does our code still work? Well, this is because Unity3D runs a different version of the .NET framework than the HoloLens does. We will deal with this in the next chapter (more or less) but for now we can fix it by adding conditional compilation directives to our code.

We need to surround all code that the Unity3D engine does not understand with the statement pair `#if WINDOWS_UWP` / `#endif`.

This will result in the Unity3D engine ignoring this code, while the Visual Studio compiler still sees the code and compiles it.

We need to do this for some using statements, the async keyword, the whole data retrieval block, and the `[Serializable]` keyword. It looks as follows.

First, the `using` statements:

```
using UnityEngine;
#if WINDOWS_UWP
using System;
using System.IO;
using Windows.Networking;
using Windows.Networking.Sockets;
#endif
```

Now, the signature line of the `Start()` method:

```
#if WINDOWS_UWP
    async
#endif
    void Start()
    {
```

I know, it does not look very appealing.

We could wrap everything in the `Start()` method this way as well. After all, this code runs only in the device and not in the Unity3D editor:

```
#if WINDOWS_UWP
    await socket.ConnectAsync(hostName, "8000");
    //... rest of the code
#endif
```

And last but not least:

```
#if WINDOWS_UWP
[Serializable]
#endif
public class SomeDataStructure
{
    public float X;
    public float Y;
    public float Z;
}
```

I warned you, it is going to be ugly. We can improve this a bit but for now it will do. If you run the app you will find it works just as before, but in Unity3D the errors will be gone.

Peer to peer

We have been using a server app that handles the connections. We could change the code in the device to also send and receive data. Due to the nature of TCP, in UWP apps we need two connections; although you can send and receive data on the same socket, there is no way to create a callback that is called when data is available.

The great thing about having a central server is that multiple devices can connect to it. You could even host that server somewhere in the cloud and share data with devices all over the world.

But what if you have two devices that are in the same area and need to share some data every now and then? Would it not be a better solution to have them talk to one and another directly? This will remove the dependency on a new machine that sits in the middle.

Well, you can. You can get rid of the server application and have all that code in the HoloLens. However, if we are going to have two devices talk, there are some smarter things we can do. We can have devices find each other and have a better way of communicating. I will show you how.

Introducing Bluetooth advertisements

If we want to get rid of the server in between, we are faced with a small challenge. We have two devices running the same app. Which one will act as the server, and which one will be the client? There are several options; the best one is dependent on your scenario:

- The first app running will be the server and the second will be the client
- All apps run as both server and client

If you go for the first option you have to know if the app that starts is actually the first one running so it can act as a central server. We will discover how to do this shortly.

If you go for the second option, it does not really matter. The moment you decide you have something to share with the world, or rather, with other HoloLens devices out there, you can see whether you can find other machines running the same app, connect to them, tell them what you want to say, and disconnect. In the meantime, you will be listening for incoming connections in case the other devices want to talk to you.

Both rely on a way to find other machines. There are multiple ways to do this. One is Wi-Fi Direct, which I will not go into. Another way is using Bluetooth.

With Bluetooth LE (which stands for Low Energy) you can transform your HoloLens into a kind of beacon, constantly emitting signals telling the world it is here to be talked and listened to. This sounds like the thing we need, so let us look at how to do this:

1. Start up a new application. You know the drill, the spinning cube again.
2. Make sure the capabilities are set. We want network options, but this time we also want Bluetooth.

Enabling Bluetooth capabilities

Setting up the advertisement

In the `SetHolographicSpace` method, add a call to the `SetupBluetoothAdvertisement();` method. Also add a `private` field of type `BluetoothLEAdvertisementPublisher` to the class and call it `_publisher`:

```
BluetoothLEAdvertisementPublisher _publisher;
```

The method we call looks as follows:

```
void SetupBluetoothAdvertisement()
{
    _publisher = new BluetoothLEAdvertisementPublisher();
    var manufacturerData = new BluetoothLEManufacturerData();
    manufacturerData.CompanyId = 0xFFFE;

    var myIpAddress = GetMyIPAddress();

    var writer = new DataWriter();
    writer.WriteString(myIpAddress);
    manufacturerData.Data = writer.DetachBuffer();

    _publisher.Advertisement.ManufacturerData.Add(manufacturerData);
    _publisher.Start();
}
```

First, we create an instance of `_publisher`. This publisher needs some data to distinguish itself from all the other publishers around us broadcasting Bluetooth signals. And trust me, there are a lot of them. I am currently in my office writing this and by simply looking around I can see the following:

- A Bluetooth keyboard
- A Bluetooth mouse
- A Bluetooth headset for my music
- My phone emitting Bluetooth signals
- My laptop next to me, doing the same
- A pair of Bluetooth speakers
- My printer, also Bluetooth-capable
- My sports watch
- Two HoloLens devices, doing the same once we have this sample done

And that is just within a one-meter radius of me.

Each company using Bluetooth should have a company ID. The Bluetooth consortium maintains a list of these IDs. Officially, you cannot just pick a number and use that. However, numbers starting with 0XFF00 are considered to be free to use, although the official statement says otherwise. I have chosen 0XFFFE as my company ID here, and that is what I set in the manufacturerData instance.

In our previous samples we had a hardcoded IP address. In this sample, I am using some code to get the actual address of our device:

```
string GetMyIPAddress()
{

    var icp = NetworkInformation.GetInternetConnectionProfile();
    if (icp == null)
        return string.Empty;
    var adapter = icp.NetworkAdapter;
    if (adapter == null)
        return string.Empty;

    var hostname = NetworkInformation.GetHostNames()
        .FirstOrDefault(
            hn => hn.IPInformation?.NetworkAdapter != null
            && hn.Type == HostNameType.Ipv4
            && hn.IPInformation.NetworkAdapter.NetworkAdapterId ==
icp.NetworkAdapter.NetworkAdapterId
            );

    return hostname.CanonicalName;
}
```

What we do here is get information about the way this device is connected to the outside world, as contained in InternetConnectionProfile. This information has details about the network adapter we are using for this. We go through the list of all hostnames we have. As you will remember, there may be quite a few of them. Here we are only interested in the hostnames that fit the following criteria:

- They are connected to an adapter
- They are of the type IPV4
- They are used to connect to the outside world

We return this hostname as a string, from which we add the data to _publisher and start publishing.

You may wonder why we use the more or less deprecated IPV4 for this instead of the much better IPV6. The answer is: Bluetooth Advertisement is a low-energy level protocol, allowing for only about 20 bytes to be sent in the payload. Since IPV6 addresses are quite large, they will not fit in the payload. IPV4 addresses are smaller in size and thus can be sent along.

Watching for other devices

This is just one side of the story. The other side is listening for incoming connections. In the `SetHolographicSpace` method, add a call to `SetupBluetoothWatcher()` and add a new field to the class:

```
BluetoothLEAdvertisementWatcher _watcher;
```

We will use this as follows:

```
void SetupBluetoothWatcher()
{
    _watcher = new BluetoothLEAdvertisementWatcher();
    _watcher.Received += BluetoothWatcher_Connected;
    var manufacturerData = new BluetoothLEManufacturerData();
    manufacturerData.CompanyId = 0xFFFE;
_watcher.AdvertisementFilter.Advertisement.ManufacturerData.Add(manufacture
rData);
    _watcher.Start();
}
```

We create the watcher and add an `eventhandler` in case we see something. Next we tell the watcher we are only interested in things coming from apps from the company identified by the ID `0xFFFE`, which is us.

Then we start the watcher.

Handling found devices

It is physically impossible to start two devices at the same time. There is always a delay between them, which means that one device will be broadcasting sooner than the other. So, one device will get the `BluetoothWatcher_Connected` event before the other one.

If that happens, you should disable both the publisher and the watcher, otherwise they will connecting again and again.

We can get to the data in the `args` parameter and read out the IP address of the sender. Once we have that, we can set up a connection like we did before. However, this time we know where the device is to be found and that it is probably alive.

Let us have a look at that.

Connecting to the other HoloLens

In the code sample where we used the server, we set up a TcpClient instance to do the network things. This time, we will do something else. In the `SetHolographicSpace` method, call the method we are about write:

```
SetupDatagramServer();
```

Also call the implementation:

```
void SetupDatagramServer()
{
    _serverSocket = new DatagramSocket();
    _serverSocket.MessageReceived += MessageReceived;
    var bindAwaiter = _serverSocket.BindServiceNameAsync("8000");
    var connectionCompletedHandler = new
AsyncActionCompletedHandler(OnConnectionCompleted);
    bindAwaiter.Completed = connectionCompletedHandler;
}
```

This time we use a `DatagramSocket`. This is a UDP-based connection. The difference between TCP and UDP is mainly that UDP is a more lightweight, loosely coupled protocol. TCP has all sorts of mechanisms built in to ensure delivery, whereas UDP just sends out the data and leaves it at that. For us, however, in this case, we can live with that. If you require TCP you are more than welcome to use it.

`_serverSocket` (do not forget to add the field to the class) has a handy event called `MessageReceived`, which is called whenever data is available.

We make sure we are listening to port `8000` and that is it. The `OnConnectionCompleted` method is very, very simple:

```
void OnConnectionCompleted(IAsyncAction action, AsyncStatus status)
{
    // We are ready to go!
}
```

We do not need to do anything here, but you could set flags, start the Bluetooth code, or anything else you might need.

That takes care of the server. So, if another device starts up and sends us messages on the UDP layer, we can receive them and do something with that. Something like the following, for instance:

```
private void MessageReceived(DatagramSocket sender,
DatagramSocketMessageReceivedEventArgs args)
{
    var inputStream = args.GetDataStream();
    using (var reader = new StreamReader(inputStream.AsStreamForRead()))
    {
        string data = reader.ReadToEnd();
    }
}
```

We have seen this before. Right?

All that is left to do is set up the other side. If we start our app and find another device broadcasting over Bluetooth, we should set up a connection. This is done in the `BluetoothWatcher_Connected` event handler.

I will give you the code first, and then we will walk through it:

```
async void BluetoothWatcher_Connected(BluetoothLEAdvertisementWatcher
sender, BluetoothLEAdvertisementReceivedEventArgs args)
{
    // Stop all Bluetooth activities
    _publisher.Stop();
    _publisher = null;
    _watcher.Stop();
    _watcher = null;

    // Get the IP Address from the publishing device
    BluetoothLEAdvertisementDataSection dataSection =
args.Advertisement.DataSections.FirstOrDefault();
    if (dataSection == default(BluetoothLEAdvertisementDataSection))
        return;

    var dataReader = DataReader.FromBuffer(dataSection.Data);
    byte[] payload = new byte[dataReader.UnconsumedBufferLength - 2];
    dataReader.ReadBytes(payload);
    var ipAddress = Encoding.UTF8.GetString(payload, 2, payload.Length -
2);

    _clientSocket = new DatagramSocket();
    _clientSocket.MessageReceived += ClientSocket_MessageReceived;
    await _clientSocket.ConnectAsync(new HostName(ipAddress), "8000");
}
```

There is a lot happening here. First of all, we stop all Bluetooth activities. We are apparently acting as the client so there must be a server somewhere. We do not need to keep watching for other devices.

We get the information about the other device in the `args` parameter. This contains quite a lot of data, but we are interested in the first `dataSection` only.

We set up a reader and read the bytes from the IBuffer within that data section. We skip the first two bytes. In case you are wondering why, do you remember the company ID flag `0xFFFE` that we used earlier? This is the content of the first two bytes, which we do not need. The rest of the buffer is the payload message, or in our case the UTF8-encoded string containing the IP address of the server.

We set up a `DatagramSocket`, set up an event handler, and connect to it. We are ready to send and receive data now!

Sharing world coordinates

So far, we have been sending random data back and forth. This is great; this means you can have users interact with each other's devices over the network. Imagine we have an app that has an option that toggles the state of a hologram. If one user toggles the state, we can send a message to the other user so that her hologram does the same.

However, what we have not done yet is share coordinates. If we want to place a hologram in the center of a table, then it would make sense if both users saw that object in the same location.

Of course, this only works if the users are in the same area. If they are remote, then you cannot do this. Remember the remark I made when we talked about loading spatial anchors, this can go wrong if the HoloLens does not recognize the room. The same goes for sharing anchors. You can share your anchors but there is no guarantee the receiving device actually understands this. You have to make sure your code handles this.

How would we do this?

Sharing spatial anchors in DirectX

You may be surprised. If you have your app set up to use TCP to share data, you have done 90% of the work you need to do to share anchors as well.

First, we need permission to share anchors. This is similar to the code we used to request access to the depth sensors. The app has declared that it wants access to the spatial capabilities and here we check to see if we have actually been granted that right. We need to do that when we send our coordinates, and when we want to receive them:

```
private async void ShareCoordinates(Dictionary<string, SpatialAnchor>
anchors, StreamSocket stream)
{
    var requestResult = await
SpatialAnchorTransferManager.RequestAccessAsync();
    if (requestResult != SpatialPerceptionAccessStatus.Allowed)
    {
        // Oops
        return;
    }

    await SpatialAnchorTransferManager.TryExportAnchorsAsync(anchors,
stream.OutputStream);
}

private async Task<IReadOnlyDictionary<string, SpatialAnchor>>
GetCoordinates(StreamSocket stream)
{
    var requestResult = await
SpatialAnchorTransferManager.RequestAccessAsync();
    if (requestResult != SpatialPerceptionAccessStatus.Allowed)
    {
        // Oops
        return null;
    }

    var result = await
SpatialAnchorTransferManager.TryImportAnchorsAsync(stream.InputStream);
    return result;
}
```

And that is it. You can call these methods and give them the streams and the dictionary containing the string identifiers and the anchors.

Should you send one or multiple anchors?

You have to make a choice. You can send an anchor when you think you need to, or you can save it all up and send a batch. Again, this depends on your scenario and your needs. But there is something you should know about this: sending a batch of anchors not only sends the coordinate systems in relation to the objects around them, it also sends information about the relationship between the anchors. This means that the relative position of the anchors remains intact during the transfer. If you send them one by one, this relationship is lost and all the system has in order to place the objects is the position in relation to the room. This could be good enough, but I have found that having more information about the objects is better. Thus, my advice to you is to bundle them together and send them off in one go, if you can. This will give you a much better experience.

Sharing world anchors in Unity3D

The way of working in Unity3D is about the same. You need to have a way to share the actual bytes, but we have covered that already.

If you want to share world anchors, and remember, world anchors are spatial anchors attached to objects in Unity3D, the amount of work you have to do is very limited. All you need to do is use a `WorldAnchorTransferBatch`, similar to the `SpatialAnchorTransferManager` in DirectX.

Let me show you.

First, I extended our *GuitarPrefab*. I have added a simple script, which has a variable in it that uniquely identifies it, so we can use that when we need the anchors. The field is called `AnchorName`:

```
using UnityEngine;

public class Identifier : MonoBehaviour {

    [Tooltip("The unique name of the anchor")]
    public string AnchorName;
}
```

To add this to the prefab you have to drag the prefab in the scene. Then you add the script to that instance. Remove the prefab from the prefab folder and then drag it from the scene back into the folder. Now remove it from the scene and remember to update all scripts that reference this prefab:

- Main camera: GestureHandler script
- Main camera: VoiceRecognizer script

It is quite cumbersome, but that is the way it is.

Sending the data from Unity3D

Open the GestureHandler script and use the new variable, but first add the field containing all anchors and their names to this script:

```
private Dictionary<string, WorldAnchor> _anchors = new Dictionary<string, WorldAnchor>();
```

And at the end of the `GestureRecognizedOnTappedEvent` method:

```
newGuitar.GetComponent<Identifier>().AnchorName = anchorName;
_anchors.Add(anchorName, worldAnchor);
```

I have added a new script to the camera in our *RockOn* app. I called it `ExportImportManager`. I will not show you how to set up the TCP connection to the server app; we did that a couple of pages earlier.

I have decided that, whenever we create a new guitar, we will broadcast this to the world and send the coordinates out there, so other apps can do the same. Here we go.

Below the two lines we just added, add a third one:

```
TransferAnchor(anchorName, worldAnchor);
```

The implementation looks as follows:

```
void TransferAnchor(string anchorName, WorldAnchor worldAnchor)
{
    var batch = new WorldAnchorTransferBatch();
    batch.AddWorldAnchor(anchorName, worldAnchor);
    WorldAnchorTransferBatch.ExportAsync(batch, OnDataAvailable, OnDataExported);
}

private void OnDataAvailable(byte[] data)
{
```

```
            // Set up the TCP connection,
            // send the data (byte[]) to the server

    }
    private void OnDataExported(SerializationCompletionReason reason)
    {
        if(reason != SerializationCompletionReason.Succeeded)
        {
            // Something went wrong....
        }
        else
        {
            // It went ok.
            // Inform the client everything worked!
        }
    }
}
```

We create an instance of the `WorldAnchorTransferBatch` and give it the new anchor and anchor name. Then we export it. We define two callbacks, such as one when all the serialization is done (`OnDataAvailable`) and one when all data is actually sent.

In `OnDataAvailable` we are given an array of bytes, containing all the anchors we want to export. Here we can set up a connection to the server that will then send it through to the other clients.

`OnDataExported` is called when all the data is sent. You may use this to inform the server, and thus all clients, that you are done sending the data. After all, data may be sent in chunks and you need to tell them when all the data is done being sent. Anchor data can get quite large.

Receiving the data in Unity3D

Receiving the data is similar. First, we need to have some TCP listener that responds to data being sent over. Once that happens, we will end up with a large `byte[]` that we need to transform:

```
private void ReceiveNewAnchor(byte[] rawData)
{
    WorldAnchorTransferBatch.ImportAsync(rawData, OnReceiveCompleted);
}

private void OnReceiveCompleted(SerializationCompletionReason reason,
WorldAnchorTransferBatch batch)
{
    if (reason != SerializationCompletionReason.Succeeded)
    {
```

```
        // Oops..
        return;
    }

    var allIds = batch.GetAllIds();
    foreach (var id in allIds)
    {
        GameObject newGuitar = Instantiate(objectToPlace);
        newGuitar.GetComponent<Identifier>().AnchorName = id;
        var anchor = batch.LockObject(id, newGuitar);

        _anchors.Add(id, anchor);
    }
}
```

When we get the raw data, we call `ReceiveNewAnchor()`. This takes that data and feeds it to the `WorldAnchorTransferBatch.ImportAsync()` method.

That method has a callback, called `OnReceiveCompleted()`. In that callback, we check if everything went OK. If it did not, we return. If it did, we go through all the IDs we are given, create a new guitar, and add it to our scene. Then, with a call to `batch.LockObject()`, we give it the anchor and set its position in our world.

If you run this with two devices in the same room you will find that, when one user adds a guitar somewhere, the other user will see it appearing at the same time. The objects will be synchronized and the experience is now truly shared.

Summary

In this chapter, we have learned about the different coordinate systems we can have. There is the normal one we have been using the whole time, called **stationary frame of reference**; there is one that stays at the same distance from the user no matter where they go, called **attached frame of reference**; and we have local systems, called **spatial anchors** in DirectX and **world anchors** in Unity3d.

We have looked at how to use TCP/IP to connect to a central server and share data. After that we learned how to use Bluetooth to tell the world the device is here and ready to talk. We also took a look at using datagrams or UDP to set up a quick connection to share data.

Finally, we explored how easy it is to share world or spatial anchors. We can now share holograms with other users on other devices, no matter where they are.

8
Speed Up Your Development - Advanced Unity3D

In the previous chapter, you saw a glimpse of the trouble a Unity3D developer has to go through. We had to make sure our code still worked and even compiled by using statements such as `#if WINDOWS_UWP` or `#if UNITY_EDITOR`.

I promised you that we would fix this, and we will do that right now. However, it will not be easy or pretty. The code will be much more readable, but you will have a lot more work than you might want to do. As usual, programming is always a trade-off between clean code and quick code. There is no such thing as clean and quick.

Framework versions

Let us examine what the problem is. I mean, why do we have to bother with all this? If you are new to Unity3D, or at least--new to it before you started reading this book, you might be bewildered with the hurdles you have to take before you can do any decent developing. The reason for this lies in the fact that Unity3D is not a programming environment. It is a multi-platform game engine and game development tool. And this is the reason why we have the problems we face right now.

The whole workflow is not geared towards developers. It is almost as if the people at Unity3D said--"Developers are smart people; they will figure this stuff out themselves. We need to focus on the productivity of the game designers".

I am not suggesting that this is what they thought. In honesty, I am sure they thought the opposite: they love developers. But they did need to make a trade-off between helping developers and helping game designers. A trade-off always means that nobody gets what they wanted, although they did get what they needed.

The biggest issue, however, lies in the fact that Unity3D is a multi-platform tool. It is not written for HoloLens only. It was written to build games for PC, Mac, TVs, mobile devices, and so on. It needs to run on different platforms such as Windows, macOS, Linux, Tizen, Android, iOS, and more.

The designers had to make a choice. They needed powerful scripting that would run on all platforms. And they found it, in the shape of the Mono runtime.

Mono runtime

When the .NET framework came out, Microsoft told the world that it was based on the open standard **Common Language Infrastructure** (**CLI**). Miguel de Icaza, a developer who early on saw the potential of .NET realized, that if the CLI was open, anyone could make their own version of the .NET framework. He knew the power of the framework, but wanted to use it on Linux. So he ported .NET.

His efforts led to the creation of the Mono framework, a version of .NET based on the CLI specifications, but running on a multitude of platforms and operating systems. This is the basis for Xamarin, the multi-platform tool. This story went full circle when Microsoft bought Xamarin, but that has nothing to do with our story here.

Mono is running on all the platforms we just discussed. But Mono is not .NET. The people at Microsoft are constantly updating .NET and C#, the language most people use to build .NET applications. Mono, being an open source initiative relying on the goodwill of volunteers, cannot keep up with the engineers working for a big company such as Microsoft. Unavoidably, they fall behind. However, the things they do write works on all these different machines. It was a logical choice for the people at Unity3D to choose Mono as their multi-platform scripting tool.

Currently, at the time of writing, the .NET framework is at version 4.6.1, with great features such as async/await, and advanced lambdas. Mono has none of those. You could say Mono still runs what .NET had back in version 3.5. Actually, that is exactly the level Mono is currently in--it supports all the features of .NET 3.5 and no features of the .NET 4.0 release and beyond.

.NET in HoloLens

HoloLens runs on Windows 10. It is constantly updated. The version of Windows 10 it runs is of course not the normal Windows version you use on your day-to-day work machine. It is a variation of the phone version, with bits of the IoT stuff in it. But the core is shared amongst all other versions. This means that most of the Windows 10 UWP apps run on all devices. Naturally, Microsoft wants us to use the .NET framework. They support the latest and greatest version in HoloLens. The moment a new version comes out you can simply install the framework on HoloLens and use it immediately. As a developer, I really love that. The new features make lives so much easier. I will give you an example. Say you want to have a string with the current time in it. Until recently you had to use this:

```
var myString =
    String.Format(
        "This is the time: {0}",
        DateTime.Now.TimeOfDay);
```

This is not too bad, but compare this to the version we can use in the latest version of the tools:

```
var myString = $"This is the time: {DateTime.Now.TimeOfDay}";
```

This is much more readable, which is something I really enjoy in code.

There are lots of things like this. I mentioned async/await before, but that is just one of the many things that make life easier.

But we cannot use it in Unity3D, since it is not supported in .NET 3.5.

Script compiling in Unity3D

The moment you add a script to your Unity3D project, several things happen:

- The file gets a .cs extension
- The file will be added to the Visual Studio solution containing all scripts
- The script will be compiled using the Mono C# compiler
- A .meta file with the same name as the original file will be added

To start with the fourth bullet point, the meta files are Unity3D's way of keeping track of what is part of your project. Every file belonging to your project will have an associated .meta file. You do not have to do anything for this; this is done automatically.

The file gets the correct extension and is added to the solution. This solution is not the one we use to deploy, but we can use it to edit scripts. The nice thing about this solution is that it is constantly being updated. If you open this solution, which is found in the root folder of your project, you will see one project, containing all scripts in an Assets folder. The moment you add a script in Unity3D and save the scene, you will see it appear in Visual Studio immediately. There is no need to build or compile anything.

The script will be compiled though, but Unity3D will take care of this. It does so using its own Mono compiler, which, as we saw before, is basically a .NET 3.5 based compiler.

Compilation errors and how to fix them

The moment you have something in your script that is not .NET 3.5 based, you will see Unity3D complaining. If we use the code we just mentioned, using the `$"{}"` syntax, Unity3D will say this:

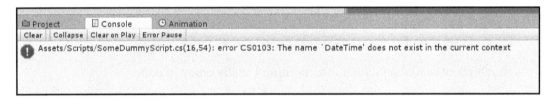

Unity3D complaining about .NET features

Unity3D does not understand what we are doing here: we are using C# 4.0 and beyond features. If we replaced the **DateTime** feature with something it will understand, it will complain about the `$` being a feature that's way too advanced.

This error stops you from working all together. Yes, you can add new GameObjects to your scene if you want to, but you cannot build the project and deploy it to HoloLens. That last part is a shame, because we know for a fact that HoloLens knows how to deal with this code: there is nothing wrong with it from the Windows 10 perspective.

Three possible solutions

There are three possible solutions to this problem. One is easy to build but very inconvenient, the second is less inconvenient but results in less readable code, and the third option is the best when it comes to maintainability but requires the most attention and work from the developer. I suggest you pick the best option for your situation.

Option 1 - do not go back and forth

This is the easiest solution, although it is not very practical. Yet, I use it during demos and quick prototyping.

Create your Unity3D project. Place all the GameObjects. Add all scripts and write some code in them. Build the project and open the final solution in Visual Studio. Only then, and not earlier, add the code that might offend Unity3D. Compile and deploy to HoloLens. If you find bugs in your code, fix them and try again. However, do not go back to Unity3D. In fact, close it down so it will not get in your way.

If you need to change something in your Unity3D project after this, you have a problem. Unity3D will load your project, but it will refuse to rebuild due to the errors. So you have one chance to get things right.

Again, for simple demos this will do. This is, of course, not very practical in a real project. So, let us have a look at option 2.

Option 2 - sprinkle the code with #if/#endif statements

The second option is the one that is being suggested as the best option. And I agree: it is quite an easy way to get the results we want. I do not think that it is the best option, but I use this one in proof-of-concept type of projects, software that I know will never be looked at again in a couple of months.

You get results fairly quickly, but the code tends to get less readable. That is OK in the short run, but will be a problem later on, which is why I do not use it in software that goes beyond the proof of concept phase.

Unity3D uses some conditional compilation defines to identify that this is actually a Unity3D project. If you open the properties of the Assembly-C Sharp project, you will see this:

Conditional compilation symbols in Unity3D

The symbols being defined are as follows:

```
ENABLE_PROFILER;UNITY_5_3_OR_NEWER;UNITY_5_4_OR_NEWER;UNITY_5_5_OR_NEWER;UN
ITY_5_5_0;UNITY_5_5;UNITY_5;ENABLE_AUDIO;ENABLE_CACHING;ENABLE_CLOTH;ENABLE
_GENERICS;ENABLE_MICROPHONE;ENABLE_MULTIPLE_DISPLAYS;ENABLE_PHYSICS;ENABLE_
SPRITERENDERER_FLIPPING;ENABLE_SPRITES;ENABLE_TERRAIN;ENABLE_UNET;ENABLE_LZ
MA;ENABLE_UNITYEVENTS;ENABLE_WEBCAM;ENABLE_WWW;ENABLE_CLOUD_SERVICES_COLLAB
;ENABLE_CLOUD_HUB;ENABLE_CLOUD_PROJECT_ID;ENABLE_CLOUD_SERVICES_UNET;ENABLE
_CLOUD_SERVICES_BUILD;ENABLE_CLOUD_LICENSE;ENABLE_EDITOR_METRICS;ENABLE_EDI
TOR_METRICS_CACHING;INCLUDE_DYNAMIC_GI;INCLUDE_GI;RENDER_SOFTWARE_CURSOR;IN
CLUDE_PUBNUB;ENABLE_PLAYMODE_TESTS_RUNNER;ENABLE_SCRIPTING_NEW_CSHARP_COMPI
LER;UNITY_METRO;UNITY_METRO_API;UNITY_WINRT;ENABLE_WINRT_PINVOKE;ENABLE_LAZ
Y_METHOD_CACHING;ENABLE_MOVIES;ENABLE_CRUNCH_TEXTURE_COMPRESSION;ENABLE_NET
WORK;ENABLE_EVENT_QUEUE;UNITY_PLATFORM_THREAD_TO_CORE_MAPPING;ENABLE_SUBSTA
NCE;PLATFORM_SUPPORTS_ADS_ID;ENABLE_UNITYWEBREQUEST;ENABLE_CLOUD_SERVICES;E
NABLE_CLOUD_SERVICES_ADS;ENABLE_CLOUD_SERVICES_ANALYTICS;ENABLE_CLOUD_SERVI
CES_PURCHASING;ENABLE_CLOUD_SERVICES_CRASH_REPORTING;CURL_STATICLIB;ENABLE_
VR;UNITY_WSA;ENABLE_DOTNET;UNITY_WINRT_10_0;UNITY_PRO_LICENSE;NETFX_CORE;WI
NDOWS_UWP;UNITY_UWP;UNITY_WSA_10_0;
```

As you can see, this is quite a lot. Yours might be slightly different. For instance, you might not have UNITY_PRO_LICENSE. There is one that is of importance to us:

- WINDOWS_UWP: This tells the system this is a UWP application

Now, if you open .csproj in the root of the folder in a text editor, you will find another set of symbols there. The most of them are the same, but not all of them. For instance, WINDOWS_UWP is missing. Instead you will find a symbol named UNITY_EDITOR.

What this means is that when the project is used in Unity3D, the symbol UNITY_EDITOR is defined and WINDOWS_UWP is not. If we open the solution that is being built then the reverse is true. We can use this to our advantage.

If you have code that cannot be run in Unity3D, you could surround it with an #if / #endif construct, such as this:

```
    void Update () {
#if WINDOWS_UWP
        var currentTime = $"The time is {DateTime.Now.TimeOfDay}";
#endif
    }
```

This code will be ignored in Unity3D, but will be usable in Visual Studio. We could also do the reverse:

```
    void Update () {
#if UNITY_EDITOR
        UnityEngine.Debug.Log("We are updating");
#endif
    }
```

This will only run if we are inside Unity3D and will not even be compiled in the final version of our app.

This sounds like a great solution, but it does have some drawbacks. Imagine the following piece of pseudocode:

```
using System.Threading.Tasks;
using UnityEngine;

public class SomeDummyScript : MonoBehaviour {
    // Update is called once per frame
    async void Update () {

        var oldPos = transform.position;
        this.gameObject.transform.position = Vector3.zero;
        await Task.Delay(1000);
        this.gameObject.transform.position = oldPos;
    }
}
```

This code does not make sense: we get the current position, reset the position to (0,0,0), wait for one second, and then restore the position. It does work, however. But not if you open Unity3D again, then you get that dreaded error again:

```
Assets/Scripts/SomeDummyScript.cs(6,6): error CS1644: Feature
`asynchronous functions' cannot be used because it is not part of the
C# 4.0 language specification
```

We just learned how to get rid of that: surround it with `#if` / `#endif`. So, now look at the following code snippet:

```
#if WINDOWS_UWP
using System.Threading.Tasks;
#endif
using UnityEngine;

public class SomeDummyScript : MonoBehaviour {
    // Update is called once per frame
#if WINDOWS_UWP
    async
#endif
    void Update () {

        var oldPos = transform.position;
        this.gameObject.transform.position = Vector3.zero;
#if WINDOWS_UWP
        await Task.Delay(1000);
#endif

#if UNITY3D
        Debug.Log("We were supposed to wait one second";
#endif
        this.gameObject.transform.position = oldPos;
    }
}
```

I do not know about you, but I am not enjoying this code at all. We need to wrap the `using` statement, the `async` keyword in the method header, and then call it to `Delay`. We also want an alternative thing to do when running in Unity3D, so we have a `Debug.Log` statement here.

I do not like this, but it does work. I have found, however, that when you start to do more complicated things such as networking, your code gets littered with these statements. They make reading and understanding your code very hard. It is time for a better solution.

Option 3 - placeholder assemblies

This option has the most work. You have to do a lot of work twice once for Unity3D, and once for the final app in Visual Studio. But it will result in a very readable code that also allows you to have fallback code to use in Unity3D.

Again, you might not like this approach. It will slow you down. If you find that to be the case, you are more than welcome to go to option 2. Option 1 is not really an option besides during conference demos.

Build your app in Unity3D, resulting in the solution, and you can open it in Visual Studio. You know: the one with the three projects.

Add a new Solution folder to the solution. I call it Plugins.

In Unity3D I, create a new folder in the `Assets` folder, called **Plugins**. In that **Plugins** folder, I have created a second folder called **WSA. WSA (Windows Store Applications)**.

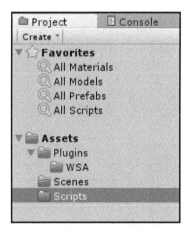

The Plugins folder structure

In Visual Studio, we will add two new projects in the `Plugins Solution` folder. I call them `MyPlugin` and `MyPlugin.UWP`. The second one is a `Universal` class library, built on the 4.6.2 framework. You can choose another version; just make sure it is one of the latest.

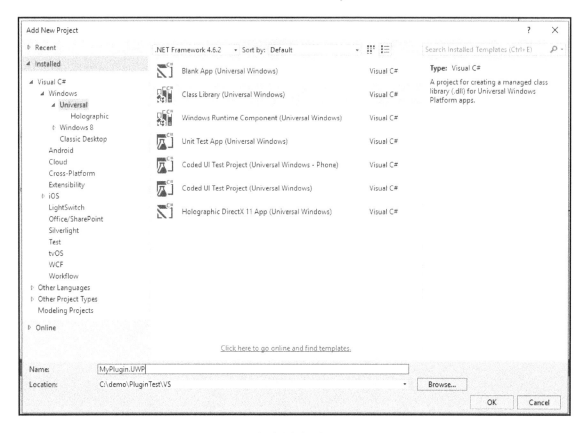

The UWP Plugin project

Create another one, also in the `Plugins` folder. This time, call it `MyPlugin`, but make sure it is *not* a `Universal` class library and that it compiles against the .NET 3.5 framework:

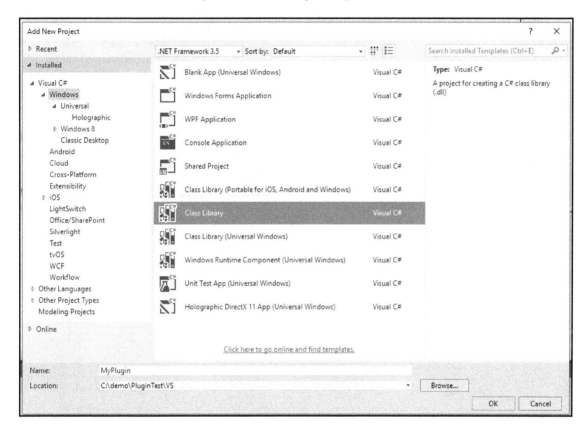

The normal class library

Do not add a reference to either project from the main projects; Unity3D will take care of that.

Delete the `class1.cs` files in both projects.

Add a new folder to both projects called `Interfaces`. In `MyPlugin` (the 3.5 version) add a new file called `IDebugHelper` to that folder:

```
namespace MyPlugin.Interfaces
{
    public interface IDebugHelper
    {
        void Log(string message);
    }
}
```

In the `MyPlugin.UWP` application, right-click on the `Interfaces` folder and click on **Add existing item**. Navigate to the interface we just created, select it, and click on the arrow next to **Add** so that the menu appears. Click on **Add as link**:

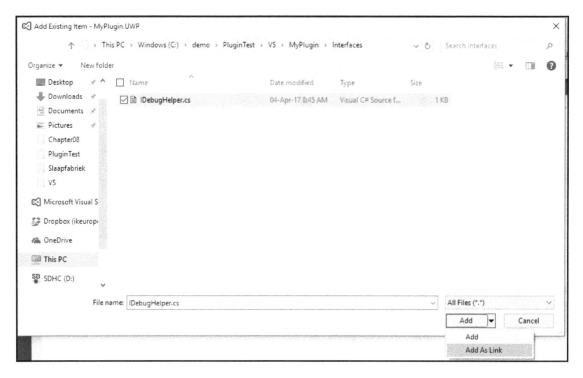

Adding the interface to both projects

This will result in having one physical file that is being shared between both projects. If we change it in one place, it will also be changed in the other.

We need to adjust the properties of each project a bit. First, in the UWP class library, make sure the default namespace is `MyPlugin` instead of the given `MyPlugin.UWP` and that the assembly name is `MyPlugin` instead of `MyPlugin.UWP`:

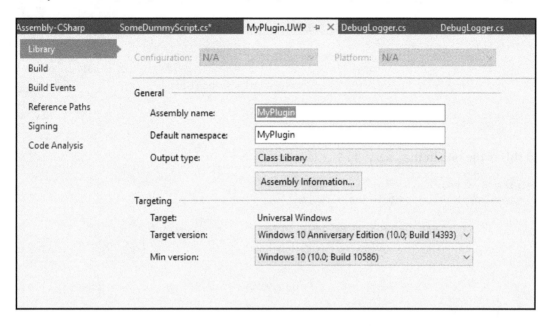

Properties for the UWP plugin

Now, we need to change the **Build Events** for both projects. In the UWP version set the post-build event command line:

```
copy $(TargetPath) ..\..\..\..\..\Assets\Plugins\WSA
```

For the 3.5 plugin, the post-build event command line should be this:

```
copy $(TargetPath) ..\..\..\..\Assets\Plugins
```

This ensures the DLLs will be copied to the correct folders in our `Asset` folder.

We will add some code to the plugins now.

I have added a folder/namespace Helpers to each project and added a `DebugHelper` class to each project. In each project I used the `IDebugHelper` as the interface and implemented it.

This is the one in the `.NET 3.5` version:

```
using System;
namespace MyPlugin.Helpers
{
    public class DebugHelper : Interfaces.IDebugHelper
    {
        public void Log(string message)
        {
            // nothing, this is just a place holder
        }
    }
}
```

And this is the one in the `.NET 4.6.2` version:

```
using System;
namespace MyPlugin.Helpers
{
    public class DebugHelper : Interfaces.IDebugHelper
    {
        public void Log(string message)
        {
            System.Diagnostics.Debug.WriteLine($"Log called: {message}");
        }
    }
}
```

As you can see, I am doing nothing in the 3.5 version. But I am using the new stuff in the `.NET 4.6.2`: I can use the handy `$"{}"` syntax, for instance.

You just saw one of the downsides of this technique: you have to do everything twice. We could reuse the interface and by using that interface makes sure we do not forget about implementing one of the methods. But we do need to define the classes and methods twice. Luckily, we only have to implement them for real in one place only: in the `.NET 4.x` version. The other can remain empty.

Now the most important thing to know about this technique is to do a build in Visual Studio. Remember that every time you change something in your plugin code, you need to build it in Visual Studio and then do a build in Unity3D. I will explain later why this is so important, but for now just build it.

If you do so, you will see in Unity3D that the `Plugins` and `Plugins/WSA` folders contain our Plugins DLL. We need to make two minor changes.

Select the DLL in Plugins and open the object inspector. Change it to look like the following and click **Apply:**

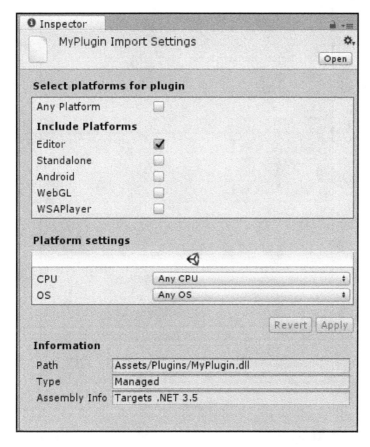

The import settings for the normal plugin

We have changed the plugin import settings and told Unity3D to only use this Plugin when we are in the Editor. As you can see at the bottom, it is seen that we are working with a .NET 3.5 version DLL, which is what we wanted.

Now, select the DLL in UWP and open the **Inspector** again. Change it:

Import settings for the UWP plugin

We have set it as a **WSAPlayer** plugin, meaning it will be used in the Windows store app environment, or, in other words, in our HoloLens. We have set the SDK to UWP and the scripting backend to .NET. Next, we had to choose a placeholder. You can click this and it will show you all the DLLs that are a candidate for this. For a DLL to be an option, it has to follow two rules:

- It must be a 3.5 version DLL.
- It must have the exact same name as the `4.x dll`. This is why we changed the name from `MyPlugin.UWP` to `MyPlugin`.
- Click **Apply**.

Add a script to your Unity3D project and add that to a GameObject. For this demo I will use the camera, and call my script `SomeDummyScript`.

Do a rebuild of your Unity3D project, then go to Visual Studio. Open `SomeDummyScript` in the `Assembly-C Sharp` project and add the following code:

```
using MyPlugin.Helpers;
using UnityEngine;

public class SomeDummyScript : MonoBehaviour {
    // Update is called once per frame

    public void Start()
    {
        var helper = new DebugHelper();
        helper.Log("Calling the plugin");
    }
}
```

We are using the `MyPlugin.Helpers` namespace. We call the constructor on the `DebugHelper` class. We call its method `Log`. It all works. Unity3D does not complain about our code, but if you run it on HoloLens with the debugger attached, you will see that the code in our `.NET 4.x` assembly is called and used.

Why does this work?

Well, the answer lies in the way Unity3D works with plugins. We have two versions of the assembly. One is marked as editor only; the other is marked as WSA only.

When we run the app in Unity3D (remember: just opening a project in Unity3D is considered running aswell) it will load the correct DLL and plug it into the `Assembly-C Sharp` project. It will add the reference automatically so the correct DLL will be loaded. In this case: the 3.5 version.

The moment we do a build and move to Visual Studio, Unity3D realizes we are building for the Windows Store environment, and thus will inject the WSA version of our DLL into `Assembly-C Sharp`. That is what we will use from then on.

If you look at the references of the `Assembly-C Sharp` project you will see the `MyPlugin` `dll` being referenced there. But which version it is depends on where you are.

This is the reason we have to do a rebuild all the time. When you make a change in the plugin code, you need to do a rebuild so they both get built and copied to the right `Plugin` folder in Unity3D. Then in Unity3D you need to do a rebuild to make sure the right version of the plugin is injected in `Assembly-C Sharp`.

Yes, it is a pain to do everything twice. But if you make a fairly nice wrapper and use the interfaces in such a way I just showed you, the pain is minimal. If you run into compilation errors, chances are you forgot to do the build-roundtrip. But your code will be much cleaner and easier to understand. I suggest you try this out.

Just to help you out a bit, I have created this handy guide. So, when you want to use the latest features of .NET in your app, but still want Unity3D to be happy with your code, here is what you do:

1. Create a folder named `Plugins` in Unity3D.
2. In that folder, create another folder named `WSA`.
3. In the Visual Studio solution, add a new solution folder named `Plugins`.
4. In that folder, add a new class library running on .NET 3.5. Name it `MyPlugin`.
5. Create another class library, but this time for UPW and the latest .NET framework. Name that `MyPlugin.UWP`.
6. In `MyPlugin`, create a folder for your interface files.
7. In `MyPlugin`, create a new interface containing all the members you need.
8. In `MyPlugin.UWP`, add a link to the created interface file. Do not copy it!
9. Change the default namespace in the `MyPlugin.UWP` to `MyPlugin`.
10. Change the assembly name in `MyPlugin.UWP` to `MyPlugin`.
11. Add a post-build event to the `MyPlugin` project, copying the result to the Unity3D Plugin folder.
12. Add a post-build event to the `MyPlugin.UWP` project, copying the result to the Unity3D `Plugin/WSA` folder.
13. Implement the actual code in the `MyPlugin.UWP` project.
14. Add placeholder code in the `MyPlugin` project.
15. In Unity3D, select the `MyPlugin` and set its properties to only be used in the editor.
16. In Unity3D, select the `MyPlugin.UWP` and set its properties to be used in the **WSAPlayer**.
17. Run the project and be amazed.
18. Quite a lot of work, but it pays off in the end to do it this way.

Performance in Unity3D

One thing to be aware of is that HoloLens is, despite its magical qualities, a fairly limited device. We need to make sure the apps we build perform well on this hardware. Usually I tell developers not to care that much about performance until it becomes an issue. Hardware is upgraded all the time, machines get faster all the time. It is usually cheaper to buy more or better hardware to solve a performance issue than to spend time developing smart tricks nobody understands or can maintain.

On HoloLens, this is a different problem. The hardware is not that advanced, at least not when you look at computing power and especially not when compared to normal desktop based devices. Next to that, we cannot swap components for faster ones. The device is what it is. So, when building HoloLens apps, you need to make sure you have performance on your mind all the time.

You should strive to have your app running on 60 frames per second as much as possible. You can check this in the portal: the performance counters give a nice indication of the performance of the system:

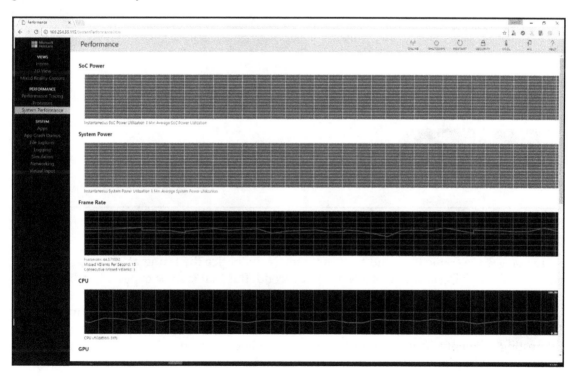

Performance counters in the portal

As you can see, my app is running and the framerate is about 44 frames per second. This is way too low; I need to do something about it. We will have a look at that later.

Next to the pretty basic frame rate counter in the device portal, we can use the advanced GPU and graphics profiling tools Visual Studio offers us. We can then use it to measure the health of the system. After all, you need to measure things before you know what to improve and to assess what the improvements are.

The Graphic Analysis tool in Visual Studio is extremely powerful. But, as always with powerful tools, it is quite complex too. Most of the time you do not need this at all, but you can find performance spots in your app if you cannot find them otherwise. If you want to use this tool, you go to Visual Studio and select **Debug** | **Graphics** | **Start Graphics Debugging**. This will load the app and deploy it to either the emulator or the device, depending on your settings. Then it will load on the following screen:

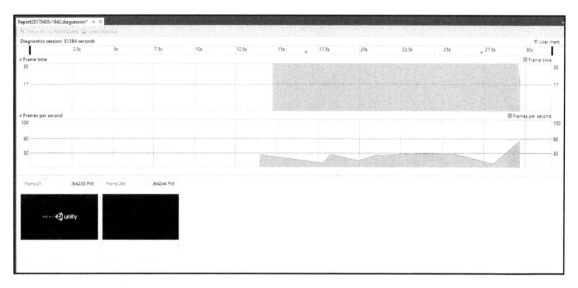

The Graphical Debugger collector screen

Here you see the frame time and the framerate. Now, notice the framerate for my app is ridiculously low: I get around 30 frames per second. But that is to be expected: debuggers tend to slow your app down and this is quite normal for this kind of debugging. After all, everything the GPU does is captured, transported to the CPU, and then over the wire or Wi-Fi to the Visual Studio Graphical Debugger that has to store that data. That takes time! At interesting moments during the runtime you can collect markers. Screenshots of those moments will be placed at the bottom part of the screen and a green arrow is placed above the timeline, indicating where the snapshots were made.

If you press **Stop**, in the top-left corner, the debugger will stop and so will your app. The data is collected and you are given the chance to dive into it.

Select one of the snapshots and the actual debugger will start up. This gives you tons of information. I have included a sample of a moment in time, to be precise, frame number 619. The screenshot you see is the information the system has about the call to `DrawIndexed` (remember that one? Yes, Unity3D also uses those APIs!). In the bottom half you get all sorts of information about the shaders, what they are doing, the data structures they are getting, and so on:

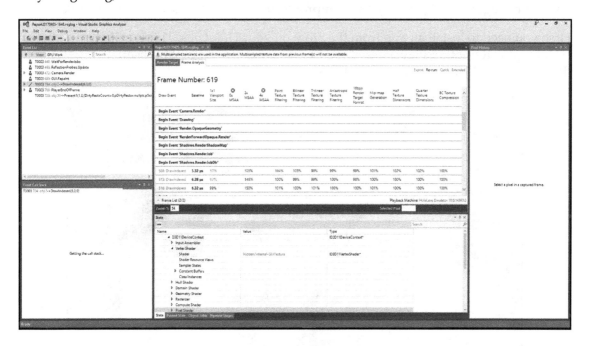

The graphic debug data

There is really a lot of information here, but it is quite hard to get a grip on it all. If you need this kind of information, I suggest you to look up resources about this typical topic and dive into it. Most of the time you will not need it, but if you do, now you know where to find it. Oh, and did I mention this also works for the DirectX Holographic apps you write as well?

Remoting in Unity3D

Unity3D itself does also have a profiler. It is actually quite useful, but to use it properly with HoloLens I need to explain the concept of remoting first.

Remoting is something that has been added to Unity3D quite late in the development of the tooling around HoloLens and it is not very stable yet. But the idea is quite nice: take the rendering power of the desktop computer, take the sensor information from HoloLens, combine those two to create the image HoloLens would display, and send the resulting image to both HoloLens and the desktop machines screen.

This means most of the hard work is done on a powerful machine instead of on HoloLens. Of course, this also means you lose one of the biggest advantages of HoloLens: you are no longer untethered. You need to have a connection to the machine that does all calculations. Still, for debugging and profiling this can prove quite useful. So, how does this work?

First, you need to install an app from the Store on your HoloLens. This is called **Holographic Remoting Player** and it is a free download made by Microsoft. If you download it and install it, you will get this screen:

Holographic Remoting Player

Not very exciting, is it? All it does is show you the IP address of your device. However, this means it is running and waiting for another machine to connect to it to do the remoting. Yes, you can write your own apps that take advantage of this, but now all we will do is connect Unity3D to it.

In Unity3D, in the menu window, there is an option called **Holographic Emulation**. If selected you will be given this screen:

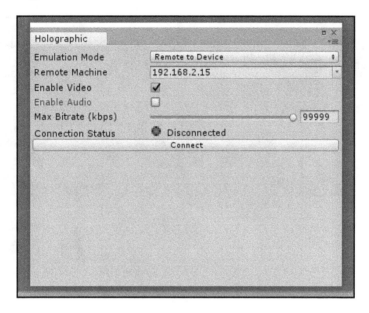

Holographic emulation settings in Unity3D

Here you can choose how to emulate (none, **Remote to Device**, or Simulate in Editor), the IP address of the device, and whether you want **video** and/or **audio**. You can select the bitrate and you can, of course, **connect**.

Set the correct properties and click **Connect**. Now click **Play** in Unity3D. You will see in your HoloLens the scene immediately. There is no need for building, deploying, Visual Studio compiling, and so on.

For debugging, this is quite handy. However, like I said, this is still early technology and I have seen it fail quite a lot. But for a quick look at how things work, this is a great feature.

Profiling in Unity3D

Go to the **Window** menu and select **Profiler**. The **Profiler** page will open. By default, the **Record** button is selected, meaning it will record data the moment your app starts. You can even profile the app while still in the editor, but that is not very useful to us.

When done profiling, simply stop playing the app and dive into the results of the profiler. Again, there is a lot of information here:

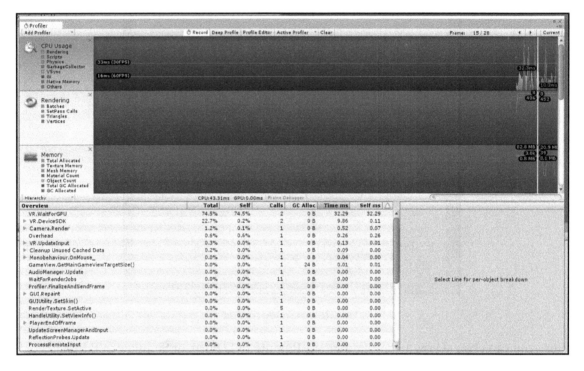

The Unity3D Profiler

You can see exactly what is going on all the time. Who does what, how long does your script take, what is drawing, when are the assets used, and so on. The CPU, GPU, memory, network, audio, physics engine, and so on, are all there.

Play around with it and see if it can help you. I found the Unity3D profiler to be a better tool to find bottlenecks in my apps than the Visual Studio Graphics Debugger. Only when things are really getting complicated I use the latter one.

Unity3D performance tricks

There are a lot of things you can do to make your app run faster, without digging deep into the bowels of the GPU or use hard to use profilers. I want to share some of the most common with you.

It is worthwhile to keep these tips with you all the time; the best way to solve performance issues is to prevent getting into them in the first place.

QualitySettings

First of all, have your quality settings set right. In **Edit | Project Settings**, choose **Quality**. You will get this screen:

QualitySettings in Unity3D

Click on the tiny triangle beneath the Windows Store logo and choose **Fastest** as the option. Yes, this will reduce the quality. But you will gain speed. You might think: "But I want great-looking graphics!" and you would be right to think so. But in reality this does not really matter. After all, with the relative low resolution, HoloLens will not notice this reduction in quality. Great quality is only observable in images that are perfectly standing still. In HoloLens, they never are: users are always moving their head a bit and the system has to fix this by anti-aliasing and moving the images a bit. This takes away any sharpness you have in your images anyway so you might as well go for the extra speed.

Polygon/vertex reduction

The device can handle about 65,000 vertices easily. Anything above that number might get problematic. There is no hard number; it all depends on a lot of things. But in general you have to be careful not to use 3D models that are too detailed or too complex. It just will not work smoothly. Using complex models, you will notice a drop in your framerate.

If you download objects from the internet you can try and search for the so-called low-poly models. They still look good, but are way less expensive in usage than the high poly models.

If you have a model, but find it has too many polygons, I suggest you use a third-party tool to reduce the number of polygons on it. Blender, for instance, has an easy to use tool for this. MeshLab, an open-source tool, is slightly harder to use, but has some options to reduce this as well while still retaining the looks of the original model.

Last but not least, there is a plugin for Unity3D called **Simplygon**. This tool used to be a third-party tool, but the company has recently been acquired by Microsoft. At the time of writing it is unclear what the future of the tool is, but Microsoft has stated it will keep it around.

Static objects

Unity3D is a great tool and does a lot of things for us out of the box. One of the things it does is constantly tracking if things have moved and if that impacts lighting, shadows, occlusion, and so on. This is all very nice, if it were not for the following things:

- Computing all this takes up a lot of time and resources.
- A lot of items in our scene are static: they do not change, or do not animate. They just sit there and need not to be checked that thoroughly

Luckily, we can modify the behavior. In your scene, select an object that is not subject to animation or a lot of movement.

In the object inspector, in the top-right corner you see the tiny word **Static** next to an unchecked checkbox. Click on the arrow next to it and observe the dropdown. Here you can specify what you want to be static:

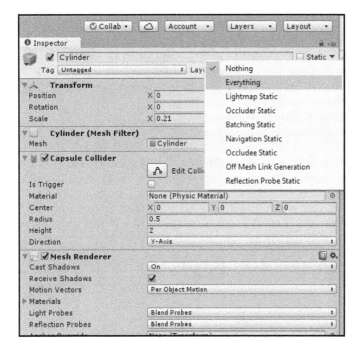

Static objects in Unity3D

Most of the time you want things to be static on **Everything**, but you can tweak it. For instance, **Occluder Static** and **Occluding Static** make sure the objects will not take any rendering time when they are hidden from view by other objects. If you want to do that, you need to set up Occlusion first. The Unity3D manual has a great topic on that, so I refer to that here.

Most of the time you will just click the checkbox and thus set everything to static, saving quite a lot of computation time.

Level of Detail

I want you to do a little experiment. Look at your hand. Notice the details. See the veins, the wrinkles, and the texture. Look at your nails. Now, find some other person, stand a couple of meters away from them and have a look at their hands. Can you see the same amount of detail? If you have very, very good eyes you might say yes, to which I say "Step back a little more". The fact is, you see more details in things that are nearer.

In computers,it does not work like that. Unity3D will treat objects the same, no matter if they are close or farther away. OK, the pixels will not be rendered in the end for all details on things far away, but they will be calculated first. This seems like a waste of time to me: we will never see those details, so why spend valuable cycles calculating them?

This is where the Level of Detail it helps out.

In short, this is a technique where you give multiple versions of your 3D model to Unity3D and tell it "Look, if this item is near, use item 1. If it is a bit further away, draw the less detailed item 2. If it is even further away, use the even more simplified item 3" And so on. This helps a lot in achieving higher speeds.

I have drawn a box in Sketchup. It is not very fancy, just a plain boring box:

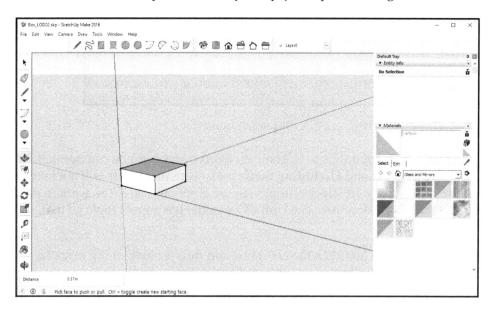

Straight box

Then I refined it. I added details to make it look a bit nicer:

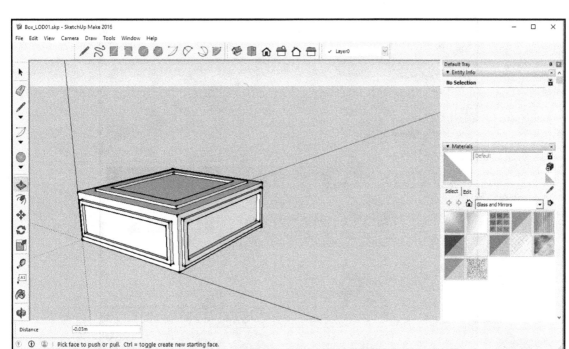

A nicer-looking box

And I added even more details in a third version.

I have added these items in Unity3D. As you can see, I gave them a special name: they are called Box_LOD00, BOX_LOD01, and BOX_LOD02. The lower the number, the more details they have.

In my Unity3D scene, I added a new empty GameObject. To this I added a new component, called **LOD Group**.

I selected the **LOD 0** item:

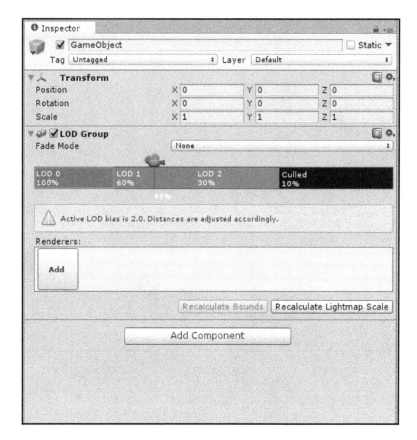

The LOD component

I dragged the Box_LOD0 item to the **Renderers** box. Unity3D asks me if I want to make the object a child object of our GameObject, which I do want. Then I clicked **LOD 1** and did the same with BOX_LOD1, and again for the last box.

The result looks like this:

LOD 0: a nice looking object

As you can see, the editor shows my nicely detailed box and tells us that we are at the Level of **Detail 0**. Now, if I slide the tiny camera in the LOD Group component towards **LOD 2**, you will see what happens. The moment we go into the area for **LOD 1** the detailed box makes way for the less detailed box, and then when we hit **LOD 2** it will render the simple plain box:

LOD in action: further away thus less details

If we were to move even further away, it would get into the culled state, meaning it will not draw at all.

You can change the number of levels, you can drag the borders between to redefine the distance at what they change, and you can change the way the objects morph into each other.

LOD is a great way to have nice-looking objects while keeping good performance in your app. You should try it out!

Lighting optimizations

I will be brief about lighting optimizations. Do not use lights in HoloLens apps. By default, you get one light and you do need that: without the light you would not see anything. But you should not use other lights. No spot lights, no sun, no other things at all. Next to that, you should disable all shadowing as well. Shadows will never be correct: in the real world shadows will not line up with the virtual shadows without extensive calculations. And those calculations are exactly what we want to get rid of. Experience has shown me users accept a mixed reality world where the virtual objects do not cast shadows, but they have trouble accepting virtual objects that cast incorrect shadows. I guess that is just the way our minds work.

Texture optimizations

Textures should be as simple as possible. That being said, you can do some nice tricks with textures to prevent your app from having to use too much polygons.

Imagine you have a brick wall in your scene. A virtual one, I mean, not a physical one. Brick walls consist of bricks with a layer of mortar between them. The mortar usually is not the same level as the bricks; you can feel the depth of them when you touch them. If you drew a realistic looking wall you would have to model that in your 3D model. But that would result in a high poly count object. And I just taught you not to do that. If you take a simple cube and put a texture on it of a brick will, it will feel and look just like that: a box with some wallpaper on it.

We want realism, but we want low-poly. How do we do that? Normal mapping to the rescue!

Normal mapping is a trick. It is a way of telling the renderer to render certain parts of our texture higher or lower than the rest. You do this by giving your material a special image, where the RGB values per pixel do not give color information, but instead will be translated into an X, Y, and Z value. These values determine the normal of the image. This means a value of (0.5, 0.5, 0.5) will be rendered with the normal perpendicular on the image. Other values give other normals.

Here is our brick wall:

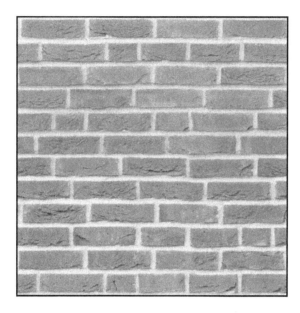

Brick wall texture

And this is the normal map belonging to the same image:

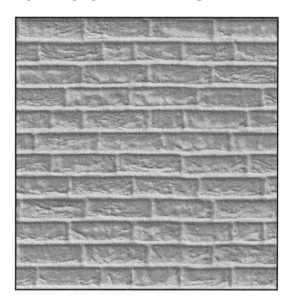

The bump map for the brick wall

Let us create a new material using these:

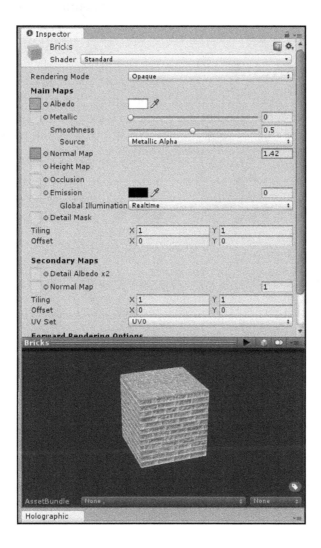

The normal mapped brick material

This material, when applied to an object will give a nice textured feel to our objects, without the overhead of all the polygons to actually render all the bumps, holes, and ridges in the wall.

Scripts optimizations

Scripts need to be well written. They run all the time, the `Update()` method is called every frame so it will be called about 60 times per second. This is true for all scripts attached to active game objects in the current scene. You can imagine that opening a connection to an Azure cloud database in an `Update()` call might not be a good idea.

It will work. However, the method will not return until all the work is done. So it will not be able to do its work in the time it has. If this script is the only one running it should do its work in 1/60 th of a second. If there are two scripts, the time is even less.

Threading

HoloLens has multiple cores. It is there for a good idea to use them as much as you can: take advantage of multiple threads to do background work, database work, network traffic, and so on. Leave the UI stuff in the main thread, but the rest should be done in a different thread.

You can use `.NET 4.x` features such as async/await and tasks to do this if you use the techniques described in the beginning of this chapter. You can also use co-routines, which are Unity3D's way of multithreading.

Say you want to do a countdown. However, you want this to happen in the background. You could do it like this:

```
using System.Collections;
using UnityEngine;

public class BackgroundWorkers : MonoBehaviour {

    // Use this for initialization
    void Start () {
        StartCoroutine(DoCountdown(10));
    }

    IEnumerator DoCountdown(int counter)
    {
        for(int i=counter; i>0; i--)
        {
            DoSomethingWithI(i);
```

```
            yield return 0;
        }
    }
}
```

`StartCoroutine()` takes a method returning an `IEnumerator`. This method will be called in a different thread. The loop starts and the first `DoSomethingWithI(i)` is called. Then it returns to the main thread. The next time there is time to do some work, usually the next frame (but that is not guaranteed!) it will pick up again after the yield statement. In this example, it will return to the loop, until we reach the condition `i==0`. Then it exits and the thread is abandoned.

Garbage collections

`.NET` is garbage collected. This means you usually do not have to worry about cleaning up allocated resources. The framework will do this for you. The thing is, you do not know when this happens. This usually takes place when the system needs to free up memory, but that is usually not at the time that is the best for your app. So you need to be aware of this: garbage collection can take some time and resources.

If you need to allocate memory for objects, it is best to do that in the start method. Do not create big objects in the Update method--when the method exists, these objects are eligible for cleaning up and thus the garbage collector might mess up with your framerate.

Keep large objects around as long as you can, and keep small objects and primitives such as integers as close to the place where you use them. Reuse database connections and TCP connections as much as possible.

Structs versus classes

I hardly ever see people use structs anymore. The reason of course is that the benefits of using them (small and lightweight and thus quick) are no longer valid, at least not as much as they were: devices are powerful enough to deal with more expensive classes. However, in HoloLens we need to take care of this. Hence the following code:

```
class WrongUseOfClass
{
    private Color _anotherExpensiveProperty;

    public string MyProperty { get; set; }
    public Color AnotherExpensiveProperty
    {
        get { return _anotherExpensiveProperty; }
        set
```

```
        {
            if (_anotherExpensiveProperty != value)
            {
                _anotherExpensiveProperty = value;
            }


        }
    }
}

struct MuchBetterSolution
{
    public string MyProperty;
    public Color NotSoBadProperty;
}
```

In normal development, the class and the encapsulation is a great way of doing things. You are protecting yourself against mistakes in the future by doing your code this way. However, it does come with a price. The struct in this case is much better for HoloLens since it is much more memory friendly and garbage collector friendly.

Shader optimizations

There is no way around it: if you want the best kind of performance you need to stay away from the standard shaders in Unity. The shaders they use are great for desktop machines, but not so great for mobile devices and HoloLenses.

Shaders are used in materials. They define how the data you supply in the shape of vertices, colors, textures, and so on get translated into pixels on the screen. Like we discussed, there are a lot of different shader types. In Unity3D we do not have to deal with all those different kinds of shader, but you will need to have a look at them.

If you look at a material in the object inspector, you will notice at the top there is this dropdown where you can define what shader to use:

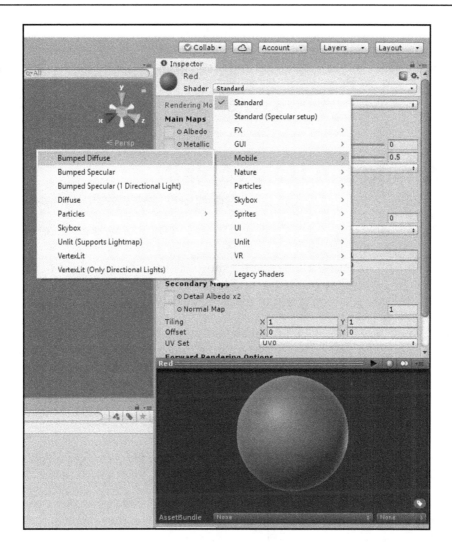

Shader selection in the material editor

There are quite a lot of shaders available. If you had to choose between them, the mobile ones would be a good bet: they are optimized for low-powered devices. You could, of course, write your own shader and use that. That way you can make it so that it is tailored towards use in HoloLens. The downside is that it is quite hard to do. Although it is not as hard as it is to write them for DirectX, there is still an awful lot of work to do and it takes a deep understanding of the inner-workings of the systems.

Luckily, there is a group of people out there that know exactly what HoloLens systems can do and how to write shaders for them. Those are the people in the HoloLens team. What they did is write some very good shaders and made them open source. You can just download them and use them.

They are part of a larger project called the HoloToolkit.

Introducing the HoloToolkit

I have long doubted whether I should include this part in this book. For these reasons:

- The toolkit is rather well documented and supported by a group of enthusiasts (of which I am just one).
- It is open source and always on the move. Things change all the time, including a lot of breaking changes that would require substantial rewrite of your code. By the time you read this, most of the things I show you will be outdated.

Yet I decided to include it. I have told you about developing in DirectX. With DirectX you can get great results and you can tweak every little thing of your app to have it do exactly what you want. However, that power comes with a price. It is a lot of work to get the results.

With Unity3D you have a tool that makes you incredibly productive. However, that speed also comes with a price: you lose some of the flexibility you had in DirectX.

The HoloToolkit takes this even a step further. The HoloToolkit can get you up to speed in your Unity3D project even faster, if you do not mind being tied to this toolset.

Everything is open source and you can tweak and change things as much as you like, but in doing so you will lose compatibility with newer versions once they come out. And they do come out a lot. So beware!

Where to get it

The sources are available on GitHub. You can find them at `https://github.com/Microsoft/HoloToolkit-Unity`. You can clone them by using this command in a Git command line:

Git command to get the HoloToolkit

Once you have done this, you have all the sources. But you also get the pre-compiled Unity3D package containing all you need.

This package can be found in your Git root folder, `]\HoloToolkit-Unity\External\Unitypackages`, and it is called `HoloToolkit-Unity-vx.x.x.x.unitypackage`, where the x in the name will be the version number. In my case it was 1.5.5.0, but that will probably be something else tomorrow.

Importing the toolkit

You can import this package in your projects. You do so by right-clicking on your `Assets` folder and selecting **Import Package | Custom Package**. You can then browse to the folder and select the `UnityPackage` file. Once you have done this you will get a dialog asking you which part of the toolkit you want. I suggest you select all of them the first time. In production apps you will probably not import all the examples, but for now this might be a good idea.

Using the toolkit

I have a suggestion--try this for a change.

Start a new Unity3D project. Give it a cool name. However, do nothing yet. Do not go through the steps you need to do to make it HoloLens-capable. Instead, import the package first before you do anything else.

Importing might take some time. There are a lot of assets in the toolkit that need to be made part of your project. Next to that, it also contains some shaders. They need to be compiled by the shader compiler, another process that takes a lot of time.

Luckily, you only need to import it once per project.

Menu items

Once it has been imported, you will notice Unity3D has another menu item, named **HoloToolkit**. In it, you find several handy things:

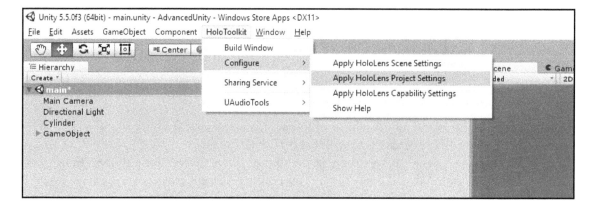

HoloToolkit menu options

If you chose **Apply HoloLens Project Settings**, the toolkit will make your project compatible with HoloLens. It will set the platform to Windows Store/UWP 10, it will set it to use C# projects and use D3D. It will also set the **Use Virtual Reality** option.

If you then choose **Apply HoloLens Scene Settings** it will set the camera to the right position, set the background color to black, set the culling parameters correct, and so on.

You can also choose **Apply HoloLens Capability Settings** to have a nice way to set the most often used capabilities.

Assets

There are a lot of scripts and prefabs you can use. Let me go through some of them.

You will want to add the following scripts to the main camera:

- Input manager
- Gaze manager

A lot of the scripts use these so you might as well have them handy.

Now, add the **CursorWithFeedback** prefab somewhere in the script. Run your app. As you can see, you now have a cursor that hugs all the objects that you might place in your scene.

Place a cylinder somewhere in your scene. Add a capsule collider to it. Add a new script to it, looking like this:

```
using HoloToolkit.Unity.InputModule;
using UnityEngine;

public class OnTappedHandler : MonoBehaviour, IInputHandler {
    public void OnInputDown(InputEventData eventData)
    {
        System.Diagnostics.Debug.WriteLine("Up");
    }

    public void OnInputUp(InputEventData eventData)
    {
        System.Diagnostics.Debug.WriteLine("Up");

    }
}
```

All we did here is add the `IInputHandler` interface to it and implemented it. Since the `InputManager` class looks at the focused object or the object the user is looking at when the tap occurs, it will try to see if it implements `IInputHandler` and call the correct functions. Easy, is it not?

Here is another fun one:

Drag the prefab SpatialMapping to your scene. Run your app. After a couple of seconds you will see the mesh from the spatial mapping. This script will even generate objects so if you turn on the gravity on your GameObjects, they will drop to the floor and not fall through. This took us all of `Chapter 6`, *Take a Look around You - Spatial Mapping,* to accomplish.

Another nice prefab is Text. This gives you a panel where you can add text to display in your app. I use it quite a lot in debug situations, but you can do anything you want with it of course.

Shaders

I promised you shaders. You got them! If you go to a material and click **Shader** you will see a new menu option: **HoloToolkit**:

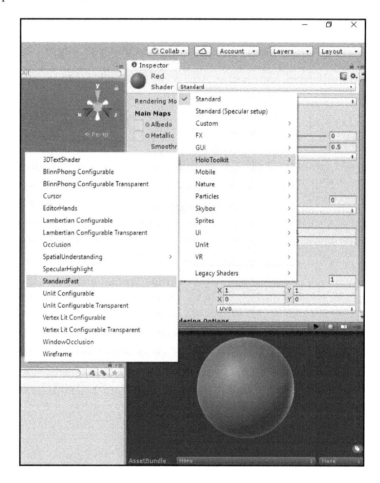

HoloToolkit comes with lots of shaders

StandardFast is a much better shader to use for normal GameObjects in HoloLens. The others can be useful if you need them. I quite like the Occlusion one.

If you draw an object in a material with this shader, you will not see it. However, it will also block out other objects behind it. This means if you create a cube with a see-through hole in it, and you place a nice game object in that hole, you can use this material on the cube to make it invisible unless you are standing in front of the object. This, in turn, means you can create fake holes in walls and floors. Just create a big object with this shader, create a hole in it, and place it in your real wall. The effect is amazing.

Sharing service

In the menu, you will also find an option to start a small TCP/IP based server that the sharing scripts talk to. This way you can quite quickly set up a collaborative app that shares holograms. As you have seen in Chapter 7, *Let's Talk! Communications Between Devices*, it is not hard to do it yourself, but it is nice that you get one for free here.

And much more

There is so much more available in the toolkit. I invite you to have a look at it yourself and try the examples. The toolkit is under constant revision and is updated all the time, so make sure you check back every now and then. It is all open source, so if you have a great idea you are more than welcome to add to the toolkit yourself!

Summary

Unity3D makes it easy to develop HoloLens apps. However, to be good at it, you need to spend some time examining its features.

Having .NET 4.x code in your app is very possible, but there are some hoops you have to jump through. You can use #if / #endif constructs or create a new set of DLLs, one for the editor, and one for the final app.

Performance in your app should always be on your mind. You can do a lot with the profiling tools in Unity3D and Visual Studio, but it is best to avoid having to deal with them. By using the tips and tricks I have shown you, you can get great results.

If you want to speed up the development time and do not mind the fact that you lose some flexibility, the HoloToolkit is a great way to start your HoloLens development. After all, now you know what happens inside of it all!

Index

O

occlusion 223, 224, 225, 265, 266, 270

P

peer to peer
  about 308
  advertisement setup 310
  Bluetooth advertisements 308, 309, 311
  connection, to other HoloLens 313
  found devices, handling 312
performance tricks, Unity3D
  about 345
  Level of Detail 348, 349, 350, 351, 352
  lighting optimizations 353
  polygon/vertex reduction 346
  QualitySettings 345, 346
  scripting optimizations 356
  shader optimizations 358
  static objects 346, 347
  texture optimizations 353, 354, 355
performance, in Unity3D 339, 340
physics 227
pixel 13, 101
Pixel Shader (PS) 103
placeholder assemblies 329
pointer 55
positioning 120
prefab
  creation code, creating 135
procedural approach 91
processors, HoloLens 11
profiling, in Unity3D 343, 344
programming shaders 103

R

ray casting 128
remoting, in Unity3D 342
Render() method 116, 117
RoboRaid app 72
RockOn app
  about 77
  developing, with DirectX 78
  developing, with Unity3D 79
  features, for implementation 77

project, building 87
project, deploying 87
rotating 121

S

sample script
  creating 44
scene
  about 44
  assets, adding to 84
script
  compiling, in Unity3D 323
  using, in Unity 126
scripts optimizations
  garbage collections 357
  struct, versus classes 357
  threading 356
sensors, HoloLens
  about 9
  cameras 9
shaders
  about 100
  adding, to project 104
  processing pipeline 101
  programming shaders 103
sharing 290
sharing scenarios
  about 295
  peer to peer 308
SharpDX
  reference 34
Simplygon 346
SketchUp 124
sound design
  about 144
  best practices 145, 146
sound
  about 56, 57, 177, 178
  concepts 174, 175
  loading 151
  playing 153, 170
  preparing 152
spatial anchors
  about 273, 274
  creating 275

www.ingramcontent.com/pod-product-compliance
Lightning Source LLC
Chambersburg PA
CBHW062041050326
40690CB00016B/2983